GEORGE DOUGLAS BROWN

GEORGE DOUGLAS BROWN

Reproduced by kind permission of J. Douglas Cairns, M.A., from an etching in his possession

GEORGE
DOUGLAS BROWN

(Author of " The House With the Green Shutters")

by

JAMES VEITCH

With a Foreword by

THE RIGHT HON. WALTER ELLIOT, M.P., M.C., D.Sc., F.R.S.

LONDON: HERBERT JENKINS

First published by
Herbert Jenkins Ltd.
3 Duke of York Street
London, S.W.1.
1952

To

T. H. HEDDLE

MADE AND PRINTED IN GREAT BRITAIN BY PURNELL AND SONS, LTD.
PAULTON (SOMERSET) AND LONDON

FOREWORD

By the RIGHT HON. WALTER ELLIOT

SINCE Andrew Lang wrote his Introduction to the first Life of George Douglas Brown, fifty years have passed. A single book, *The House With the Green Shutters*, has carried its author's name across so long a span; and his name is still alive, still strong on the wing. What is the reason for this vitality?

The reason lies primarily in the book; but also in its writer. George Douglas Brown typifies a figure of perennial interest in the life of Scotland. He is the very embodiment of "the lad o' pairts." Here was an illegitimate child from the humblest surroundings, a brilliant schoolboy, borne by the sheer power of mind from parish school to Ayr Academy, from Ayr Academy to Glasgow University, from Glasgow University to Balliol. After six years of hack-work he wrote the novel of his generation and awoke to find himself famous. He died at thirty-three, of some obscure and sudden sickness, at the very threshold of the career towards which he had worked with a single eye all his life long. Even as a documentary of the life and thought of student Scotland, so great and so typical a part of our people, Mr. Veitch's presentation would earn our gratitude.

But this is also the record of how a great work of letters came to be born. The startling fact is, that the book which so swiftly attracted the attention of all the literary world, remains, after fifty years, worth all that was said of it, all that was hoped from it—and more. The tolerant, humorous, faintly patronising note of Andrew Lang's appreciation seems strangely out of date, today. George Douglas Brown came, at one step, without strain, without a sign of overreach, to the circle of the eight or ten Scots authors into whose company any man of letters, of any time, from anywhere in the world, would be proud to draw in his chair.

He was born in the very homeland of three such men: Boswell, John Galt, Robert Burns; in Ayrshire, the fertile county, low between the moors and the sea; sentimental, noble, gross; learned; infinitely alive, infinitely curious; gossipy, quick-witted, drunken; at once Scotland and Ireland, at once Highland and Lowland. If you look for its archetype, dig up Boswell, recall Auchinleck. No two men would have hated each other more than Boswell

5

and George Douglas Brown. No two men would have understood each other better.

His mother, Sarah Gemmell, was Irish of the second generation, a dairy-worker on his father's farm. Yet this was no question of boy-and-girl light-of-love, or an affair between the village Lothario and a dairymaid. She was thirty-eight, a mature, capable woman, and this was her first child; he, a travelled man; with two brothers at one time or another professors of English in Paris, and a sister who had married money from Australia. It was the family, by all accounts, who stopped the marriage, and though the fact of George Douglas Brown's illegitimacy burnt itself into his whole life, there was a curiously lasting association between Sarah Gemmell's son and his father. And it is on record that young Brown, overhearing, as he sat on the top of the station waggonette, the characteristic Ayrshire comment "Aye, auld Broon's bastard—ye ken, Drumsmudden," burst out: "I'd rather be auld Broon's bastard than the son o' any man in this brake."

Drumsmudden, or 'Smudden, as auld Broon was usually called, giving him, in our Scottish fashion, his territorial designation, was one of those small fiery dark men very well known amongst our turbulent people. The physical make-up of his family was vigorous, but not enduring; they tended to burn themselves out at an early age; and this, as much as any obscure illness, was probably at the root of George Douglas Brown's early death. The leaping flame was a symbol of all his days and nights, and of all his habit of work. He was the true son of his father, in build, in looks, in ways of thought; and in his passionate assault upon learning, once it had taken his heart, most characteristic of all.

It was the cardinal fact of his life that he was educated above all in the classics, and above all, in Greek. The dominie of Coylton Parish School, John Smith, saw him through his six elementary standards. When young George Brown left school, he started work as a pit-head boy, cleaning coal as it came up the conveyor belt from the pit at Trabboch. But John Smith had kept track of him; followed him up, and eventually got him into Ayr Academy under William Maybin, of Queen's University, Belfast, the Rector (Headmaster, for English readers, not a clergyman)—a classicist to the bone.

George Douglas Brown finished his schooldays "superior to the fellows in a class which was far above the average merit" according to William Maybin himself. He sat the Bursary Competition at Glasgow, and also, for this was life or death to him, at Edinburgh. He came out sixteenth at Glasgow (the future Viscount Horne, by the way, was eighteenth) and nineteenth at Edinburgh. His way was clear to the University. After that, in the wide Scottish fashion, he read everything, learnt everything, thought everything. "Everything in the world I can read," he boasted, "except algebra, the Elements of Logic, and the speeches of Mr. Gladstone." Naturally, also, he could not abide Tolstoy, whose pyschology, he considered, lost itself in a morass of words.

Even Dostoevsky he disliked for his exaggeration and obscurity. His love was for the French, and Turgenev, on whom he modelled his first work. This book shows how he was fortunate in his teachers. He found in Glasgow, first, Ramsay and Sir Richard Jebb. And then?—Gilbert Murray. Murray succeeded Jebb, young Gilbert Murray, professor at twenty-five, fire-new from Oxford, pouring the whole Mediterranean from a cup of gold. Gilbert Murray invited him to Castle Howard; Gilbert Murray drove him up to success at the Blackstone Examination in Greek, for which he won the Cowan Gold Medal. He took a First in Classics, he won the Eglinton Fellowship of £100 a year, wealth indeed to a Glasgow student in those years. He went in vacation to teach Greek at Ayr Academy; and then—honour of honours, joy of joys—he acted for a time, though only a short time, as Gilbert Murray's assistant in the Greek Class at the university.

After that it was almost an anti-climax that he should win the Luke Prize in Ancient History. And then he won the Snell; which took him to Balliol.

During all this time, as Mr. Veitch tells, he soaked and drenched himself in Ayrshire landscape, and in Ayrshire life. His mother's health became poor; he had to mother her in turn; at the end, nursing her cost him his First at Oxford. But also, during all that time, something else was brewing. The genius of Scotland, which swings like a pendulum, endlessly from horror to sentiment, and to horror back again (altogether unlike the compass-needle of England, vibrating always towards sanity and the middle road) was rising high to a new turn. It had exhausted the Kailyarders; it was about to rush to the opposite extreme. Of all that swing, Brown was the forerunner and interpreter. "I will write a novel," he said at Oxford, "and tell you all, what Scottish village life is like." It was a grim picture; bitten into metal with strong poison. George Douglas Brown's village of Barbie, straggling down the Ayrshire slope from the House with the Green Shutters, is no more what Scottish village life is like than is Barrie's village of Thrums, by Kirriemuir. Reality lies somewhere between the two. But our pendulum cannot halt at any centre. If it did, the tick of the clock would stop also; and Scotland would be dead.

We have seen it swing, in our own time, from Hugh McDiarmid's poetic and eager idealisation of Lenin, to the bitter satire of Eric Blair, better known as George Orwell, a Scot of the Diaspora, in "1984", the great de-bunking of the Kailyard of the Left.

Meanwhile, George Douglas Brown began to be bored even with Oxford, even with Greek. He had thought other men's thoughts long enough. It was time he began thinking his own. He left with a Third, knowing well enough that at that time he was worth no more, "even by heavy cramming I could not have scored more than a second. . . . I shall have to spurt to get a third or a fourth." In fact, he did not even sit, on the first morning, and was almost dragged to the examination, in the afternoon, by the Master, who had taught him in Moral Philosophy at Glasgow, and had no mind to see the whole affair go by default. He went to London, dug his pen in his ink-pot, and began to write shockers, and stories for boys. This was as should be. He had to leave Scotland, to see it whole. He enjoyed London, its roar and its fury, "there is only one place to live," he would say as he came in from its surrounding ring; he loved Bayswater and its inhabitants. He loved to walk in the parks, which he thought much more alive than the "flat Oxford landscape." But all the time his mind ran on the rock whence he was hewn, the pit from which he was digged. At length he went to a cottage in Haslemere, Surrey, to sever himself from everything but memory. He bought a stock of large black-covered exercise books. There, one autumn night, he wrote the first chapter-heading of the book which had haunted him so long. By the following October it was published; and his work accomplished.

The House With the Green Shutters is two things: a drawing of Scottish life and character so intimate as to be quite effortless, and a tragedy above time or surroundings. Here was the fruit of his watching, of all his reading. Here was the shadowing of all the ways, the first Homeric phrase which ever struck through to his imagination. Here was the array and discipline of the great Greek dramatists; here, too, the Greek sense of terror in nature "lonely as a night in the hind-harvest," he once wrote, "when there's a cauld yellow licht alang the bare stibble and the wind takes an eerie sough aboot the gloaming." Here was the inexorable quality of the myths; nemesis, necessity, the stroke of the gods upon men, innocent or guilty.

Here, too, in the style of true tragedy, his small feckless characters— the silly mother, her son, hounded by the Furies, her sickly daughter —suddenly begin to take on the very shape of man at grips with destiny, and to challenge Omnipotence. "Ruin and murder," says Mrs. Gourlay, as her life falls about her grey head, "ruin and murder; and madness; and death at my nipple like a child! When will Ye be satisfied." Then she goes to her end, by her own hand, without a falter, while her daughter hurries behind to keep her company; but first she reads aloud, "giving it out as from a pulpit," of all things, the thirteenth chapter of First Corinthians:

"Though I speak with the tongues of men and of angels, and have not charity, I am become as sounding brass, or a tinkling cymbal."

George Douglas Brown had finished a master's job. He had achieved the katharsis, the purge of the spirit, the tranquillity at the far side of things. He had said what he came into the world to say. Then he died. At the time of his death he was only working upon *Hamlet*; notes without any great inspiration or discovery. It may well be that he was fortunate in the occasion of his death. He had written an act out of Aeschylus, in Ochiltree. It is not given to many to do as much.

8

CONTENTS

But first, I pray yow of youre curteisye,
That ye narette it nat my vileynye,
Thogh that I pleynly speke in this mateere,
To telle yow hir wordes and hir cheere,
Ne thogh I speke hir wordes properly.
For this ye knowen al so wel as I,
Whoso shal telle a tale after a man,
He moot reherce, as ny as evere he kan,
Everich a word, if it be in his charge,
Al speke he never so rudeliche or large;
Or elles he moot telle his tale untrewe,
Or feyne thyng, or fynde wordes newe.

—*The Prologue, Chaucer's* Canterbury Tales.

INTRODUCTION

When a novelist undertakes the writing of a biography he is apt to entangle fact with fiction. I should like, therefore, to make it clear that this book is a straightforward attempt to present Brown the man and the writer. Where dialogue occurs in the narrative I have been at pains to ensure that it actually took place as depicted, and in several instances I have been able to verify it from several independent sources. To maintain accuracy, I have omitted episodes about which there are conflicting statements: for example, the original cause of Brown's weak eyesight. Certain it is that he injured his eyes in boyhood, but it is impossible to ascertain whether the mishap was caused by home-made fireworks or an explosion in a school science experiment.

Among the many people who have given me generous and invaluable help I wish particularly to thank Miss Jessie M. McQuarrie, daughter of the late Mrs. Elizabeth McQuarrie (née M'Lennan), for the loan of Brown's notebooks, his long-lost study of *Hamlet*, and many other unpublished manuscripts; Mr. A. S. Neill, who abandoned his own intention to write a biography of Brown and very kindly presented me with all his material, including Mr. Francis Neilson's letters from America and Mrs. Tessa E. Bradley's albums of letters and cuttings; Sir Ernest Barker for his collection of letters; Professor Gilbert Murray for reminiscent notes; Mr. Tom Smith, grandson of Mr. John Smith, Coylton, for his late father's letters and recollections; Mrs. Isabella M'Lennan Russell for her sympathetic encouragement at all times; Mrs. Isabelle B. Gemmill (née Smith) and Miss Maggie Stevens for their Coylton schoolhouse memories; Reverend Hugh R. Thom for his late mother's reminiscences and Coylton anecdotes; Mrs. H. D. Wood (née Brown) for sending cuttings from South Africa; Mrs. Florence Rousseau Emanuel for albums and information concerning her late husband's friendship with Brown; Mr. David Maughan for sending letters from Australia; Miss Lettice Milne Rae for her late mother's correspondence with Brown; Mr. Charles Jackson for letters and books; Mr. Archibald D. Thomson for undertaking research at Glasgow University; Mr. John McVie for magazine cuttings; and Mr. J. Douglas Cairns, M.A., for the Frontispiece.

I also wish to thank the following people who, either in interviews or letters, gave much of their time and patience: Mr. and Mrs. William McCance; Mr. and Mrs. John Harper; Mrs. Jean Nimmo; Mrs. Janet S. Fraser; Mrs. Grace Mair; Miss Ninian Muir; Miss M. E. Allan; Mr. Robert R. Rusk; Mr. D. C. Gemmell; Mr. J. M. Begg; Mr. George Humphrey; Mr. James S. Stalker; Colonel D. C. Cameron; Mr. Archibald Jamieson; Mr. R. A. Rippon; Mr. Myer S. Nathan; Mr. Robert Bowman; Mr. Vernon Sommerfield; Mr. Montague B. Ashford; Mr. D. E. Easson; Mr. Robert Donald; Mr. J. Morrison; Mr. James Thomson; Mr. Oliver Crombie; Mr. P. W. Bennet; Mr. John M'Lennan Boyd; Mr. V. H. Collins; Mr. Archibald Menzies; Mr. J. P. Gibb; Colonel J. Jamieson; Mr. Jack Tosh and Mr. James MacIntyre. If I have overlooked any correspondent I trust that he or she will excuse the omission. It only remains for me to mention the warm-hearted assistance which I received from the late Mr. William Menzies, Edinburgh, and the late Mr. Robert Wright, Ochiltree; and the fact that in the summer of 1931 the late Lord Tweedsmuir (then John Buchan) gave me the account of Brown's humorous description of what might happen when a distinguished Scot returns home.

PART ONE

THE EARLY YEARS

I

With the passing years Ochiltree does not change much, and of a starry night or at Hallowe'en ghosts never lose their way about its quiet, familiar streets. For this couthie little Ayrshire village, slanting off the Cumnock road, is neither in the world nor out of it. Omnibuses and motor-cars have taken the places of brakes and gigs, and in the direction of Burnock Street new houses stand in regimented rows. But the railway station remains a mile and a half distant; folk still forgather at the ancient Cross; and there is an age-old tranquillity in the green kirkyard.

Mauchline and Auchinleck being close neighbours to the parish, this proud trio have been termed the very core o' Kyle. From the farm of Mossgiel Robert Burns saw "the corn fields o' Ochiltree"; while to Auchinleck House triumphant James Boswell brought Doctor Johnson before the completion of their Tour. History clings to Ochiltree itself as lichen to a slab of rock. At Ochiltree House, where the Burnock joins the Lugar at the Leddy's Green, John Knox found his second wife in seventeen-year-old Margaret Stewart, and, because she was of royal blood, he thereby set a pretty problem as to whether he was moved by politics or his libido. Over one hundred years later John Graham of Claverhouse married Jean Cochrane, the niece of Sir John Cochrane, who for a time was the proprietor of the same Auld Hoose. Other events more deeply affected the life of the people. From the Cross Sir Robert Colville and his men marched over the Border to stain Flodden Field with their blood, even as Covenanters from west and south afterwards rallied at the same point before marching north to ill-fated Rullion Green on the blue Pentlands.

Today the rattle of swords is heard no more; instead there is the sad sound of a whetstone against a scythe; and when horses' hoofs drum along the roadway, it is but huntsmen in quest of the brush. To the villagers the local flower show is more important than front page headlines, while the presence of a stranger causes keener speculation than the outcome of the latest diplomatic mission. The cynic, unaware of his own short-sightedness, is quick to gibe at such parochialism; but in this very trait lies the warm, human intimacy of every small community.

If Ochiltree is content in its own backwater, it was even more leisurely, with its long rows of cottages stretching up the brae to Gallowlea, during the last century. The snuff-box makers and tailors would pause at their work to watch a waggonette bound for Ayr, eleven and a half miles to the west. They might see the minister in the back seat, and then, my certie! tongues would wag: what was taking him to Ayr?

Towards the end of 1868 they were not unduly excited about the General Election or the issue of the disestablishment of the Irish Church. The fact that Gladstone was to become Prime Minister for the first time did not shake the Cross. There were other matters of more pressing interest: the curling prospects on Plaid Loch and the annual reunion of Ochiltree Schoolfellows on Hogmanay. Everyone knew, of course, that the woman Gemmell—Sarah Gemmell—was going to have a bairn.

A little above medium height, she was shapely in spite of being big-boned, with strong, plain features, which were softened by an unblemished skin and reddish hair parted in the middle and drawn carefully behind the ears. More important was the flame of Celtic fire that often burned in her blue-grey eyes. As she walked up the brae, she carried her head high; too high, to be sure, for some people's liking. More shame and less pride would have befitted this illiterate daughter of an Irish labourer; but it was plain that she expected no sympathy and despised pity. When an unmarried woman becomes pregnant, there is often much speculation about the sire, but in Sarah Gemmell's case there was no doubt, and lascivious rumour was denied its fling. Brown o' Drumsmudden was responsible for her condition.

He was a coarse, rough-tongued man, George Douglas Brown, although there was no want of intelligence in him. He was short and lacked that solid build with which farmers are generally associated. He had dark, sharp features and a fine brow. He was elemental, with his feet deep in the Ayrshire soil. "He's clever, too," the bodies would have told you; "for they're a brainy lot, the Broons."

His father, George Brown, married Margaret (or Peggy) Nicholson, and to them at the farm of Benthead in the parish of Sorn were born seven children. Alec (1802) and John (1805) died in infancy, but there was more smeddum in the others who followed: John Nicholson (1806), Mungo (1809), Francis Nicholson (1811), George Douglas (1813), and Helen Hood (1815).

It was a hard life at Benthead, with mean food, grudging earth, and the snell winds of winter fair like to strip the flesh from their bones. They knew that to escape from such drudgery and heartbreak they must first seek knowledge, and consequently, in the shelter of a dry-stone dyke or by the light of a kitchen candle, they

16

taught themselves to read and write. John Nicholson's tombstone in Sorn kirkyard illustrates what this meant. "A self-taught man," it records. "He supported himself from the age of eight, attended Sorn School only eighteen months, devoted his leisure hours from daily toil to the pursuit of self-acquired knowledge." True, Mungo got no further than farming Bogwood, near Mauchline, and becoming factor to the laird of Nether-Place; but John and Francis were more ambitious. Leaving their native country, they established themselves as teachers of English to some of the first families in France. John attained the position of Professor of English at the College of St. Barbe in Paris, and at his death in 1841 he left the incomplete manuscript of a political treatise. Ten years later Francis returned to Scotland and occupied many posts, including French master at George Watson's College, Edinburgh, before his death in 1865.

Helen married Ivy Campbell Sloan, a Scot who, fortunately for her brother George, amassed a fortune in Australia. For George alone remained at Benthead. Left fatherless while still a boy, he was forced to help his mother to complete the lease of the farm. On leaving Benthead and still looking after his mother, he settled in Sorn and did odd work with horse and cart. Dour and independent, he was a man with iron in his soul. When it appeared, indeed, as if he must remain a jobbing contractor, Helen and her husband returned from abroad and built a home for themselves at Catrine. There they took old Mrs. Brown, and George, with their financial aid, was enabled in the early sixties to become a farmer at Drumsmudden. His farm was not extensive, being about two hundred acres of rough grazing, with a byre for thirty cows and outbuildings for the production of butter and cheese; but it gave him standing, and it pleased him to know that men referred to him as 'Smudden.

In the district around Ochiltree he soon became a character. Never had anyone been known to swear with such blasphemous and colorific invention. Stand up to him, and he admired you; cringe, and he despised you. He was fond of a dram and good company, and if business took him to Cumnock or Ayr it was invariably late before he set out on his homeward journey. His trap had bright yellow wheels, and Mr. H. B. M'Lellan, who was agent of the Cumnock branch of the Bank of Scotland, laughingly told him that his machine was altogether too kenspeckle. "As soon as people catch a glimpse of it," he pointed out, "they say, 'There's 'Smudden awa' hame—late as usual!'" Brown declared that he did not care a damn; but, when he next met M'Lellan there was triumph in his eyes. "By God!" he roared. "Ye were richt, banker. But d'ye ken what I've done? I've painted the wheels as black as a coffin. The deevil himsel' wullna ken them noo!" He had his own vivid gift of expression, and on one occasion, when he had a guest who' was making a very poor meal, he said, "Man, stick in like a soo[1] in a pratie[2] pit, and no' sit there mumpin'[3] like a rabbit." Yet there was more to Brown's talk than mere robustness, and from time to time he gave evidence of being well informed and deeply read. Long afterwards a neighbouring farmer, with whom he had had many quarrels, remarked, "He was the most original man I ever met." In actual business he was very quiet and reserved, almost watchful, a side of his nature that was aptly described by the Cumnock banker when he termed him "a still man."

To his farm came Sarah Gemmell, and even if he lacked polish Brown knew a comely woman when he saw one. Although she was a skilled milker, he might not have complained if she had not been. Her tawny hair and smooth skin, ay, everything about her stirred him. She had a character to match his own: the same unyielding pride, quick temper, and ability to recognize and admire strength in another. She possessed, too, the much more fateful trait of Celtic sensitivity. Thus they were thrown together, the hard, talented farmer and the ignorant, warm-hearted peasant woman, in the environment of this quiet countryside.

The outcome was inevitable. Sarah realized that she was pregnant, and when she told 'Smudden, she fully expected that he would fulfil his duty and marry her. He himself was prepared to do so, but when his sister Helen and her husband appeared, they were furious that he had allowed himself to become involved with a—an Irish servant. Had they not financed him and done all in their power to give him a real chance in life? "Hell, ay." Brown reflected darkly. "That's true enough." But was this a time to cast it up? Was it just to be torn between his indebtedness to them and his duty to Sarah? While he deliberated, the domestic pot came to the boil. Helen could not conceal her feelings from Sarah, and while she acknowledged that her brother would have to pay for his mistake, there was scornful condescension in her manner. Sarah hated to be patronized, and in her highly strung condition she was swift to anger. Who did the Browns think they were? She was not going to tie herself to a man on sufferance. Inwardly she hoped that 'Smudden would assert himself, but for once he did not demonstrate his force of character, and she whipped herself to fresh fury. If only she had remained calm and dignified, the marriage would have taken place; as it was, interference and her own temper wrecked the prospect.

Knowing at the back of her mind that she was defeated, Sarah then packed her belongings, banged out of the farmhouse, and took the road to Ochiltree. For the time being she lived in a little white-washed cottage on the brae. As the weeks went by, she displayed a philosophic fortitude that proved to friend and enemy alike that

[1] Sow. [2] Potato. [3] Nibbling.

she was content to meet her destiny. Nothing mattered now that she could feel the child stirring in her womb.

And on 26th January 1869, her son was born. While he lay with red, puckered face beside her, the news quickly passed from door to door. "Sarah Gemmell's had her bairn. . . . What'll 'Smudden have to say now?"

But he did not have very much to say. Little over a fortnight later he and Sarah visited the local registrar's office, and there, in black and white, the brand was laid upon their child.

2

It did not take Sarah Gemmell long to estimate her plight. She was thirty-six, a more than usually awkward age at which to have an illegitimate child. Yet as she nursed the baby at her breast she felt no resentment towards him; instead, a warm tenderness permeated her whole body. She did not possess the intellect to indulge in metaphysical inquiry into origins and ends. All that she understood was that here was flesh of her flesh, her real reason for being.

For four years the brae was her son's world. Everyone knew the lively, dark-eyed laddie as Geordie; everyone, that is to say, who recognized his mother. Most of the villagers became tolerant and even sympathetic towards her; they admired her independence and blamed 'Smudden for failing to make her his wife. Others, rigid in their morality and forgetful of charity, preferred to ignore her. But Geordie did not notice their contemptuous faces. Great, feathery-legged Clydesdales, clip-clopping past the door, were more exciting than human beings. Nevertheless, he soon found that there was more to life than horses. One morning, after his mother had given his face an extra hard scrubbing, he was taken to Mr. Aird's school and placed in the infants' class.

To give him more opportunity Sarah knew that she must find the wherewithal, and as dairy work was her sole accomplishment, she secured a position as "bower" or "boo'er" to a Coylton farmer, James Dickson o' Duchray, this meaning that she rented his cows at so much a head per annum.

Like its inhabitants, the parish of Coylton and its eight hamlets, Coylton, Hillhead, Joppa, Woodside, Craighall, Barbieston, Little-mill, and Rankinstone, are rich in character. A strip of country about twelve miles long with an average breadth of two miles, its scenery varies from the low-lying fertility of the north-west to the bleakness of the Craigs of Kyle in the south-east. Flowing along the eastern border, the Water of Coyle turns at Bonnyton and brawls north towards the Laigh Brig o' Kyll. Here it runs westwards over

19

the dancing linn behind Sundrum and on between leafy banks and holms to its union with the River Ayr below Milncraig on the far boundary.

For Geordie, then, the flitting to Duchray, five and three quarter miles west of Ochiltree, was high adventure. The farm yard was oblong, with an exciting hayloft immediately to the right of the entrance; along the left ran the byre, with outbuildings on the opposite side; while at the end, adjoining the milk-house, stood the room and kitchen in which he and his mother were to live. A short distance apart was the farmer's residence, Duchray House. James Dickson was a just, upright man, although to small boys there was about him an awe-inspiring quality. Scorning an overcoat even in winter, he invariably wore a black suit and top hat, and as he stalked about on his long legs he was not unlike one of the rooks that foraged in his own fields. He was shrewd, and he knew the worth of Sarah Gemmell. Whatever there was to say against her, she was a skilled dairy worker, a thrifty, hard-working woman, who was obviously devoted to her bairn.

In May 1875, Geordie was enrolled at Coylton School, conveniently situated less than a mile away. As he walked down the Manse Road, which turned and twisted between high hawthorn hedges white with blossom, he passed the village pump on his right and the manse and glebe of the Reverend James Glasgow to the left. Beyond the kirkyard and Caley Hay's house, he lingered by the open door of Wullie Campbell's Smiddy. Firstly, the heavy, sickly scent of hawthorn . . . now the acrid smell of hot iron. Was there any other place like this Manse Road? But the schoolhouse lay ahead, dourly waiting to receive him, and he went on, a quaint little figure in a waistcoat and jacket buttoned to his neck and wearing trousers that were much too long.

The dominie, John Smith, scrutinized him keenly. So this was Sarah Gemmell's love-bairn. He noted the head, big enough to have brains all right, the broad, high brow, determined little jaw, and firm mouth. And the eyes? They did not waver; they held his with . . . what? Resentment? No, the laddie was not sullen. Suspicion? A wee bit, perhaps, as if he had already been hurt at some time or other. But John Smith was not satisfied that he judged him whole. He had a feeling that here might be an old head on young shoulders. Time alone would tell. If Geordie Broon had it in him, he would bring it out. There was no doubt about that.

A "Hutton Bursar" of Hutton Hall Academy in the parish of Carlaverock, Dumfriesshire, John Smith had assisted when seventeen at Annan Burgh School. A year later, in 1851, he had successfully competed for entrance into the Normal School, Glasgow, and had remained there as a student until his appointment to Blairmains School in the autumn of 1852. In those days the ambition of all young teachers was to open a parish school, and in January 1855, on seeing Coylton advertised, he had promptly applied. Following his appointment, he had opened in April of that year, and thus began his real work. A happy man with a great zest for life, he could have gone far in his profession—nay, in his calling—but there was no need. He had the wisdom to know that, no matter where he went, he would never be more complete than he was here in the auld schoolhouse o' Coylton. He had an ideal wife in Elizabeth McLennan, and, in addition to teaching, he was clerical handyman to the whole parish. He measured fields into lots for public sale, assisted farmers with their accounts, and was Registrar of Births, Marriages, and Deaths. While he made his pupils work hard, he never spared himself. For instance, children who were backward in Euclid received private tuition for an hour each morning before school began. In after years it was not only a long line of doctors, lawyers, ministers, colonial officials, bankers, and teachers who remembered his faithful service; at his jubilee in 1905 miners and farm servants left the pits and steadings to meet at Coylton to do him honour. One of the finest dominies who ever paced a schoolroom floor, he was indeed their Mr. Greatheart.

Under his influence, Geordie's progress was rapid. He had a quickness of mind that, with the exception of mathematics, made light of the curriculum. Later on he displayed an outstanding gift of expression, and a week seldom passed but the dominie read one of his essays to his class-mates. When he carried home his prizes, Sarah was pathetically proud, but some people sourly observed, "It's weel kent where he gets his brains." John Smith alone saw deeper. He was aware of a rare spark that would either burn itself out or would one day burst into flame.

Known as "Grog" to the other boys, Geordie brought an eager enthusiasm to their games, but in the main he preferred the companionship of books. The first volume that he ever possessed—a copy of the *Poetical Works* of Robert Burns which had been given to him by an old herd—remained his favourite. He even made tentative attempts at verse. There was inspiration in the knowledge that the bard had been an Ayrshire man, breathing Ayrshire air, and that he had lived his tragedy and his triumph against this same familiar landscape.

With his high order of intelligence and sensibility, however, a great deal more than poetry occupied Geordie's mind. When he realized that other laddies and lassies had two parents, he put the questions that Sarah had dreaded. Why did he not have a father? Why was he called George Douglas Brown? She told him simply and honestly, hoping that the knowledge would fade, but he never forgot anything. He not only picked up oaths and curses; he understood what they meant. The whole art of swearing was to use the words in their proper sense. He heard rough-tongued men refer to him as "'Smudden's bastard," and there was no doubt what the hateful term implied. Because his mother was unmarried, he was not the same as other children. And when he saw 'Smudden driving through Coylton, his face clouded. In his deep, secretive manner, he hated the small, dark man, hated him for being his father and yet for not being his father.

Fortunately, to counteract his brooding introversion Geordie had a tremendous resilience of spirit, and Coylton parish, with its worthies, was an enchanting place in which to live.

Most people were kindly, and he was never turned away from their doors. He was fully alive to the rich gallery of character around him. Every eccentricity, every foible and trick of speech were stamped upon his brain. He had, for his age, an uncanny insight into human nature. He saw it, too, against the fascinating background of the countryside. He had a quick ear for the mavis singing high up in a storm-tossed tree, and when he was guddlin' trout in Coylton Burn he noticed kingfishers flashing by like sapphires in the sunlight. To Coylton, he was a bright laddie, with plenty of high spirits; but he had queer moods, and in their grip he invariably sought refuge in the hayloft at Duchray. There he found the solitude he craved. He was alone, so utterly alone that, when footsteps or voices sounded in the yard, he felt as if he were a being apart. He read classics and penny dreadfuls with equal avidity; for words and phrases delighted him. When darkness crept down, he lighted a stump of candle and read on until his eyes smarted. He did not realize that he was putting a dangerous strain upon them. Nothing mattered but the printed page, and often, when Sarah called him to bed, he did not hear. Amongst the straw, with mice scampering unheeded across the floor, he dwelt in his own private and exciting world.

At school he was now outstanding, and by 1881 he had passed through the six elementary standards. Even his childhood sweetheart, little Agnes Mercer, did not distract him from his desire to learn. His essays, very often embellished with original verse, continued to impress the dominie; but there were times when John Smith tugged his short beard and speculated upon what would become of his strange, brilliant pupil. By a remarkable abnegation of self, Sarah Gemmell had scrimped and saved to clothe, feed, and educate him, but there was a limit to what a woman in her circumstances could do.

Geordie himself knew the full extent of his mother's sacrifice. Every long, hard day in the byre and milk-house, where she frequently worked bare-footed, was dedicated to his support. When money was scarcer than usual, he never went hungry, and yet by some miracle she kept free from debt. Despite the stigma of his birth, she taught him, by her example, charity and self-respect, the result being that there existed more than a sympathetic understanding between them. Almost subconsciously they had placed in each other a complete and sacred trust that was, in very truth, a spiritual bond.

None the less, Geordie felt that his mother had borne too much, and he insisted that, for the present at any rate, he must find work. In spite of her dismay, Sarah agreed, for she was fully aware that facts had to be faced. The world, their world, was changing.

3

Geordie was just another laddie looking for a job, and he had no choice. To the pit-head at Trabboch, where one of the first conveyer belts in Scotland had been installed, he went to pick dirt and stones from coal. To those who scrabbled alongside him prose and poetry were unimportant, and during the midday breaks he slipped off alone to eat his "piece" and to pore over a book. Once, his gaffer came upon him and casually asked what he was reading. Geordie told him, and the man stared in astonishment. He understood neither books nor this sallow, dark-eyed laddie; but he was certain that the pit-head was no place for one who loaded his mind with so heavy a weight. Then he shrugged, feeling slightly foolish, and walked away. After all, what could *he* do about it?

When he returned home in the evenings, his face black and his hands blistered and bleeding, Geordie showed a cheerful front to his mother. He did not let her suspect that he saw himself as an outcast, a misfit, in the wilderness to which society had condemned him. He believed that he was doomed to a life of degradation against a background of cruelty, poverty, and ugliness: a bleak and terrible prospect when in his heart he detested ugliness and cruelty most of all. Then, at the thought, his lips tightened and a dour look came into his eyes. He recalled the words that Shakespeare put into the mouth of Polonius. "This above all—to thine own self be true." Ay, reflected Geordie, there was a maxim for anybody who called himsel' a man. He derived comfort, too, from the words of his own Robert Burns.

> "*He'll hae misfortunes great an' sma',*
> *But ay a heart aboon them a'.*"

Let that suffice. He was what he was, and he would go his own way.

Eventually his mother gave up her work as "boo'er," and to Geordie the departure from Duchray was a tremendous wrench.

23

He knew that there was part of him here that nothing would ever take away.

For a while he and his mother lived at Kayshill Farm, Trabboch, but she was convinced that "craw-picking" at the pit-head was not good enough for him, and they accordingly moved to Ochiltree. There, although thankful to be freed from Trabboch, Geordie underwent a period of agonising self-torment. If he saw two people standing together on the brae and glancing casually in his direction, he felt sure that they were discussing him, that the one was re-marking to the other, "Ay, that's Geordie Broon . . . 'Smudden's bastard, ye ken." The charity of outlook that his mother had im-bued in him was at war with bitterness and suspicion. He was the badge of lust, the personification of what smug, self-righteous people, with gloating eyes and smacking lips, called sin. And his hatred for the man who was responsible, the man whose name was his, burned within him with a new intensity.

In the village school, under Mr. Andrew, he proved that he was anxious to work. Yet when he saw boys hurrying off to the train to go to the Academy, he realized that, if he were of their company, he would be terror-stricken. They would talk about him and have everyone else—strangers—talking about him behind his back. His sensitivity (both a blessing and a curse) made his emotional ex-periences larger than life.

Three months later fortune seemed to smile when his mother secured a temporary position as housekeeper at Cronberry Farm on the Auchinleck estate. The tenants, Howatson Bros, had moved to Patna, and it was arranged that she should stay until their successor took over. Unhappily, the village of Cronberry was not another Coylton. Small and ugly, this huddle of miners' houses was situated where the fertile country around Cumnock gave way to the dreich moorland that stretched towards Muirkirk.

Periodically Geordie suffered from a sore throat, and this place, with its rawness, seemed likely to suit him ill. For over nine months, however, he attended school. The master, James Hyslop, was an unimaginative, well-meaning, hard-working man. He expected his pupils to repeat the populations of various Scottish towns and other dry statistics, and if they failed to do so he relied upon a leather tawse to stir their wits. How unlike the Coylton dominie! For truancy or wanton mischief John Smith favoured a supple hazel rod cut from Sundrum Woods, but he never punished a pupil for dullness. As he watched Hyslop's flailing arm, Geordie was not intimidated. His prodigious memory kept him out of trouble, so that he could afford to regard the master with cynical amusement. Yet every hour in school was so futile that he was glad when the new tenant arrived at Cronberry Farm. "I'm leaving Hyslop's school," he told John Harper, one of his friends. "He canna teach me onything; mair like me teaching him."

Fortunately the Coylton dominie had not forgotten Geordie. By the clash of the countryside he had kept trace of him and his mother, and he knew that, if the laddie's gifts were not to be wasted, some action would soon have to be taken. As before, he pondered over Sarah's financial resources, and finally, to settle his mind, he paid her a visit. Geordie was there, a searching look in his dark, luminous eyes. And Sarah? She was more drawn and care-worn than she had been at Duchray, but her Celtic fire still burned within her. Of course, she wanted Geordie to carry on with his education. She would make ways and means.

Promising to talk to Mr. Maybin, rector of the Academy, John Smith seized the first opportunity to do so. William Maybin, a graduate of Trinity College, Dublin, was a robust, vigorous man, with greying reddish hair and a full, bushy beard. To teaching, especially to his beloved classics, he brought fanatical enthusiasm. His critics sometimes whispered that, if a pupil was not a classical scholar, Maybin had no interest in him, but there was an essential bigness about this Ulsterman, and on a later occasion, when he recalled pupils who had been killed in the South African War, tears ran down his cheeks.

Knowing his man, the Coylton dominie did not mince matters. He told the blunt truth about Sarah and her struggle against poverty, and how Geordie's outstanding ability was in danger of coming to a dead end. As a result an interview was arranged, and Geordie and his mother duly appeared at the Academy. Sarah was awestruck, but the Irishman in Maybin soon put her at ease. To his questions Geordie gave quick, intelligent answers. He liked this hearty, bearded man, and somehow the thought of entering the Academy already seemed less frightening. Then Maybin went on to explain about fees. Aware that £2 12s. 6d. was a formidable sum for Sarah to find each term, he indicated that he would lighten it. This was indeed a fortunate gesture, for without such generosity Geordie's schooling could scarcely have continued.

For convenience and economy Sarah realized that it would be necessary to live near Ayr, and without much trouble she secured a vacant cottage at Crofthead. No one was very surprised at this turn of events. It was to a place like the Academy that her big rummle o' a laddie belonged. Bedding and sticks of furniture were stacked on a farm cart—"a gey puir flitting", as noticing bodies observed—and once more Geordie and his mother slowly moved across the Ayrshire countryside, away from Cronberry, past Ochiltree, through Coylton, and westwards to Crofthead and the future.

essays, Mr. Cormack handed it to the rector. Maybin let his wife see it, and she was so enthusiastic that she remarked upon its worth to Geordie. "Oh," he said confidently, "I can easily write a far better one." How he did so is recorded in Maybin's own words.

"George came under my own personal instruction in the Vth class. I was accustomed to gauge the quality of the pupils by an essay to begin with; and, on the occasion when he joined the class, the subject which I set for a home-written essay was 'Burns.' Brown's essay was quite a unique performance, standing absolutely alone, without any second, in point of merit. The thought was so mature, and the expression so finished that the essay read like a magazine article rather than the crude production of a schoolboy. I was staggered for the moment. 'What book have you read for this essay?' I asked the writer. 'None,' he answered, with some edge. 'Is this essay absolutely your own work?' 'Yes, sir,' he answered, with surprise and some perceptible irritation. I had obviously wronged him by the suggestion (it was no more) of a suspicion, and I put the matter right by a frank apology. One other incident in connection with his essays I remember. I had proposed as a subject 'The High Street of Ayr on a Saturday Night.' Brown's essay was a perfect portraiture of the scene. In particular I recollect that he drew a crowd to hear the song of an Irish ballad singer. The ballad was his own. It was thoroughly Irish. I only wish I could remember it. What I do remember is that the whole picture was instinct with movement."

Perhaps because he had a clever family of his own, two boys and four girls, Maybin knew very well how to get round young people. In reminiscent mood, Geordie often told how one afternoon he was put down step by step to the foot of the class. He plunged deep into the sulks until Maybin, in a soft, gracious Irish tone, brought him out with "Come now, George."

Above all Maybin was a born teacher, and although, when he held forth in that great beard of his, Greek became a living, splendid language, he gave his gifts, rich voice, humour, enthusiasm and vitality, to every subject on hand. Small wonder that Geordie sat there, eyes aflame, spellbound and inspired before him: he had discovered his perfect mentor.

5

On 9th November 1885, Geordie wrote another essay on Burns. Rather annoyed this time, Maybin scribbled above the title, "This was not the subject appointed"; but to be fair he awarded ninety-two marks.

"The key-note to Burns' genius" (wrote Geordie) "is his deep knowledge of humanity in general, and of the workings of the Scotch heart in particular. His own noble nature was continually breaking through whatever clouds adverse circumstances had gathered around it. There is nothing overstrained, nothing far-fetched, nothing egotistic, in the productions of his rustic strength. Mankind to his deep-thinking soul was an open book, from which he read to the world his lessons of true manly nobility. . . . Burns may be said to have died from want of sympathy. . . . He gave the brightest efforts of his genius to the world, and found no one who was able thoroughly to know him, and realize him. The people could appreciate his genius, but what could they give in return? Absolutely nothing. Burns was an alien in his own land, as re-garded the majority of his fellowmen. True, he could, and did hold, converse with his own Scotland's grey old hills, and her lakes, and her rivers; and he communed with the brackens on her mountains, and the daisies in her fields, and he watched the heart-stirrings of her peasantry; but when he poured his golden grain at the feet of the litterateurs they could make him no intellectual recompense."

In Class VI in the following year Geordie tackled Tam o' Shanter, and in the course of this essay he declared:

"Burns never wrote out of his circle. His circle was 'God's uni-verse, and what tasks there are in it'; and instead of leaving it to create ideal men and women, he painted the men and women of his own time, as he saw them, and as they were. And thus it is that we find characters such as Tam o' Shanter and 'rough, rude, ready-witted Rankine' scattered so abundantly over his writings. Such men were, for Burns, imbued with a deep and peculiar interest. They were the representatives of an age that was passing away, the last of the old school of Scottish farmers, hard-riding and hard-drinking, yet pawky and intelligent withal. Every thew and sinew of Burns's body was interlaced and interpenetrated with their old-world lore, their pawky humour, their patriotism, and their rugged independence; and the hand, drawing its material from the fulness of the heart, handed down to us those cameos of Scottish literature of which the brightest is Tam o' Shanter.

"Every line is brimming with humour, and his descriptive power, especially in the scene at the Auld Kirk, has never been equalled. The introduction of the Satanic piper at the midnight revel of the witches must ever be regarded as one of the brightest strokes of Burns's genius. It is when treating of the great enemy of mankind, that all the intense humanity of Burns's character as a poet and as a man comes into play. He 'humanized' even the devil. Imagine the Satan of John Milton 'garrin'' the roof of Pandemonium 'dirl' with a strathspey, while his followers foot it merrily to his enlivening air. By sheer power of imagination Milton compels us to study the character of his Satan: by the more genial humour of Burns's genius we are forced to laugh at his conception of 'Nick wi' the resistit phiz.'"

Considering it to be worth ninety-two, Maybin wrote, "I wish you had gone more into detail in criticizing the poem. What you have said is well said—very well. A fuller essay of equal merit as regards treatment would have merited ninety-five, say." He also criticized the second paragraph. "The ideal, too, is surely in God's Universe in the largest sense; the thought of man exists as a fact in God's Universe and as a factor of it. Surely God's Universe is in some respects wider than the 'circle' of the Ayrshire ploughman and poet."

Maybin's remarks were invariably pungent. To an essay on Goldsmith's *Deserted Village*, he gave ninety-five and counselled, "Take care: guard against a certain vagueness of expression which arises from misty conception. Get your pictures clear before your own mind; then try to transfer them to paper. As it is, you have a certain pleasure in nursing a mystic, dreamy kind of reflection or imagination; and this induces a corresponding vagueness of expression. Nothing is gained by obscurity of any kind. BE CLEAR THEREFORE."

While he undoubtedly valued and endeavoured to follow such advice, Geordie remained unpredictable. If a subject did not appeal to him, he simply selected one of his own choice. There was in Class V the outstanding case of an essay which ended:

"It is the winter of the year 1666. Night has fallen on the streets of London, and the fierce gusts of a rising storm sweep, with a wild whistling noise, along the deserted thoroughfares. Onward speeds the shrieking wind, buffeting intoxicated cavaliers, and causing crazy wooden tenements to creak and groan in the blast. Gathering all its forces, it dashes against a humble, though strongly built, dwelling, and, for a moment, drowns the voices of two men, who are engaged in conversation within. The elder is a man with whom Time has evidently dealt unkindly, for, though his haughty bearing bespeaks an unconquerable will, his hair is silvery, and never again to those great lustrous eyes will return

> *Day, or the sweet approach of even and morn,*
> *Or sight of vernal bloom or summer rose,*
> *Or flocks or herds, or human face divine.*

That man is John Milton, and his companion is his Quaker friend Ellwood. And there, while the storm rages without, he relates, in tones rich with the melody of his youthful associations, why he attempted to sing of the mysteries of Creation, of the Godhead, and of the horrors of Hell. He tells of youthful projects, of his 'long

30

choosing and beginning late', and of one memorable spring morning, when he first resolved to sing

> *Of man's first disobedience, and the fruit*
> *Of that forbidden tree, whose mortal taste*
> *Brought death into the world.*

And then he shows how Satan, like that great bridge of his imagination which joins the Mundane Universe to Hell, is the link between the Finite and the Infinite, between the Known and the Unknown, and how his part in the Universal plan, as set forth in *Paradise Lost*, is to be the expounder of all these vague questionings, regarding existence anterior to the creation of the Mundane Universe,

> *Which dodge*
> *Conception to the very bourne of Heaven,*
> *Then leave the naked brain."*

"Shall I give you nought or one hundred?" wrote Maybin underneath. "o, if I judge by the subject-matter which has only the most distant connection with the subject set for the essay—'the Character of Satan'—one hundred, if I judge by the style, which, for a boy, is, I am bound to admit, beyond ordinary merit. My dear Brown, I must again solemnly press you to 'keep to the text.' You are not bound to find a subject: what you have to do is to write well on the subject proposed—to say what you have to say in a style suited to the subject. The purpose of all writing is to mirror exact thought in clear expression. You know I have great hopes of you if you will only have the patience of self-discipline: otherwise I cannot hope or promise anything. Let me see that you understand in your *heart* the advice which from the heart I give you. W.M. P.S. I will be illogical enough to give you ninety-five."

During the summer vacation of 1886 Maybin arranged for Geordie to spend a holiday in Ireland, the result being an essay in which he gave an account of his experiences. He related how he had climbed Slieve Crube, about seven miles from Ballymurphy, and how, during a downpour, he had been given food and shelter in the home of an Irish labourer.

"Meanwhile" (continued Geordie) "the tea and home-baked bread had been rapidly disappearing, and Pat began to discuss, as a topic of interest, the agrarian disturbances in Ireland.

"'Ye see,' he remarked, 'there are some vices that resimble vartues enthoirely, an' an Oirishman's got three av these in partikler. In the fust place, he's quick in his instincks, an' the same feelin' that meks him do a kind act quickly, meks him hit his neighbour a bat on the head on the laste provocation. Thin, he's

31

moighty susciptable in every pint, good an' bad, an' whin you blarney him into belavin' that sich a wan's aginst him, he's up in the air loike a barrel av gunpowther. Agin, on the other han', he's a stickler fur his cause, an', whin his cause is his counthry's good, sure he's tinderwood, an' no mistake. Now, a craythur like that is as asy led right as wrong, but, whin roarin' spakers an' flamin whisky git hould av him, it's nuthin' but blood an' murther, an' it's devil a lie I'm spakin'.'"

Although his eyes continued to trouble him, Geordie was reading as voraciously as ever. Again and again Maybin would query a quotation with "Have you read Emerson?" or "Have you read Carlyle?" And Geordie would smile to himself. He had read more widely than the rector realized. He wrote with ease upon "Satan's Expulsion from Heaven," "The Creation of the Starry Universe," "Satan's Arrival at the Newly-created Universe," "Milton's Theory of the Universe," and "The Circumstances Attending the Fall of Man." To "A Contrast between the Characters of the Monk and the Clerk of Oxford," he brought a note of authority.

"Chaucer, like all character-painters of the highest genius, is gifted with a wonderful power of condensation." ("It is hardly condensation," said Maybin.) "He is often able, in a few words, to hit off the essential peculiarities of the character he is describing. This is a necessary law of his genius, for it naturally follows that a lightning-like power of reception should be accompanied by an equally prompt and vivid power of reproduction. In addition to this, Chaucer is endowed with another faculty, to which, we may safely assert, is owing the exquisite finish and delicacy of touch that lends such a charm to his characters. He is a logical painter. In all his portraits, we find that he has drawn the general outline in the first few lines, and from thence has proceeded, by the most delicate touches, to fill in the minor tints of light and shade. The qualities here referred to are both exhibited in their highest perfection in his portraits of the Monk, and of the Clerk of Oxford. The quiet sarcasm of the opening lines in the Monk shadows forth completely the picture he is proceeding to work out with such a masterly hand. And in the opening lines of the Clerk of Oxford, we have a complete picture of the student's assiduous application to study, in spite of his threadbare poverty. The individual peculiarities of the men, moreover, are hit off in the after description, by words and phrases, which are possessed of extraordinary power and vividness in themselves, and which blend in singular unity with the general idea of the character."

Maybin, while condemning "a tendency to plethoric expression here and there," adjudged the complete essay "remarkably good." In another one, "The Lady of the Lake," which was written shortly afterwards, Geordie revealed strong and independent views.

"I enjoy a good dinner, but I don't want to receive instructions from Betty in the culinary art; I admire a fine sunset, but I want no scientist to come up and lecture me on the principles of atmospheric colouring; and if poetry is a bright streak amid the darker shades of life's picture, I want no critic to disillusionize me by any 'hewing and hacking' whatsoever. Critics deal only with the secondary aspect of poetry. They rub out the bright colours and show us the blank bare canvas. And for this reason Scott needs little criticism. In him we find none of the cunning subtleties which distinguish the tight-laced, well-balanced, antithetical rhymers

> *Who stop a hungry chaplain in his grace*
> *To talk of unities of time and place.*

"In The Lady of the Lake, as in all Scott's writings, we find illustrated the sentiment to which he gave utterance amid the wild solitude of the Border moorlands. 'I think I should die,' he exclaimed, 'if I did not get away from the garden scenery of Edinburgh to gaze on my own wild wastes, at least once a year.' In Scott, therefore, though we find neither Byronic raptures, nor clearcut Pope-like precision, we find the mountains and the lakes, the men and the women of Scotland, painted with a genuine Scotch love of the beautiful. Scott's lines, moreover, 'express no meagre shrinking, no unlaced excess.' His mind reflects his pictures as clearly and distinctly as did Loch Katrine 'the tufted knolls' that were traced in her dark-blue mirror.''

Maybin let himself go. "Criticism rather calls one's attention to colour among other things. Do you not mean that criticism is conscious, sometimes self-conscious; and the unconscious is frequently greater and better than the conscious? Had you considered the subject in its totality, I should have given you as near 100 as possible. I give you 92 to call your attention to a characteristic defect. You will consider this in a friendly spirit. You must prune—not destroy and not deface and not stint—but *prune* your style. P.S. "Putare" to think is literally to *prune*. verb. sap. N.B. Your illustrations are sometimes a little too homespun or homely. For a time avoid Scotch."

Avoid Scotch! And only a week or two before, in "Our Soldiers and Sailors", Geordie had gone all Irish!

Beginning with a lively picture of market-day in Ayr, he had gone on to describe the departure of a company of soldiers, one of whom had sung the following lay of the family Mahone.

> *I'm an Irishman, lads, as ye know,*
> *A Paddy in blood and in bone,*
> *For long ere the deluge did flow,*
> *My fathers were kings in Tyrone.*

c 33

When the big flood began to git frisky,
My ancestor ould Maurice Mahone
Shipped himself—and a keg of good whisky
In a tight little craft of his own.
But thro' not steering right, with his swilling,
A big tree smashed a hole in his boat ;
(And, it's troth, I'd be moighty unwilling
The language he used then, to quote.)
So he tossed up an ould Irish shilling,
Which in value is now worth a groat,
And leaving her rapidly filling,
Astride of his keg went afloat.
Right onward then paddled bold Paddy,
Nor once in his voyage did flinch
Till, coming to Mount Aednavaddy,
He moored, without cable or winch.
(Of this hill a queer fact's to be noted,
That it's crumbled away, inch by inch,
Since the day when ashore Maurice floated
Till the battle of Ballynahinch.)
And so, boys, in honour of Maurice,
'Tis a mark of the family Mahone,
As fixed as firm Plaster of Paris,
That they never make murmur or moan
So long as they've lots of good whisky,
That strength'ner of blood and of bone,
That has kept them so hearty and frisky
Since the days when they ruled in Tyrone.

Almost as an afterthought, Geordie had added a tribute to "our own Jack Tar," and, eyes twinkling, Maybin commented, "What with the High Street on Market-day, with the lay of the family Mahone, and with the closing apostrophe to Jack Tar (eloquent, indeed, but isolated from the body of the Essay and with a tendency to fustian), 'Our Soldiers and Sailors'—the subject of the Essay— have been, apparently, all but forgotten. Take care, and don't *grow to wood.* Compare your own with Currie's[1] and with Edgar's and try, all three of you, to benefit each by the merits and defects of the others. P.S. As the song is original, I have added ten marks— your mark being now ninety-five—but, remember, I do not bate a jot of the appended critique."

To fix his thoughts on paper, as he had been urged to do, was more important to Geordie than to form words in a style to please a calligraphist's eye. This aim was noticeable in "The respective influences of Town and Country Life on the Character," to which Maybin appended the observation, "Most of the t's are perfectly

---

[1] J. R. Currie, Geordie's class-mate, had a distinguished medical career and in 1923 became Professor of Public Health at Glasgow University.

formed, but there is still a sufficient number of undotted i's to give one an uneasy impression of slovenliness."

"The majority of mankind" Geordie declared at the outset "are destitute of character in the truest sense of the word. Each individual has, it is true, ways of action peculiar to himself, but, in most cases, these have not been influenced by his surroundings; they have been totally generated by them. Divest 'society' of the peculiarities of conduct arising from surrounding circumstances, and you will find that the greater part of the human family is composed of those who, as to their character, may be compared to square blocks of polished granite. One block may be larger or smaller than another; but they are all completely square; they are all perfectly polished; they are all granite. The so-called different characters of these persons are exactly like the varieties of moss which may be found growing on the same kind of rock in different localities; they are entirely the result of time and place, and not a natural outgrowth. The only one, then, who is capable of having his character influenced, in any way, is the man who, though he may be destitute of what the moneygrubber calls strength of character, in the midst of his sinning, his struggling, and his failing, has deep-down in his inmost soul a well-spring of truth and beauty which, permeating his every aspiration, enables him to be true to Nature and to himself. . . ."

Those undotted i's? Maybin shrugged and, marking 90, added, "Very promising."

Following on with "Over the Moor," Geordie gained a full one hundred. In this essay, which went on to describe a holiday in a neighbouring village, he began on a note of self-revelation.

"Talk not to me of the indulgence of doting parents, or of the sly ways in which maiden aunts conceal the peccadilloes of their youthful nephews. I know an old dame, with gold-rimmed spectacles, and a bob-cap white as her silvery hair, who surpasses them all. 'Grannie' she is called,—a kindly old creature, known to many and beloved by all. Well I remember how disconsolate I was, when I realized the sad fact that I had no Grannie to supply me with unlimited quantities of 'candy', and to nurse me well, when her sweets had made me sick. I believe that was the first real sorrow I ever had. I felt like an outcast; I had no Grannie; parents were common enough sort of persons, but a Grannie,—she was an inestimable possession. At length there came a bright sunshiny day, on which the cloud of sorrow that had enveloped me was dispelled. My bosom friend, Jim Arnott, to whom I had confided my trouble, had a Grannie, and he forthwith agreed to give me half of her, just as we shared everything else. When we intimated our intention to the old lady, she ratified the agreement by a kiss, and gratified the desires of our souls by an abundant allowance of toffee.

Henceforth I was my own man again. I had found a Grannie,

35

and was happy. And a true Grannie she proved to us in many a trouble. When we were branded (not undeservedly, I fear) as the worst boys in the whole village, she stoutly maintained that the 'callants, though steerin' eneuch, were a hantle sicht better than the feck o' them that misca'ed them.'"

If Geordie was familiar with his own countryside and its characters, he was also at ease when Maybin set a Shakespearian subject. Although he did not interweave quotations into his essay on Macbeth, he knew most of the play by heart, and concluded:

"In a happier sphere, and amid different surroundings, Macbeth might have been a good—nay, a noble character. In every scene of the tragedy, we are made to feel his intellectual superiority over the other characters. But evil influences from without fostered the evil promptings within, and he was led, by his wife, down to the very nethermost depths of Hell. The storm of fiendish hate and ambition raged more fiercely in Lady Macbeth than in her husband, and her punishment is more awful in proportion. She can rest neither day nor night: her life becomes a complete blank—a vast expanse of nothingness, and she dies of a broken heart. But, although Macbeth's life has become as empty and desolate as his wife's, yet his death is that of a warrior, and he falls, amid the clang of broadsword and shield, with his 'back to the field, and his feet to the foe.' We cannot refrain from a feeling of pity at the hell-racked state of his mind, and, as we turn from the last tragedy of his tragic life, we cannot repress a sorrowful thought about 'what might have been.'"

In an essay on Shakespeare himself, Geordie and the dominie were in complete accord. "This is a very compact and well-ordered sketch," said Maybin. "You are taking my advice. You will find subjects enough for original treatment. This sketch is the very thing I wanted."

Maybin's patient guidance was having results. While his comments were keen, he offered that constructive advice which is less easy and consequently of greater value than destructive criticism. Week by week he pencilled his injunctions on Geordie's pages. "You will yet be able to write well if only you will resolve to be orderly and accurate ... The first aim of writing is clearness ... Try to get more terseness of expression." He was equally as quick to commend a vivid phrase: "Down they go through the avenues of night," for instance, in "Satan's Expulsion from Heaven"; and, in "The Faerie Queen," "The winds sigh soft and low through the blood-red blossoms that are pulsing with an unseen life."

Yet when he penned those lines Geordie did not require Maybin to emphasize their worth. He knew instinctively that they were good, for he was exercising something that he had found in the old hayloft at Duchray: the enchantment and power of words.

6

In school hours (and especially during uncongenial periods of mathematics) Geordie's thoughts often strayed back to the cottage at Crofthead. He wondered what his mother was doing and how she was feeling. Of late, she seemed to have lost her driving energy; her complexion had an unhealthy, yellowish tinge; and he guessed that her constitution was beginning to crack.

When at length she was forced to stay in bed, he was filled with dismay. He wanted to find a job, but she urged him to carry on "wi' the learning." She did not understand how heavily the scales were weighed against him. Her illness could not have happened at a worse time, for his studies were becoming more intensive. Next year would decide whether he was fitted or not for the university.

With dogged determination he tackled the immediate problem of how to look after his mother and, at the same time, attend the Academy. He rose at five o'clock, lighted the fire, made his bed, and tidied up the house. Later, as he prepared breakfast, he concealed the fact that he was harassed and that, with the Academy opening at nine, he had to keep an eye on the clock. Time was a thief who had to be outwitted. Finally, with a tender smile and the promise to hurry home, he was on his way. He consoled himself with the knowledge that in his absence a neighbour would see to his mother's wants.

Somehow, giving little or no hint of the strain that he was undergoing, he lived through each long, anxious day. When late afternoon brought release, he tore off to Crofthead, there to find his mother as he had left her, a lonely, stoical figure in the shadows of the box bed. She never failed to muster a pleased smile, and as he built up the fire and made tea, he told her about the day's happenings, even inducing her to laugh outright at one of Maybin's sallies. In turn she declared that the hours had soon passed. From time to time someone or other had looked in, and when she was alone the birds outside had sung to her. As he listened, Geordie was moved almost to tears; for he knew that out of this innate simplicity was born her fortitude and faith.

During the evening he had logs to saw and other odd jobs to do. Then he attended to his mother and, with many gentle touches, made her comfortable for the night. After she had drifted off to sleep, he arranged his books on the table, trimmed the lamp, and worked into the "wee, sma' hoors" at algebra, history, and Greek. When his eyes, red and inflamed, could scarcely see the page, he rose and tiptoed outside to draw the cool air into his lungs and to listen to the sounds of night. Beneath the starry sky he ought to

PART TWO

THE VITAL YEARS

I

The young man paused, pen in hand, as he filled in his matriculation slip. Through the pince-nez clipped to the bridge of his nose his dark eyes narrowed suspiciously. Why did the University authorities require to know about his father? Was there, could there be, an ulterior motive? Reluctantly and with a tightening of his lips he completed the form.

No. 1701. Matriculation Album. 1887–8
Natio Rotheseiana[1]
George Douglas Brown. Age—18. Birthplace:
Ochiltree,
Ayrshire.
Father: George Douglas Brown, Farmer.
Arts—Classes—Latin, Greek.
Address (Lodgings) —(1) 293 London Road, Glasgow.
(Home) —(2) 21 Crofthead, Ayr.

There was nothing in these facts to betray him, nothing that could give anyone an opportunity to deride or jeer; but that in itself was no safeguard. There were other students at Gilmorehill, and even while he knew that they would be busy with their classes and ambitions, he could not quell the suspicion that they would gossip and tell others about his stigma.

Apart from this (which as a handicap existed only in his own mind) he had the satisfaction of knowing that he was not unworthy. In November, 1887, by passing the Preliminary Examination in Junior Latin, Junior Greek, and Mathematics, he was admitted to the Senior Latin and Senior Greek classes under Professor Ramsay and Professor Sir Richard Jebb respectively. In the Bursary Competition, he took sixteenth place and was awarded the Cowan Bursary of £35 for two years.

Despite the fact that he was thus fairly launched upon his academic career, the discipline of regular study was impossible to acquire. He often worried about his throat, which pained him with increasing frequency, and he knew all about that insidious depression that accompanies nervous disorders of the stomach. When he

[1] Added every third year for Rectorial elections.

43

went out late at night and saw the moon, pale and remote above the high tenements, he longed to be back in his beloved Ayrshire. A man could walk there beneath familiar stars. He pictured the scene in every detail: the whiteness of stubbled fields, shadows flung across empty farmyards, and those sounds and smells that made night exciting and alive. He had but to shut his eyes to hear the peewits and to feel the smell of half-decayed turnips behind a dry-stone dyke.

Yet he was equally as susceptible to outward influences in the city. He afterwards remembered in detail his lodgings on damp Sunday evenings. Drab furniture and cold gas-light and, outside, greasy pavements, the clinkum-clankum of kirk bells, the sound of crowds moving below in the street, one or two hurrying to the end, and then silence and the grimy, sprawling city all round.

As the session went on, he threw himself with terrific concentration into sudden spells of work. Haphazard though it might seem, this method suited his temperament, and the results were reasonably sound. He took fourth place for general eminence in Senior Greek, and in Senior Latin he was ninth for general eminence and second for Latin Prose Composition.

He made arrangements to return to his lodgings, which had the saving grace of cheapness, and then, with a light heart, he went off by train to Ayrshire. Overjoyed to see him, Sarah had to be assured that he was well, that the strain of studying was not too much for his eyes, and that his landlady looked well after him. And he held her close and told her that everything was fine and that, for them both, a good time would come.

After his months of loneliness he was ready to laugh and talk. He sought out his cronies, exchanged Rabelaisian stories in the stables, and helped on the farms. What comparison was there between a Glasgow dray-horse in Renfield Street and a massive, feathery-footed Clydesdale on the Ayr Road? Everything here was vibrant and alive. The trees did not droop with the shabby listlessness of those in Kelvingrove, and the sky behind Crofthead was bluer than he had ever seen it above Gilmorehill.

Spending a good deal of time in the company of Tom Smith, who was still at Ayr Academy, Brown was often invited to share supper at the old schoolhouse at Coylton. His satisfaction was profound in the knowledge that he was truly and whole-heartedly accepted. The Smiths stood for loyalty; he had no fear that any one of them sneered behind his back. This knowledge brought contentment of spirit, and on his way home, usually after most people had gone to bed, he gave himself up completely to the enchantment of night.

Back at Glasgow University, however, his blackness of mood returned. He wondered how much his mother was keeping to herself; her health was still far from satisfactory; and he did not like to think that, for the time being, she was working at Coylton.

44

He brooded over his matriculation slip, for while it was a mere chit to other people, he magnified it out of all proportion. What did his father mean to him? He might as well . . . Ay, damn it! Why no'? And on the raw edge of impulse Brown made his decision.

No. 1514. Matriculation Album. 1888-9
George Douglas Brown. Age—19. Birthplace:
Ochiltree,
Ayrshire.
Father: Dead.
Arts—Classes—Logic, Senior and Private Greek,
English Literature.
Address (Lodgings) —(1) 293 London Road, Glasgow.
(Home)—(2) Woodlands, Coylton, nr. Ayr.

He had killed his father . . . on paper, and time alone would show if he had destroyed all thought of him in his mind.

With his strong likes and dislikes, he viewed the work ahead with mixed feelings. Professor John Veitch, who occupied the Chair of Logic and Rhetoric, did not appeal to him. A pity, perhaps, when Veitch was at heart a solitary—and a poet. Brown, however, was not altogether to blame. Veitch had very little hold over his students, his persistent critical style repelled them, and not until later years did they look back and recognize his power. In any case, Brown, with his passion for Greek, was more interested in Sir Richard Jebb's successor: a man called Gilbert Murray. Brown was drawn to him at once, for no one since Maybin had so excited and fired his intellect. Like Maybin, too, Murray soon realized that Brown was not essentially a scholar.

"Yet such," he afterwards wrote, "such was the general force and artistic power of his intellect, he was certainly the best or second best of the classical undergraduates in Glasgow at the time of my first arrival there as a professor. If I may characterise his work more particularly, I should say it was marked by very remarkable vigour of mind, together with a sort of impatience and irregularity—the qualities that often accompany an artistic temperament. He was the reverse of plodding or punctilious. He worked furiously hard for long spells, sat up late, read fast and voraciously, and remembered what he had read. I recollect once thinking it impossible that he could have read through a certain book—Harrison's *Mythology and Monuments of Ancient Athens*—in the time that he had had it, amounting to a few hours. I asked him some questions, and found he remembered it as accurately as I did. I had spent several days over it. At other times, when the mood changed, he was startlingly lazy."

Apart from his friendship with Professor Murray, Brown's

inclination was to remain rather aloof. He took no share in the proceedings of the Dialectic, the Philosophical, or the Alexandrian Societies, and he did not contribute to G. U. M., the 'Varsity magazine. For the present it satisfied him to experiment in verse in an effort to make words reflect the intensity of his impressions. That was why his Browning was so well thumbed. The vivid descriptions of material objects, as in *Childe Roland*, meant more to him than the poet's philosophy.

In more prosaic moments it occurred to him that he had been long enough in his present lodgings, so he moved to new quarters in Dumbarton Road, which were more convenient to Gilmorehill. One morning, as wind and sleet swept up the Clyde, he received a parcel from his mother, and in the evening he wrote to her on a page torn from one of his exercise books.

> Mrs. Cameron's,
> 359 Dumbarton Rd.,
> Glasgow.

Dear Mother,

You cannot believe how glad I was to get such a snug looking brown-paper parcel when I came home from college this stormy morning—just the sort of morning for a top-coat to arrive. It is a good thing that I did not get another, or I would have been quite overstocked with top-coats—an unusual thing for me. It fits me to a nicety and is very comfortable.

You will excuse this paper as my stock is done, and I do not want to go out for more to-night. By-the-by I am afraid that you will not get this on Friday as I am later in the day of writing than I intended. I have really no news except the joyful tidings that it is only a fortnight and a day till the holidays. I am afraid that I shall need some money before then. I always pay my lodgings on Monday and I have as much as do this on first Monday (the twelfth) but after that there are eleven days until the holidays. Do not put yourself about this however as I will be writing before I need to pay again, and perhaps the landlady would let me off till I come back after the holidays.

I am getting on very well at College, and I do not feel so lonesome as I used to do. I hope that you too are keeping up your heart for the 'good time coming' at Christmas. Wishing you all joy till then

> I remain your dear boy
> Geo D. Brown.

After the Christmas holiday his methods became increasingly disorganized, and although he was occasionally brought to book there was faint hope of reform. Once, when called upon to explain his absence from a Greek class, he smiled to himself as he filled in his excuse card. "Was consulting a doctor for a cure for insomnia during lecture time." Knowing his man, Professor Murray

46

appreciated the joke; but if it had happened in Logic John Veitch would not have been amused.

At the end of the session Brown stood second in Senior English to A. D. Blacklock, and in this subject he undoubtedly enjoyed the animated style of Professor Nichol and the late hour of the afternoon at which the lectures took place. C. C. Edgar, who knew Brown at Ayr Academy, Glasgow University, and later at Oxford, left this shrewd comment on record: "He was unusually susceptible to the season, the weather, the hour of the day, the look of a street and so on: ordinary things which leave no impression on the ordinary mind were to him full of a definite relish."

Brown was glad to escape to Ayrshire, but his mother seemed fairly well, and there was much to be done. In order to work up his classical composition, he therefore accepted Gilbert Murray's invitation to spend part of the vacation in Yorkshire. Murray was staying at a fine old house, Castle Howard, and here, Brown was assured, conditions for study were ideal. But the environment was entirely new to him; he could not easily assume its garb of elegance and refinement; and he amused his host by pointed comments on the difference between details here and life in a humble but and ben. On the surface, he appeared to forget the true purpose of his visit.

"I had expected him to work extra hard," related Murray, "and he seemed hardly to work at all. He was a charming companion, with his straight look and sunny smile, and vigorous and original views on all manner of things. There was something manly and truth-loving about his intellect. Everyone liked him in the house. But just at that moment he seemed unable to work! He was intoxicated with the summer, and used to lie for hours in a boat, sometimes with books, and sometimes without. I have no doubt whatever that his mind was really hard at work, thinking and recuperating all the while."

Certainly the change did Brown good, for he returned to Crofthead in excellent spirits. Maybin roped him in as a temporary assistant at the Academy, and he taught Greek—and taught it well— for the six weeks between the opening of school term and the resumption of his University classes. Tom Smith said that "it was really amazing the amount of Greek he could remember and quote freely." Nevertheless, Brown was aware of the real issue. He knew that Maybin was allowing him to acquire experience for the time when he might become a fully qualified teacher. A wry thought! As the centre of his life's work, the schoolroom was no more attractive than it had been two years ago.

Yet when he considered the future, Brown did not guess and fear as Burns had done. His mother had settled down again at Crofthead, and he experienced no despondency when he boarded the Glasgow train. He had a feeling that the session would go well.

Before filling in his matriculation slip, he was shamed by the recollection of how, last year, he had declared his father to be dead. Surely rancour had swayed him in a mean, unguarded moment. Or was it simply that his outlook had broadened? Was he now seeing life in clearer perspective? No matter. He would rectify the wrong that he had done.

No. 967. Matriculation Album. 1889–90
George Douglas Brown. Age—20. Birthplace:
                              Ochiltree,
                              Ayrshire.
Father—Farmer.
Arts—Classes—Senior and Private Latin, Moral Philosophy, Natural Philosophy, Mathematics.
Address: Crofthead, nr. Ayr.

After all, Brown realized, a few strokes of the pen one way or another did not alter facts, and throughout the past year the ageing man at Drumsmudden had never been banished long from mind.

2

Brown loathed tenement life. He made a fresh move, this time to a house at 2 Gilmore Street, but his room was no more satisfactory than the last, and he only tolerated it because work was pressing in upon him.

At the opening of the session he obtained the Stewart Bursary of £15, tenable during the Gown Course, but he knew that he would not shine in those classes that were necessary to complete the Arts Curriculum. True, his work in Moral Philosophy, under Professor Edward Caird, showed gradual improvement, but Professor Sir William Thomson, who became Lord Kelvin, did not evoke in him any feeling for Natural Philosophy.

In the Greek Black Stone Examination, however, Brown was on familiar ground, and he gained the Cowan Gold Medal. He hastened to tell his mother—and even dated the letter, a detail which he usually ignored.

                              2 Gilmore St.,
                              Partick,
                              Glasgow.
                              Dec. 2nd, 1889
Dear Mother,
    I write to inform you of the happy news that I have won a Gold Medal worth ten guineas. I did not know about it till Edgar told me on the night before we had to give in our names. I went in

quite unprepared and came out first in the written examination. A fellow Duncan was second and Edgar third. We three were then chosen to undergo a public examination before four professors and as many students as liked to come and look at us. I had only 2 clear days to get up the work I professed but went in and was the only one of the three who finished what was set him, so there's no doubt of my getting the Medal though it has not yet been published owing to our Greek Professor being away getting married.

I am going to leave my lodgings and would like if you could send me up a pound to clear off with the landlady. I mean I'll leave the day we get our holidays and will leave my big trunk the three weeks at the station. It will be a good deal cheaper than if I had to pay for my room all the time. My landlady is honest enough but a slut.

I was glad to hear about your cow.

Be sure and send the pound soon and also two shillings worth of stamps[1]
I'll be home on Saturday the 14th. G. D. B.

On the promised date Brown returned home to share with his mother a quiet Christmas. It was good to sit with her by the fireside and to know that he was back in the heart of his own countryside. He was aware that to some people in the district he was a mystery; but there were others who thought of him only as a friend. One evening, while Tom Smith was paying a visit, a farmer called at the cottage.

"Man, Geordie," he began portentously, as Sarah showed him into the kitchen, "I've got a bit job for ye."

Brown's eyes beamed through his glasses.

"At this time o' year?" he asked.

"Ay. There was a plooin' match at ma ferm a day or twa syne, and I want ye to write oot a report for the papers."

As the farmer went on to describe the event, Brown scribbled the necessary notes. There was much about "the best rig-oot," "the best start," and "the best feenish."

"Noo, Geordie," adjured the farmer, "whatever ye do, mind and pit this in the paper. 'Thereafter a very pleasant evening was spent in song and sentiment.'"

Brown solemnly assured him that he would not forget . . . and he never did. He often reminded Tom Smith about that concluding phrase.

On his return to Glasgow, his first concern was to get lodgings, and this time, still in the convenient district of Partick, luck was on his side. Mrs. Currie at 7, Clarendon Street, gave him a room that combined cheapness and cleanliness, a room where he could study without discomfort. Yet even by Spartan economy he knew that he could not hold out indefinitely. He tried to devise schemes for

---

[1] For some reason, which has never been explained, Brown always had an intense antipathy to buying stamps at a post office.

making money, but though he occasionally wrote to his mother to ask her opinion about them, they never materialized. They were mirages to urge him on across a desert of impecunious existence. Eventually, in this same year, he reached the rock of his reward. On completing his Gown Course he presented himself for examination in Arts, and graduated Master of Arts, with first-class honours in Classics. In the examination open to deserving students who had taken this degree, he then obtained the Eglinton Classical Fellowship, which offered him a choice of following a course of study in the University or giving assistance there in teaching.

That evening Brown scarcely noticed the tea which Mrs. Currie brought in. His only outward sign of excitement had been the swift way in which he had strode down from Gilmorehill. Now his sole desire was to pour out his news to the one person who mattered. He wrote quickly, as if the very speed of his pen would hasten the delivery of his letter.

> Mrs. Currie's,
> 7 Clarendon St.,
> Partick,
> Glasgow.
> Wednesday evening.

Dear Mother,

I am *first* all over both for the general fellowships, the Scott Scholarship, and for Honours. I shall, therefore, get the Eglinton Fellowship of three hundred pounds—that is one hundred a year for the next three years. You are not allowed to hold the Eglinton with another; else I should be eligible for the Scott also. I have also, as you will see from the accompanying list, got first-class Honours. You may judge of their value from the following circumstance. Before I came up the Rector told me he would be better pleased if I got Honours than if I got *any* of the Fellowships or Scholarships.

I have abandoned the plan of raising money which I mentioned to you; and on the strength of my recent success have written to the Rector asking for the loan of four pounds. I have no doubt he will give it to me and this with the private teaching which I hope to Heaven I'll get will tide me over till I receive the first half of my Fellowship in the shape of fifty sovereigns soon after the New Year.

I hope this is plain enough for you to read but I have great temptations to write hurriedly. By the bye the Scott for which also I was first is worth £160. And now blessings on you, your cow, your calves, your hens, your dog, your cat, your kitten

> from your ever affectionate son
> George Douglas Brown.

To conform with the conditions of the Eglinton Fellowship Brown returned to Glasgow University, but in one deep, fundamental matter success had not changed him. Again, with sullen brow, he meditated upon his matriculation slip. Last year he had

50

been charitable and had done "the right thing." This time he was dominated by the thought that a principle was involved. Why should he, a bastard son, acknowledge the father who had done nothing for him? What he then wrote was inevitable.

No. 1938. Matriculation Album. 1890–91
George Douglas Brown, M.A. Age 21. Birthplace: Ochiltree,
Ayrshire.
Father—George—Deceased.
Arts Classes—Senior and Private Greek (taken as a public class).
Latin Prose.
(Lodgings)—c/o Currie, 7 Clarendon Street, Partick, Glasgow.

This slip revealed more than the see-saw of his emotions. By taking Latin Prose he recognized the weakest point in his classical scholarship.

It was fortunate that his landlady was long-suffering—or easy-going. As the session got under way, he suffered from indigestion and insomnia, the result being that his hours became more capricious than ever before. Edgar often found him breakfasting in the afternoon, while many nights he never went to bed at all.

"This same year," declared Edgar, "he read through a great quantity of novels, partly to beguile his sleeplessness, and partly, I believe, with an interested consciousness that character painting was a subject for which he had himself a unique taste and talent. He had a keen appreciation of traits of character both in the authors he read and in the people he met, and his observations were always full of freshness. Revelations of vulgarity and self-importance seemed to touch an exposed nerve in him; but there was mostly humour in his criticisms, and never any maliciousness or desire to depreciate. There was nobody against whom he told a better story than against himself."

Brown was indeed conscious of his gifts. Although he had not abandoned verse, he was prone nowadays to experiment in prose. He did not attempt a finished incident or picture. Instead, he sought to create vivid, original phrases, always with an eye to the right word, to express his meaning. What he experienced, he wanted others to feel, otherwise there seemed to be no true purpose in writing. In writing? Owing allegiance to his mother, he knew that he dare not risk the hazards of literature.

In any case, he soon had very little spare time in which to coax words into a pattern. Gilbert Murray's class assistant died, and Brown was invited to fill the vacancy. The work in itself gave him no difficulty, but he could not overcome his abhorrence of routine. "One felt," said Murray, "he was not cut out for anything in the shape of a schoolmaster. The clock-like regularity that comes naturally to some men, and is so necessary in the teaching of a

51

Scottish University, was evidently a matter of considerable effor to him."

When left by himself to study in accordance with his topsyturvy methods, Brown had few compeers. He now smoked a pipe, and in his room, thick with blue reek, he could absorb more knowledge in an all-night sitting than most students could do in a week of disciplined grind. In 1891 he gained the Luke Historical Prize of £12 for the best Examination in Ancient Greek and Roman History, and then, in his own way, he went on to the outstanding feat of his entire academic career. On 25th April he won the University's premier award, the Snell Exhibition Scholarship, which, with its £130 for three years, obliges the holder to reside and study at Balliol College, Oxford.

In his hour of triumph, however, Brown left Glasgow, which at one time he had disliked, with curious misgivings. He had set the heather rather than his heart on fire. He was glad, intensely glad for his mother's sake that he had succeeded; but once over the Border, he would be a long distance from Ayrshire. To counterbalance this reaction, he took a fierce, secretive pride in the fact that he had reached the heights, that he, the poor illegitimate, possessed brains to match the best o' them.

Yet in his holiday at home that halcyon summer, he was the Geordie Broon that the people around Crofthead and Coylton had always known. When he leaned upon a five-barred gate or hunched his shoulder to the wind to light his pipe, he was more the countryman than the scholar, albeit his great Scots head, his penetrating eyes and massive brow, indicated intellectual power. No one could accuse him of conceit or what, in Ayrshire, is swiftly recognized as "swelled-heidedness." And when he was asked how he felt when he knew that he had won the Snell, he shrugged his shoulders.

"Oh," he said. "The pipe just dropped out o' my mouth."

3

In the act of walking by, early one evening, Brown paused to talk to Mrs. Thom at her house in Coylton. As a boy he had come here to see her baby's toe-nails, and he now knew her so well, this kindly woman whom he could trust, that he did not hesitate to confide in her.

"Guess where I'm going tonight," he began; and, looking into his eyes, she saw a curious mixture of resolution and trepidation.

"Geordie!" she responded in a hushed voice. "You—you don't mean you're going to Drumsmudden?"

He nodded grimly.

"I've got one or two matters to settle before I leave for Oxford," he said. "I must have his signature to these papers."

He patted an inner pocket, and Mrs. Thom stared at him in consternation.

"Oh, Geordie," she pleaded, "mind what you're about. Whatever he says, don't do anything you'll regret."

He made no promise. Bleakly he resumed the long tramp to Drumsmudden. To his strained nerves the whole countryside beyond Coylton was instinct with a sense of awful anticipation. Now . . . at last . . . he was going to meet, face to face, the man who had fathered him and rejected him, the man who had blasted his whole life. He knew that for a long time he had waited for this hour. Some vague intuition had forewarned him that it would come, and his lips tightened at the thought. No matter what happened, he would not be found wanting. 'Smudden, with his rough tongue, had a formidable reputation. He had once roared at a worker, "I'll gar your brains jaup red to the heavens"; but this time he would not be dealing with a shrinking orraman. He would be matched by the strength of his own flesh and blood.

As he drew near to the farm, Brown's pace did not slacken. He was his mother's son, and he would let 'Smudden know what the last twenty-two years had cost her in health and hard work. Without her self-sacrifice and faith—and for all this man had cared—he would still have been "craw-picking" at Trabboch pit-head. On the other hand, this very fact gave him an advantage, for he could stride up to the door in the certain knowledge that there was no debt to pay. He did not owe the Snell Exhibition to 'Smudden's bawbees.

At the house he met with none of the incivility that he had half-expected. He was shown into a room where a fire burned in the grate, and a minute later he heard a slow, heavy footstep. When his father came in, Brown realized that there would be no ill words, no sordid recrimination. Hatred and bitterness left his being as snow slides from a dyke in a thaw; for he gazed into the face of an old man.

On 'Smudden's side there was no awkward pause, no moment charged with truculent intent, and as he sat down and invited Brown to "draw in a chair", he obviously did not regard him as a ghost out of the past. Before this witness of age, with its courage and pathos, Brown saw his father in focus for the first time. 'Smudden was not the monster whom he had imagined but a plain man of the earth: one who, with a mortal's share of faults and virtues, was essentially human. Because of this, Brown wondered how much he regretted, and certainly, from an occasional word or two,

53

it was clear that he had not forgotten Sarah. Perhaps up here, with the wind and the rain and the sun on his face, it had been easy to remember.

From this evening Brown saw more deeply into human nature. If he did not altogether forgive, he understood, and when Mrs. Thom inquired how he got on he told her quite simply, "My father is just like anybody else."

After one or two more visits to the farm, he sometimes discussed 'Smudden with Isabelle Smith.

"He's the best swearer I've ever heard," he said. "But"—thoughtfully—"there's more to him. All that's good in me is my mother; my brains come from my father."

Which meant that he was indebted to the old man after all.

It made no difference to Brown's relationship with his mother. At this time, in fact, he became particularly concerned about her. On several occasions he had surprised her in the act of drying white cloths by the fire, and once he had seen her unbuttoning her dress and folding one of them over her bosom. She had said that it was nothing for him to worry about, but he had been disturbed in mind ever since. The "wee cloots" clung to his thoughts as he had seen them clinging to the kitchen chairs, and it was against their background that he pictured his mother as he travelled over the Border and down through England to Oxford.

He was keen to begin work, but he did not find the prospect enticing. He guessed that conditions would be completely different from Gilmorehill. He would be expected to live in college in circumstances of some affluence, and that, he knew before he got there, was beyond him. He had been forced to accept a loan of money from Professor Murray,[1] and he owed a sum to William Maybin. To such men, his word was his bond, but he wanted to repay as quickly as possible. Independence was important.

He matriculated at Balliol College on 20th October 1891, the month in which William Robertson Nicoll brought out the *Bookman* and the same year in which another complex Scot, James Matthew Barrie, gave his winning and anomalous novel, *The Little Minister*, to a large and gullible public.

Ere the month was out Brown realized that the soft autumn air of this thousand-year-old city would not suit his health, and he was older than most of his contemporaries. If he could have captured some of Oxford's detachment, he might have grown accustomed to her way of life. There was not much traffic to disturb the Broad or the High; for she was still a world of her own, and it was easy, at sight of ancient gables, to believe that little had

---

[1] "I offered to supplement his scholarship by a small sum," Murray wrote. "He had told me something of his circumstances at the time. He looked me straight in the eyes, rather sternly, and said, 'I'll pay ye back!'"

changed since the Middle Ages. But even in the Balliol quadrangle with its great, autumnal trees Brown was incapable of surrender. Oxford could never claim him as it was to claim John Buchan after a similar beginning.

To his mother, however, Brown was careful not to give cause for worry.

Balliol,
Monday.

Dear Mother,

It is a great shame I have not written to you before but I knew you would be sure I was all right. I have not had any money from Glasgow yet but when it comes I will send you plenty. Meanwhile I will send you a pound to buy odd things with. Take plenty of good food, plenty of sleep, and persevere with your medicine. I was bilious for a while but I am all right now.

Your aff. son
George D. Brown.

No hint that even here, hundreds of miles from home, he experienced misgivings and distrust. When two or three students were together in the quadrangle, he watched them askance. Though, as a "Sneller," he was bound to attract attention . . . was it his scholarship that they were discussing? With no means of knowing, it was inevitable that he should think the worst. The meetings with his father had brought no concrete change. From himself there was no escape.

4

Brown got cheap, inconvenient rooms on the ground floor in the Garden Quadrangle. To qualify for the degree of Bachelor of Arts, it was necessary to prepare for two principal examinations, Moderations and Greats, and he intended to set about the task in his own manner. He did not suppose that the tutors who were to supervise most of his studies, J. L. Strachan-Davidson, the courteous Senior Dean of Balliol, and gallant, paralysed Evelyn Abbott, with his wheel-chair and gift of quiet scholarship, were greatly impressed in the first few months. While, in fact, the Dean cautiously decided that he displayed "good sense and intelligence," there were disquieting reports that he was rather dull and "ambitious, but lacking knowledge of books." To Brown, who had an uncanny knack of knowing the minimum amount of work that would get him through an emergency, the important point was that he knew his own capabilities. What irritated was the boredom of familiar subjects, and, in a letter to Gilbert Murray, he bitterly complained about the weariness he felt in his classical work.

Fortunately, he soon made two trustworthy friends: Montague Rousseau Emanuel, a handsome young Jew, who became a barrister of the Inner Temple, and David Maughan, destined by the middle of the twentieth century to be the Father of the Australian Bar. With the exception of dinner in hall, meals were taken in one's rooms, and Brown, being unable to afford to entertain on a large scale, relied on his own small circle. Late in the evening Emanuel, Maughan, and a few others met for cocoa, and Brown's prodigious appetite for sultana cake usually proved to be a precursor of indigestion and an accompanying fit of the blues.

Nevertheless, he responded to the able men with whom he thus came in contact. He sharpened his wits and developed a magnetism that made people aware of him, so that when he walked into a room one felt that here was a tremendous, vital force. It warmed his heart to be called "G.D." or, quite simply, Brown. He would argue as long as there was body left in an argument, either with his feet planted wide apart and his back to the fire or excitedly pacing to and fro. Sometimes, he would snatch up the poker to emphasize his meaning, while the burning light in his eyes would remind his listeners of what Sir Walter Scott wrote about Burns:

"There was a strong expression of sense and shrewdness in all his lineaments; the eye alone, I think, indicated the poetical character and temperament. It was large, and of a dark cast, and glowed (I say literally *glowed*) when he spoke with feeling or interest. I never saw such another eye in a human head, though I have seen the most distinguished men in my time."

Yet Brown could be roused only by certain subjects. He had no interest in politics, and Maughan hazarded the opinion that "In so far as he had any political views, they would be those of the Liberal or even the advanced radical of the day: he had a strong humanitarian side and a leaning towards the under dog."

In religious matters he was even more reticent, but he was "down" on ministers and had no patience with dogma. Maughan was near the truth when he recognized that it was Brown's "deep spiritual quality which made him, in my opinion, a religious man."

On literature and poetry Brown was always at his best. He spoke with the authority of wide reading, and if, for example, the conversation turned to Keats, he was ready to pause over a favourite quotation.

> *Charm'd magic casements, opening on the foam*
> *Of perilous seas, in faery lands forlorn.*

"Maughan," he often said. "I love those lines."

Jestingly on occasion, Emanuel and Maughan guided the talk to current Scots fiction, whereupon Brown either shrugged his shoulders or made a disparaging gesture.

56

"No one pictures the real Scottish village life," he declared. "I will write a novel and tell you all what Scottish village life is like."

This was not a reckless boast. Brown was neither amused nor annoyed by *Auld Licht Idylls* and *The Little Minister*; he had his own ideas, and already he was seeking to develop them.

He experimented with names in his notebooks. For a village he wanted something that expressed "Scotchness" in the very sound. No doubt in which country one would find Mauchline, Auchinleck, and Ochiltree. Then he thought of Coylton, Hillhead, Rankinstone, Craighall, Barbieston and—and, in a flash, he had what he wanted. Barbie! There it was, simple, yet full of atmosphere. A good name for a village. He began to picture Barbie. It would be on a brae, with a long, white gullet of a street stretching down . . . and a house, an important house, at the top. In his usual form of " doodling ", he wrote his name several times: G. D. Brown, George Brown, Geordie Brown, George Douglas Brown. Ay, Barbie was not merely a good name; Barbie was a village with possibilities.

The thought made Brown homesick. He was glad to get out of Oxford at Christmas and to return home. A man wanted to dance on the seat of his compartment when the train crossed the Border. He found his mother apparently well, but she could no longer deceive him. He understood the significance of the "wee cloots." In the evenings he usually walked to the Coylton schoolhouse where the dominie and his family gave him the sympathy and encouragement he needed. When he first appeared, Maggie Stevens, the faithful and outspoken maid, was dubious. She had regarded him as a young man who had always been willing to give her or any other lassie a turn at the country dances. Now he was back from Oxford and probably ready to look down his nose at the likes o' her. She therefore kept out of his way until she had a fire to attend in the study where he was browsing over a book. As she was leaving, he glanced up.

"Steek the door, Maggie," he said. "It's cauld in here."

And she nodded and smiled because she knew in her heart that she had misjudged him.

Before he returned to Oxford, however, she was near to screaming. When he was invited to stay overnight at the schoolhouse, he and Tom Smith talked until long past twelve o'clock. Throughout the evening Maggie had fortified them with pots of strong black tea, but at last Tom firmly decided that it was time to call a halt. Maggie thankfully retired to her room, undressed, and tumbled, dog-tired, into bed. She had almost fallen asleep when she was jerked back to wakefulness by the crunch of footsteps on the gravel outside her window. This indication that Brown was on the prowl faded away, and Maggie sighed in relief and turned over on her side. She heard the cry of an owl afar off . . . stillness . . . and then crunch, crunch, crunch! So it went on, with Brown coming and going, until heaven knew when; but to poor Maggie, who could scarcely crawl to the kitchen in the morning, the last straw came when she had to take breakfast to him in bed.

"Sit up!" she rated him. "Here's your tray. Why can ye no' gang to your bed and sleep like ither folk?"

"How d'ye mean?" asked Brown, yawning.

"Ye jist aboot drove me demented wi' your carry on last nicht."

"But ye should have gone to sleep."

"Sleep!" Maggie expostulated. "How d'ye think I could sleep wi' you stamp, stampin' aboot fit to wauken the deid?"

"Och, ye needna blame me, Maggie," said Brown, with a laugh. "It maun have been your conscience."

How could she understand that under the spur of his insomnia he was forced to seek solitude? Hours of argument and discussion set his brain afire; afterwards it was essential to be alone.

Near the end of his vacation he paid another visit to the Smiths. He was not surprised to hear voices and laughter from one of the rooms, for the old schoolhouse was a happy place. When Tom explained that his cousins, the M'Lennans, had arrived from Glasgow, Brown's interest remained mild. All he knew was that Mrs. Smith's brother, James M'Lennan, was a partner in the Glasgow firm of Alexander Bryce M'Lennan, wine and spirit merchants, and had reached a degree of importance in civic affairs. A man o' position, Deacon-Convener M'Lennan.

Then Brown was introduced to the company, to one M'Lennan after another, until he met Isabella. Oh, it wasn't the first time that he had looked into a lassie's eyes! But this girl, with her grace and beauty, was different. During the evening he became aware of her spirit, intelligence, and that quick, warm sympathy which, to him, was an essential part of a woman. Her gaiety, too, was infectious: she had a gift of laughter that made him lighter in heart than he had been for a long time. With her by his side, he could reach up and touch the stars . . .

On the road home his mind was filled with the thought of her. He recalled the graceful movements of her beautifully shaped hands the delightful, unexpected mannerisms, and indeed everything about her. She was for him that rare combination: an ideal and a reality.

When he resumed his studies at Oxford, he thought a great deal about her. He wanted to see her again, and at the first opportunity he was back in Scotland. To his delight, she was on another visit to the Smiths, and he felt that she was genuinely pleased to see him. He had grown a moustache, which suited him, and when not in use his pince-nez dangled from a thin black ribbon. Such small details made him seem older than twenty-three, but he was youthfully buoyant and full of confidence. No depression or dyspepsia when he was in Isabella's company!

Tom Smith saw that Brown was attracted to her, and later on he mentioned the fact in a letter. Brown smiled and sat down to reply. The hush of eventide, hanging over Balliol quadrangle, encouraged him to write at length.

Balliol College,
Sunday.

My Dear Tom,

I am enjoying a well-earned repose to-day, and as the scrawl I sent you was somewhat perfunctory I despatch this at the heels of it. Mind, although I shall be too busy to write again to you at length, I expect two big screeds at least from you in return for these two. I forgot to notice some things you mentioned in your note, so here goes.

Yes I liked your cousin Isabella very much indeed. I thought her a girl of spirit and wit, with a keen sense of fun and a still keener sense of personal dignity; a clear-eyed dainty girl withal who was good to look at. I like that sort of "moue" she makes—the pouting tilt-up of the chin—when talking.

I know the passage that struck you in the "Ode to the Nightingale." It goes on

> —Call'd him soft names in many a musèd rhyme,
> To take into the air my quiet breath.

Thanks awfully for your offer about the dimes; but I'm in funds just now and shall be, I hope, till next summer. If I can oblige you with a quid let me know and you shall have it. The bally eighteenpence you mentioned may keep till we have a "nicht wi' Downie."

Maughan, Emanuel, and I breakfast with each other by turns every Sunday morning. We went into the Parks to-day at 11.30 when they were filled with 'Varsity people and well-dressed women —not a muldoon to be seen. Blue spaces in the sky; a soft wind that bathed you, and breathed the freshness of last night's rain; and silhouetting Keble and other large buildings there came down on the yellowing trees a large *diffusing* light—mellow and soft but too clear to be called a luminous haze. And then the handsome girls with their easy stately poise! There was one dainty rogue with brown wavy hair that came round behind the smallest and prettiest ear in the world, a pure pale brow, eyes brown and clear as a mountain-pool, a slightly aquiline nose, red lips and a freckle or two on her pale cheek. She had some puffy green stuff on her shoulders, a slim waist; and in holding up her skirt shewed a peep of a white petticoat and two trim little ankles. And the "*action* o' the bit hizzy" as Wull Lindsay would say! My interest in her was purely impersonal of course—I admired her as a living picture of the beautiful.

The weather is balmy and mild: from a slope you can see the flat landscape stretching for miles beneath a faint clear—half-blue —haze. A cock-crow in Scotland is something cheery—"a rousing craw"—here it is subdued and far-away: you hear the sound miles off, one would think, and a vague feeling of sadness comes over you. But the distinguishing feature of this flat country is the pathetic sense of vague, far-off, lonely horizons and illimitable distances. But it's high time to dry up.

Yours vy. sincerely G. D. Brown.

5

Brown was never afraid to speak his mind, and when he became a member of his College's literary debating club, the Arnold, squalls were frequent. H. W. C. Davis, the history scholar, was frequently in violent conflict with him, although they never bore each other malice. Sometimes Brown would walk out in the course of a debate, "but," said Davis, "these ebullitions occurred at a time when his nerves were unsettled, and they never lasted long."

In his first and second year, Brown was indeed a keen supporter of the Arnold, and for a term he officiated as President. One of his best lectures was on Robert Burns. When he ought to have been doing other work, he had been making copious notes on the poet. He had a fair idea of their worth, and as a reminder for the future he wrote one word across the top of the first page: "Printable?" After College Hall one evening, between thirty to forty members of the Arnold gathered to hear his address. His throat had been sore of late, but to-night it gave him no trouble, and after dealing with the early life and upbringing of Burns, he warmed to his subject.

"Burns is unique," he declared, "in the *matter* of his work. He was born and lived and died among the people. Others have described peasant life from above, Burns knew it from the inner and the under side.

"It is said that the gloomy anger which he showed after the Edinburgh visit was due to the fact that he failed to obtain a post which would save him from the drudgery of farming. We may be thankful that such was the case: what Burns lost, literature gained.

"Because he never left the country and the country life, he sang of them always from actual observation, never from jaded reminiscence. He lived what he wrote, more perhaps than any other author, and hence his matter is unique, being new and fresh, and racy of the soil."

Standing with the ease of a man who was perfectly sure of himself, Brown amused himself by tossing up a pellet of paper as he spoke.

"Burns's range is limited because he knows only peasant Scotland: but within that range he is illimitable because not a feature of it has escaped his observation. It is his sympathy then that keeps the personal element in his work so healthy. His hypochondria never infects his general verse. . . . It is true also that Burns with his fiery practicality rarely bothers himself with the so-called 'problem of existence,' a vague consciousness of which is at the root of Byron's misery. It is thus that Byron appears the most potent force, though he has no more natural fire than Burns, and his power is of a far less varied nature."[1]

As he poured out his knowledge of Burns, Brown became more excited; his brow gleamed in the gas-light, his voice reached a higher pitch.

"It is absurd to say that he failed because (to use the cant phrase) he did not grapple with his doubts. Burns's misery (when he is miserable) is that of a fiery nature coming into contact with this world, not that of a nature speculating on the world to come. He has little of the 'yearning that cannot be uttered': he cares nothing for the infinitudes and never gave a thought to teleology. On the contrary it is the closeness of his grasp on actual life, the relation of things as they are, that gives him his force in literature."

After this lecture Brown whipped himself to the effort of writing to Tom Smith, and in the opening paragraph there was a marked resemblance to what he had said about Burns.

Balliol,
Wednesday.

My Dear Tom,

I am suffering from dyspepsia, insomnia, hypochondria, and all the horrors of Hell. Usually I never bother much with the Infinitudes, but when my liver gets out of order I speculate on the Primal Cause, the nature of God, the end of Man, and other questions of teleology which metaphysics have never answered and never will. And "that way my madness lies," quoth Hamlet the Dane.

Well to speak the truth I am ill—both in mind and body: besides I was vivisecting Burns for the Arnold Society: these are my reasons for delaying to answer your letter. The paper was critical rather than panegyrical and I seemed to make the men understand Burns in spite of the fact that they have no more conception of Ayrshire than a Hottentot has of Paradise. I don't suppose many of them know how a woman's dark eye glistens looking up to your face in the moonlight.

No Tom: I've plenty of the needful at present, thanks all the same, though, for the offer: and remember that when I have, and you haven't, you can draw on me.

I suppose the eminently respectable and practical——is speculating now on the prophets of Israel and anon on the profits of a parsonage. Eh, whow me, Tam, it's a hell o' a worl', a hell o' a worl'

[1] Compare with the article on Burns in *Blackwood's Magazine*, August 1896.

a'thegither. ——'s a by ornar douce sponsible man—verra respectable, verra. Still an' on, Tam, still an' on—ye unerstan me fine, withoot sayin' ony mair. I like a *man* who can forget occasionally to be a prig and a Philistine.

Yours most sincerely,

Geordie Broon.

P.S. I hardly know what I have written for my brain feels as turgid and raw as a frosted turnip when it's boiled. I have had only 9 hours sleep in 3 nights.

For a while Brown was attracted to the Milton, a University literary society of senior men, but even in it his views were often unpopular. Not that he cared. He derived considerable benefit from the rough and tumble of debate.

To economize, he moved out of college to rooms at 9, Walton Crescent, whereupon his interest in both the Arnold and the Milton diminished. On walks by the Upper River to Godstow and Wytham, he often complained to Emanuel and Maughan that he had made a mistake in coming to Oxford. As he had known all along, he was not cut out for teaching, and late at night, when sleep was impossible, he took refuge in his notebooks. That village . . . Barbie . . . Suppose he tried to describe it.

Tam the Miller lived in a roomy house at the top of the steep brae of Barbie. ·

The house was grey and old, and when it was bathed in the quiet sunshine and there was a faint perfume from the wallflowers on hot afternoons, it used to make me kind of lonely when a boy.

Except when the school skailed or in the evening, the half-mile street was deserted. All through the drowsy afternoon that long white gullet of a street slept in the sunshine without a soul stirring—except, maybe, when away down the brae an old wife in a white mutch crept across with a can of water. I have mind yet how the sun used to hit against the glinting sides of the Barbie water-cans.

Barbie, as the folk said, was "jist a' brae thegither." From the other side of the water you saw the whole of it lying plain and naked to the view—a "sheuch" o' hooses sloping down the brae from the meeneral well to the brig o' Barbie. But there it stopped—there was no body to this long crooked arm.

It was Jock Logan who fixed Barbie for ever as the "single breistit toun." He was sprauchlin' up the brae drunk at the time—in fact, he was taking the breadth o' the road, as the Barbie folk said.

Jock was a great hand at description, but he came from another parish and was suspected as a "gey queer yin."

Had he been a native, he would have been admired as an "unco droll yin." For the Scots is a language of fine distinctions.

Brown closed his notebook and went out to walk the deserted streets. He did not fret about his insomnia; he was thinking about the house at the top of the steep brae of Barbie.

6

To return home was always an event in Brown's life. He liked to hear his mother remark that it was as if he had never been away; for, unlike many students, he never required to readjust himself. While Oxford (willynilly) was having its effect upon him, it did not show in what an old member of Balliol neatly described as "the tranquil consciousness of effortless superiority." William Maybin, the Smiths, and cronies like Davie Downie did not notice any difference in his manner.

Yet there was change in the countryside itself. Brown's father was no longer at Drumsmudden. Rather tactlessly perhaps, Mr. George Reid, the factor, had refused to renew the lease on the grounds that the farm required a younger man. 'Smudden let it be known that, in his opinion, the move was entirely vindictive. When Reid had asked him, a Liberal, to vote for the Tory cause at an election, he had bluntly refused, and this, he maintained, was the outcome. In Ochiltree and farther afield, the matter had been hotly discussed, and on a dark night in March 1892, sympathizers had gathered in a field at Drumsmudden and burned the effigy of an individual who had been labelled, "A Scots Landlord's Evicting Machine." To be sure, the demonstration had had no effect. 'Smudden—who was 'Smudden no longer—had been forced to go. He had taken the farm of West Newton in the Parish of Loudon, where he was now, an old lion at bay, fighting to the end.

Brown naturally admired the stand that his father had made[1]— whether in the hot air of the Arnold or in the open sweep of Ayrshire his sympathies always lay with a fighter—but he did not deviate from his mother's side.

One evening during the Long Vacation of that year, Tom Smith called at the cottage. He had been studying for an examination, and arising out of it he impatiently remarked to Brown that Wordsworth was prosy. Later in the evening, as the sun went down beyond Arran, they climbed the hill behind Crofthead. When they reached the summit Brown quoted:

> *The holy time is quiet as a Nun*
> *Breathless with adoration.*

Tom Smith quickly turned towards him.
"I like that, George," he said. "Who wrote it?"
"Your prosy friend Wordsworth," replied Brown.

[1] See Appendix.

Moving down the hillside, they discussed a growing tendency to paraphrase poetry in examinations.

"I think it's absurd," said Tom. "Beautiful poetry ought to be left in its original form."

Brown nodded in agreement.

"Imagine," he said, "those lines in *Vox et praterea Nihil* set to be paraphrased:

> *'Like air touch'd harps in flowery casements hung;*
> *Like unto lovers' ears the wild words sung*
> *In garden bowers at twilight; like the sound*
> *Of Zephyr when he takes his nightly round*
> *In May, to see the roses all asleep.'"*

When Isabella M'Lennan and her sisters were on holiday, Brown was often at the schoolhouse. Isabelle Smith watched uneasily. She understood him and her cousin, and she wondered how their friendship would end. Brown was so obviously in love. . . .

He paid scant heed to Lizzie M'Lennan in the background, for he regarded her as a schoolgirl. Yet there was one occasion that they did not forget. Word was received that a friend of the Smiths and M'Lennans had been murdered in Africa, a native, with a grudge, having stolen a rifle and shot him. Lizzie, to whom he had been a romantic hero, was numb with shock. She was sitting alone and dry-eyed when Brown found her, and, understanding how she felt, he straightway began to talk about the murdered man. He pictured the scene: the dark, watching face. . . the crack of the rifle . . . the slumped body . . . red blood in the sand. At first Lizzie heard him as if from a great distance, but Brown went on talking so that every word became a slap across her face. She stared at him in horror until, at the very moment when she felt that she must surely scream, hot tears blinded him from her sight. For a moment or two Brown hesitated; then, as sobs racked her body, he quietly left the room. He knew that she must hate him.

Throughout the summer the schoolhouse buzzed like a beehive. Apart from the presence of the M'Lennans, old pupils called to see the dominie, and meals were required at such unexpected hours that chaos was prevented only by the combined efforts of Mrs. Smith and tireless Maggie Stevens. It was now understood, too, that Brown could rely upon a bed whenever he decided to stay overnight, the inevitable consequence being that no one was ever quite sure when he might arrive. If Isabella M'Lennan was likely to be around, he took a certain amount of care of his appearance; but more often he came along in an old suit, dusty shoes, and with a couple of days' stubble on his chin. He enjoyed the company of dogs, and one evening he turned up with a collie puppy at his heels. After supper and a long bout of talking, he put the animal

64

in a shed at the back of the house and went to bed. He had a feeling that he would sleep well for once, but he had no sooner undressed than the puppy started to howl. How it produced such high-pitched wails at twelve weeks was a mystery. Brown put on his trousers and padded out to the shed where he was greeted with delighted whimpers. He carried the pup into the house and shut it in the study, and to his relief there was no further disturbance. Not, at any rate, until Maggie entered the study in the morning. As she surveyed the carpet, her eyes opened wide. Then she took one look at the culprit, gazing up at her with soulful expression, and tore off in search of the dominie.

"Come and see this!" she cried. "It's owre much!"

John Smith followed her to the study.

"You're quite right, Maggie," he said, nodding grimly. "Geordie will have to clean this himself."

Which meant that there was no breakfast in bed for Brown that morning.

Episodes both sombre and gay thus filled his summer, and no child ever returned more reluctantly to school than he did to Oxford.

"Oxford is as damnable as ever—except for one's chums," he wrote to Tom Smith. "The Dean has already jumped on me for coming up late."

Emanuel and Maughan wondered why he had come back; it was obviously not to study along established lines. He preferred to tell them of his exploits in Coylton and to give humorous sketches of old worthies or to go a-punting on the Cher. When alone, he read modern authors and reflected that, if he put his mind to it, he could depict character far better than they did.

By 1883 he had done so little preparation for Moderations that he was faced with a formidable spell of work. True, Moderations was repetition and a continuation of what he had already done, but large doses of the two great classical orators, Demosthenes and Cicero, were more than he could stomach. Finally, as H. W. C. Davis recorded, "he made up his mind as to the minimum amount of reading which would get him a First in Moderations, and ploughed through it in seven or eight weeks. It was a great feat. He worked almost continuously the whole day and every day, only submitting occasionally to be dragged out for a hurried walk." Brown had no intention of losing his First. He was wily in his choice of subjects, taking up, for example, four plays of Euripides (a somewhat unusual course) because he considered that in the short time he had left himself he could more easily master them than the customary three dramas of Sophocles, or two of that poet in conjunction with the Agamemnon of Aechylus. His reasoning proved correct.

After obtaining his First, he triumphantly joined his mother at her temporary home in Ochiltree, the Crofthead cottage being under extensive repair. In the afternoon he was pottering about in the front garden when Tom Smith came upon the scene. Knowing his man, Tom spoke about every subject under the sun except Oxford, and finally Brown bent down to pick a weed.

"I got a First in Classics," he remarked; and as he straightened himself Tom grasped his hand.

"Congratulations, George," he said warmly.

"I see ye had the sense no' to ask me about it," responded Brown. "I can't stand this damned keekin' and spierin'."

His brow darkened and cleared almost at once.

"Come in and see my mother," he went on. "She doesn't understand, you know, but she's tremendously pleased all the same."

Sarah smiled at the sight of him, and he turned laughingly to Tom.

"There you are," he said. "She'll give us an egg for our tea all right."

In Ochiltree he could not forget that he was in the place of his birth, although he had good friends down the long brae. People like Bob Wright and his wife were possessed of that simple, home-spun sincerity which did not permit them to say one thing and think another. When Brown called at Mrs. Wright's house next day, she stood back, arms akimbo.

"Ye ken what I'm gaun to tell ye, Geordie," she scolded. "Ye're an absolute disgrace. Ye're no' being fair to your mother when ye gang aboot in thae auld claes."

When he paid another visit the following afternoon, he was elaborately dressed in morning coat, high collar, and tall hat; but Mrs. Wright was still displeased.

"I might've kent it, Geordie," she said. "Ye either gang to yin extreme or the other. Never a happy medium."

He laughed and nodded as if to acknowledge that she was not so very wide of the mark.

Meanwhile he was anxious to give William Maybin the news about Oxford, and at the earliest opportunity he set out for Ayr. The waggonette which ran from Ochiltree seemed to him to be the most convenient mode of travel, and he was in time to get a seat at the top, just below the driver. Soon the brake was filled, and as the horses moved off a farmer next to the door at the far end surveyed the passengers. His expression bespoke his thoughts: a stranger in the brake!

"Wha's he that i' the front seat?" he asked the man beside him. Brown listened intently.

"Man"—he heard the reply—"d'ye no' ken wha that is?"

"Na, I canna say I do."

"That's auld Broon's bastard . . . ye ken . . . 'Smudden . . ."

If ever there was a glower in a man's eyes, it was in Brown's at that terrible moment. He did not stop to reflect that the crude-tongued farmer had stated a simple fact without any intention of malice.

"I'd rather be auld Broon's bastard than the son o' any man in this brake!" he ground out between his teeth.

His words had a shattering effect. Not a man dared to speak above an undertone for the rest of the journey.

By the time he reached Maybin's house, Brown had himself under control, but the incident was branded into him, and he afterwards sought relief by telling Isabelle Smith what had happened.

"Never mind, Geordie," she told him gently. "Such men are far beneath you. Just—just never mind."

But she knew that that was empty solace to a man who had been crucified.

It was her cousin who brought the laughter back to his voice. Dear, sweet, sympathetic Isabella M'Lennan! He knew beyond all doubt that he was in love with her and that no one else could make life seem so radiant.

Meanwhile he was still soaking in the atmosphere of the country-side. He continued to keep his ears open for vivid and unusual words, and at night, when Ochiltree was asleep, he committed them to paper. He planned to begin writing in earnest as soon as he got back to Oxford. There was, of course, the "Greats" part of the classical course to tackle; but if he delayed any longer the ideas and characters that were crowding his mind would become a disordered phantasmagoria. Instinct told him that he must not run that risk.

7

At Oxford Brown had found a Scot who was entirely to his liking. In his second year, this young man, William Menzies, who had already been a student at St. Andrews and Edinburgh, was his temperamental opposite. Whereas in argument Brown became excited and paced the floor, Menzies sat quietly, offering subtle reflections "in a sort of meandering mumble." Chiefly because they were both so well read in English literature, they respected each other, although their views did not necessarily coincide. Not long after term began, Menzies adversely criticized Thomas Hardy, and Brown was up in arms in a trice. Words poured from him in a trenchant flood, so that instead of Menzies attacking Hardy it ended by Brown vigorously attacking Menzies. They could afford to let themselves go, because they knew that they would not quarrel.

When Brown complained about indigestion, Menzies suggested

that he ought to cut down on sultana cake and take up cycling. Brown retorted that he had never ridden a bicycle in his life, and, rather unthinkingly for once, Menzies offered to teach him. A week or so later, after many back-breaking struggles to hold Brown upright on a borrowed machine, he gave up in disgust. For some reason—perhaps because of his weak eyes—Brown lacked all sense of balance.

He had gone back to his rooms in Walton Crescent, but he often visited his friends in college. He and Menzies were together one evening when a new man was introduced: the grave-eyed and able Ernest Barker. Inevitably he and Brown were drawn together. His father's wages being about eighteen shillings a week, Barker had come up the hard way. From a small country cottage in the north-east corner of Cheshire, he had gone to the village school and then to the excellent Grammar School in Manchester, and, like Brown, he owed much to the wonderful and indomitable spirit of his mother.

That first meeting was a memorable one for Barker. He was instantly aware of the magnetism in Brown's personality, and was impressed by the bold forehead and quick, glinting eyes, all the more piercing when Brown took off his glasses and had to make an effort to see. It was, however, his voice that Barker remembered most clearly, for Brown's tone, which was generally high, ran up to a shriek that somehow suited his own intensity. "I hear him rather than see him," Barker claimed, "and it is some high-pitched, 'Why, damn it, man, that's grand stuff,' that I hear." In his book of early memories, *Father of the Man*, he finally summed up Brown by saying, "He shone with the brightest flame of personality among all the men I knew."

While Brown always made a strong impression, he was not widely known among the undergraduates. Hilaire Belloc held glittering court in rooms at the foot of the staircase in Fisher's Buildings, but Brown was not cut out to be a courtier. He remained in, and was faithful to, his own circle. Besides, he had a tendency to treat certain people with a reserve that was almost suspicion. In a letter to his mother he gave his views on the line of conduct to follow in such company.

9 Walton Crescent,
Oxford.
Tuesday.

Dear Mother,

I am getting on all right. I know that is what you are chiefly concerned about so I stick it down first and foremost. I hope everything is going on well at Ochiltree with you and all your concerns. Life here is really so even and uneventful that there is not very much to write about. I enclose a licence for the dog which you must keep and have to shew when called upon.

I am glad you went to see the D——s and had a pleasant visit. I hope you did not talk much about me. You know I don't like being talked of before people of whose perfect friendliness and sincerity one isn't sure. To be quiet and reserved is the best policy when visiting swells.

Your aff. son
Geordie.

There was beyond doubt much of himself that he did not give away. In talking about his mother and Ayrshire, he never made any mention of his father. Yet when he accompanied Menzies to a theatre to see a mid-century Victorian play, he laughed aloud at a scene in which the father delicately informed his daughter, "You are a nature child, that is to say, you are a child of nature." After leaving the theatre Brown continued to take an immoderate delight in the episode. Again and again he stopped short and, turning to his companion, proclaimed, "'You are a nature child, that is to say, you are a child of nature.' Damned good, eh, Menzies?" Menzies was mystified by his mood, but years later, when he learned about Brown's illegitimacy, the events of that evening came back to him in their full significance.

As the term dragged on Brown grew less and less inclined to study. Lectures on Ancient History bored him, and after one on the Babylonians he remarked to an astonished undergraduate who had been taking careful notes, "Doesn't it depress you to hear of all the works of all those dead kings?"

The great Jowett[1] had died before Barker came into residence, but Brown often spoke about the Growler with amused contempt. "When I saw the veins on his forehead working," he said, thereby revealing his morbid faculty for visualization, "I knew that he was fairly twitching for an epigram with which to dismiss me." On another occasion he had found in the Master's *Plato* the advice to fix one eye on the problem immediately before him and to cast the other abroad upon the universe. On the margin Brown wrote: "Oh, Master, how you must squint!" The volume was a Balliol library copy, and the librarian, on observing the annotation, ordered him to purchase a new one. Brown liked to relate that type of story, but there was another evening when he was not so ready to laugh over his reminiscences of "the Jowler."

"How unfair it is," he said, "when someone dogmatizes as Jowett used to do. Unless a man is assertive his whole nature may be crushed by such bigotry. For example, if he's imaginative, metaphysical, and in an essay expands his views or ideas to a bigoted hard intellectualist, he is pretty sure to be snubbed and, if timid, self-distrustful, to be crushed. The intellectualist, finding him wanting on his pet side of knowledge, sets him down as a fool—all of

[1] Jowett's opinion of Brown has not been preserved.

which is damned unfair. The intellectual bigot is only showing his own narrow-mindedness and imperfection."

Becoming bitter in his condemnation of Oxford, Brown once declared, "What it needs is a cataclysmic intellect to vitalize life and thought"; but, paradoxically, he was ever ready to observe and uphold its traditions. When anyone made a pun or a classical quotation during dinner in hall, he was penalized for the offence by being sconced. In other words, he was mulcted by the chairman of the night in a mug of beer which went round the table. The culprit could, of course, stand up and "floor his sconce," which meant that, if he had sufficient stamina, he drained the cup. He was then entitled to sconce the man who had accused him. Sometimes appeals were sent up in writing to high table, and once, when one happened to be upheld by the Dean, Brown was furious. Outside he told Menzies that he was going to have the matter thrashed out, and though Menzies tried to dissuade him, he followed the Dean to his quarters and was closeted with him for a quarter of an hour. When he rejoined Menzies, who had waited in gloomy apprehension, he wore a look of grim satisfaction.

"It's all right," he said curtly. "I damned well told him what I thought."

But Menzies never learned what actually occurred.

In his attitude to Oxford Brown was thus a contradiction: he could be flippant one day, acidulous the next, and all the while remain surprisingly loyal. He was reading his own melancholy into Oxford, and—as Barker realized—he was fated to undergo bouts of depression wherever he went. His nerves were often in such a raw state that he was oppressed by a strange sense of suffocation, a complaint from which he frequently suffered in later years. At the same time, all this was not without value as an intellectual ferment. His senses were so keen that they presented him with pictures far more accurate than would otherwise have been the case. Consequently, when he wrote, he sought to capture physical sensations. He tried to get not only into the brain but into the very nerves of his characters.

Off and on that term he worked at a long sketch of country life, and because he wanted a sound, critical opinion, he finally read it aloud to Menzies. Unaware of Brown's desire to be a writer, Menzies was impressed by the artistry and strength of the sketch, and at the end of the reading, which took nearly an hour, he was sincere in his praise.

" It was Turgenev's *Sportsman's Sketches* that started me off," said Brown. "I thought I'd try something on similar lines."

He had been reading deeply in Russian literature, and he soon let Menzies know that he had little time for Dostoyevsky or Tolstoy. In psychological analysis, Tolstoy and Dostoyevsky both failed at the critical moment, the one by losing himself in a morass of words, the other by exaggeration and obscurity. Turgenev remained poised, his intellect perfectly balanced, as one writing in terms of French art; and Brown, realizing this fact, seized upon it for his own use. He was also reading French literature—he had given one of Renan's books to Barker—but though he admired Balzac he was never dominated by the French novelist in the way that many critics afterwards assumed.

In Menzies' company he now talked almost continuously about Ayrshire characters and scenes. At first Menzies found his anecdotes amusing, but gradually they came near to boring him. There was about them too much of a muchness for his searching, Socratic mind. He did not wound Brown by saying so. Instead he wondered what it all meant . . . and the answer was not yet. When the term ended and Brown returned to Ochiltree, he wrote a brief description of his journey.

"How glorious after wearying your verra soul in that flat Oxford landscape—on a lovely afternoon it aye minded me o' the wan pathetic smile o' a bit lassie deein' o' consumption—how glorious to travel up Nithsdale (stampin' on the carriage flair in verra delight to be back again!) watchin' the mist curlin' alang the hills and the great clean broon muirland water foaming and tumbling; maybe seein' some fisher, the swing o' his great shouthers showing him the Scot dowp-deep in the water, making the rod bend prettily."

Brown guessed that many villagers now were wondering what he was going to do with all his learning. For himself he did not want money or a job; he wanted time.

8

The year 1894 began reasonably well. In January Menzies was sufficiently in funds to organize a traditional Burns Supper for a small party of friends. Brown proposed the Immortal Memory and, as Menzies fully expected, gave an excellent critical estimate of the poet's work. With several bottles of whisky, "the night drave on wi' sangs and clatter," so that by twelve o'clock one or two guests had lost interest in the proceedings. Like Menzies, Brown could not afford to indulge in habitual drinking, but when the occasion arose he was able to take his whisky with the best of them. In the early morning he was still above the table and reciting whatever the others requested, and when the spree ended around two o'clock, he led the survivors outside to give a long-drawn rendering of *Auld Lang Syne* in the moonlight. The Dean, returning late from a visit, obviously understood the reason for the row; he passed, unheeding, as if he had suddenly become stone-deaf.

In March Brown was in Scotland, helping his mother to remove from Ochiltree to Crofthead. She was so glad to be back in the cottage, now completely renovated, that he went off in high spirits to visit various friends. When he arrived in Coylton and learned that Tom Smith was sitting examinations in Glasgow, he wrote the following letter in the vernacular.

Munday.

Dear Tam,

We are a' sittin thegither cheek by jowl bletherin awa like Biddy McAnally when the soo piggit. Bella's on ma richt, Mary's on ma left, and the snores o' Maggie Steen are sughin out through the kitchen door. I hae been stravaigin aboot the kintraside an' as Hugh McMillan wad say "have taken up my domicile for the night at the schoolhouse." Thanks for your last letter which I o't to have answered before but they put us through our paces at the last you know and leave little time for anything. However I faked up an excuse and got home about a week before the end of term and have transplanted my household gods to Crofthead—for the benefit of the sea air. Man it's glorious tae hae the big quate fiels, and the peesweeps, and the mavises an' the Arran sunsets at yer door instead o' the damned yammerin' and skirlin' o' the weans aboot Ochiltree. I was up at a pairty at McTeedieston on Friday nicht. When twal' o clock came we had champit tatties, ham, deuk, grapes (o' a kin's) lemonade for the lassocks and whisky for the men, and Will Lindsay nae less tae ladle it oot till us. A' the——s were there —Billy scunnerin' me tae ma bowels whammet in my inside an' Bess liltin' awa' like a mavis in a dauchy gloamin'. I cam daunerin doon the road on Seturday mornin', gaed straucht tae Ayr, roon by Affleck and feenisht aff wi' a nicht wi' Downie. A fair programme, I'm thinkin. I hae verra little min' o' ony mair tae write the noo and so subscribe masel yer sincere frien

Geordie Broon.

At Oxford again Brown's temper was uncertain. As he had done several times in the past, he suddenly gave up smoking and mooned about, sucking an empty pipe. When men whom he did not like crossed his path, he was quick to show his animosity and, with a few farmyard oaths thrown in for good measure, made a number of enemies in a short time. He forgot that everyone did not possess the sympathetic understanding of Barker, Menzies, Emanuel, and Maughan.

Behind his brusqueness he was hiding deep anxiety about his mother. She had been cheerful since her return to Crofthead, but he could not forget the stark fact of her disease. When he found it possible to send money, he enclosed a brief note.

Balliol College,
Tuesday.

Dear Mother,

I write in a great hurry. I send you a five-pound note and 3 postal orders for 3 pounds. The orders are in Davie's name and he will go to the post office and get the money. One of the pounds is his own: you are to use the rest.

And do for any sake take care of yourself, dear mother, and be well when I come back.

Your son
Geordie.

Yet he knew—and she must know—that she could not be well when he got home.

He was perturbed, too, by the amount of work that pressed upon him. He grumbled about it in a letter to Tom Smith, and then by way of relief introduced a Rabelaisian verse that was popular with undergraduates at that time.

Balliol College.

My Dear Tom,

I scrawl you off this in a hurry just because I haven't time to write at length (as I meant to do all week) and yet don't want to keep you waiting for an answer. I'm in scrapes, I can tell you, because I came up this term with so little work done. The work is coming rolling in on me like Atlantic billows—swamping me and leaving me gasping—each towering wave bigger than the last. I have to reread the *Ethics* and make analysis of it, ditto the *Republic* of Plato (X books in both: there are 354 pps of translation in the *Ethics*) whole of Thucydides, whole of Herodotus, Cicero's *Letters*, 6 books of Tacitus, some Plutarch, Aristotle's logic—the *Posterior Analytics*, Mills' *Logic*, Selections from Locke, Berkeley, and Hume—the ancient authors of course to be read in the original, analysed and the history of philosophy extracted from them. There's some smaller stuff but that's all I remember just now—oh, Bradley's *Logic*'s another—besides lectures, etc.

I've got till the middle of June, *and I mean to work*. The worst of it is I'm getting interested in the stuff and can't vamp it as I would for a merely cramming exam. Fortunately, my health (barring a damnable cold) and my spirits are both of 'em ripping. This is a stupid, hastily written and "sprieky" sort of scrawl. But one of the reasons I like you, Leviathan, is that a fellow can open out to you—shew you his mind in its night-shirt, as it were—without the risk of being sneered at.

Love to the girls,
Yours ever sincerely
G. D. Brown.

It's 12.15 Saturday morning. I'm trying to write an essay on the value of Aristotle's conception of the mean as a moral ideal. Ah me miserum—Damn it, it's a big letter, after all.

Yours,
G. D. B.

While he believed that he was "getting interested in the stuff," Brown had, of course, no leanings towards philosophy or history, the two subjects conjoined in Greats, and he certainly could not, as Barker subsequently did, enjoy them both impartially.

During that last summer term his mother's condition worsened, and in the autumn she was removed to a Glasgow infirmary for an operation. After it, as she hesitated between life and death, he gave up all thought of work. He calculated that with luck a late, superhuman effort would see him through; but early in 1895 news reached him that his mother was to leave the infirmary, and he had a premonition that she was being sent home to die. With pale, set face, he explained to the Master, the tall, white-bearded Caird, and said goodbye to Menzies and the rest. He had made his decision— and went off to nurse his mother at Crofthead.

This time—even when he sat beside her, her comfort and her staff in the long watches of the night—Sarah was too ill to wonder why he was not at Oxford. He dreaded what was to come, albeit he knew that it must come; for death was in life a constant shadow. Today, despite her pain-racked body, his mother had her being. Tomorrow, what then? There—and be damned to divines, dons, and philosophy!—there was the ultimate, inexplicable mystery.

Hopefully, as the weeks wore on and the birds sang to the resurrection of the spring, Sarah rallied a little, and Brown felt free enough in mind to write to Barker.

Crofthead,
Near Ayr.
Sunday.

Dear Barker,
Forgive my apparent neglect in not answering your letter. Believe me it was due to no coldness of feeling or want of sympathy on my part. I like you to write to me unreservedly and I don't think you can accuse me of not returning the confidence. But I have been wretchedly worried for a while. My mother was lying at death's door for some weeks and is still very ill, while I myself have had a bout of toothache, insomnia, and neuralgic headache for a week. Between sitting up at nights and mental and other worry I haven't done a page of honest work since I came home. I'll come down with an awful *dump* in Greats. I have experienced in the past the pleasant danger of hearing my keel scrrunt on the shallow bar as I glided into the smooth haven of a first but this time I'll drift broadside on and stick there a helpless and useless hulk. All of which brings me round to say that you'll now see why I didn't write to you before.

I had intended to send you a big and full and, if possible, interesting letter but after last night's hot restless misery I cannot make my brains stick together. Thank heaven I'm not in town to-day with its brain-shattering eye-wounding annoyances—rasping noises and hot sun beating down on red bricks and white glaring pavements. I went up Crofthead Hill about three o'clock; away to the South Carrick Hill sloped grandly to the Firth—softly veiled[1] in a warm delicate haze; larks everywhere and the great mild melancholy sunshine. It was the kind of day that reconciles you to existence. But for all that I was glad to escape to this cool dark room with the earthy barnlike smell that clings to old fashioned rooms on a hot day.

One thing I owe to my insomnia—the enjoyment of some glorious moonlight skies. About a week ago there was a *white* night of marvellous beauty—the sky all muffled up in a great milky cloud-fluff—a glorious white canopy full everywhere of a soft clearness—no cold austerity of a bare and starry firmament but a veiled and tender sky shedding a kindly wooing light upon the dusky earth.

Look here, Barker, did you say in your letter that I took more delight in my love letters than in idylls of nature? Why, Barker my friend, I differ from Burns hugely for I prefer a landscape to a sweetheart, (though I admit that the one enhances the other sometimes of a summer evening); at Oxford I kept a journal in which I noted sunsets and things of that sort with religious accuracy.

I send you some rhymes which you once said you liked rather (No. 11), and also some other verses (No. 1) which I wrote two years ago and found the other day in the pocket of an old coat. (They are not written to my loyal lover and comrade.) When I rediscovered them I was inclined to swear that they were really love-poetry but I'm a very bad judge of my own compositions and I'm not so sure now: at any rate I like them better than No. 11 which is perhaps too neat to be altogether noble. Give me an honest even if a merciless opinion.—I have mentioned my loyal little comrade . . . what a dear wee lady she is!—"the charmingest dainty wee lady, half lyric and all repartee" as I once wrote in her album. You will do me the credit of believing, Barker, that I don't tell you all this because I plume myself on having made a conquest. Ma foi, ce n'est pas le premier temps, cela! Besides this is a mean form of vanity from which I think I'm remarkably free. And if you will take my advice, Barker, you will never womanize. Even at its best it is but noble sentimentalism and has a bad effect on a fellow's character.

My head is too muggy and achey to admit of my writing more to-day. I'll finish my garrulous nonsense to-morrow.

I am very ill at ease when I think of the four years I spent at Oxford. I hated the physical and intellectual atmosphere of the place but if I had rendered myself more amenable to its discipline I should have corrected some faults of which I am only too conscious. Arnold quotes from Goethe something like "Wer grosses will, must

[1] I mean the Hill was " veiled " of course.

sich zusammen—raffen'' and I for one need pulling together most damnably. Laziness, hypochondria, and devil-may-careness have all been developed in me much more than they were four years ago—in fact both inwardly and outwardly I'm in a bad way. I could write more but the postman is due and I must dry up—probably to your great relief.

Yours ever,

G. D. Brown.

P.S. I know that it's almost an impertinence to remind you that this letter is strictly confidential. Write to me as freely as you like about anything. You, you know, are now lying beneath the trees of the term after Mods in the barge of a First with your heels up and a cushion below your head, and have time—great kindly time to do what you like with—while I—ah me!

No. 1.

All the Beauty and the Grace
That abides within thy face
Flashes forth with glad surprise
When thou lifst thy glorious eyes—
Those dark shining eyes that move me
Even more and more to love thee.

Dark thou art as summer night
When it shines with dusky light
And the earth seems fairer far
Shimmering 'neath the evening star—
Happy hour when I can move thee
For a little while to love me!

Blue-eyed girls with golden hair
Are as languid as they're fair
Thou'rt a maid of warmer worth
Wild with wit and mad with mirth—
Sweet my darling wouldnst thou prove me
Take my love and learn to love me.

No. 11

To a lady who reproached the Writer for Unbelief

I believe not: would I did,
That I might, when thou dost bid,
Swear, "By Heaven I love thee."
But since Gods are idle dreams,
And my only Heaven seems
Where thy beauty sheds its beams,
Let me swear a nobler oath,
Sweeter pledge to bind us both,
"By thyself, I love thee."

Here's something else—an excerpt from my scrap-book—for
your scalpel—to refute your sneer at Scotland.

Melancholy Oxford

The weather is balmy and mild: from a slope you can see the flat
landscape for miles beneath a faint clear half-blue haze. A cock-
crow in Scotland is something cheery—"a rousing craw"—here
it is subdued and far away: you hear the sound miles off one would
think and a vague feeling of sadness comes over you. But the
distinguishing feature of the flat country is the pathetic sense of
vague far-off lonely horizons and illimitable distances.

Heigh-ho it's Sunday and I ought to be reading Thucydides.
Life's a damned nuisance. If it's a joke the Deity has a very
poor sense of humour. But I daresay you've heard me say that
before.

As an afterthought Brown enclosed some lines which he had
written on college notepaper at one time.

In Summer Term

How good
When the head is dazed with the heat
When the limbs are tired and the eyes
Ache in the pitiless glare
From the white-hot dust of the roads
To escape to an old fashioned room
That is spacious and shaded and cool
Where the far-off noises are husht
And the multitudinous leaves
Whose greenness curtains the view
Scarcely ripple and
Hang in the down-beating glare.
How good
Lying at ease on a couch
Big, with a slope in its back
Suiting the curve of your spine,
To long on the thirst-soothing tea
That haply a Barker has made;
Glancing anon at a book,
To enjoy the delicious cool.
And how good
Lazily sucking a pipe
Lazy with half-shut eyes
Content acquiescent in life
To forgive your natural foes
Pardon the master D Eau

After receiving Barker's reply, Brown wrote the following:

It's almost unnecessary to   Crofthead,
congratulate you on your first—   Near Ayr.
nothing else was expected of course.

Dear Barker,

I myself was very much out of conceit with these verses even when I sent them. But you and I seem to differ as to love songs for the lines you thought the best I thought about the worst. I was better pleased with "Flashes forth with glad surprise when thou lifst thy glorious eyes" etc., for the girl could raise her great dark eyes in a flashing way that glorified her face and surprised and delighted the beholder. I think, too, you're wrong about the comparison with evening. I did not say that she was like the evening *because* I saw her then, in fact I thought the sudden apostrophe of the "happy hour" not a bad tip though perhaps artificial. As a whole you're right—for the whole affair ("affaire" rather) was artificial and hardly worth thinking about. I'm not working twenty-five hours a day, the more's the pity. It's all very well to spurt but when you're trapped up in the beginning of your spurt as I was this time you simply lie there and kick your heels and wait for the inevitable. I'm in a slab of unholy resignation and can't even work up a funk. I'm going to begin my work to-morrow.

You say, "pity me, for this I wrote immediately after receiving your letter." Well, Barker, if one can diagnose by the excrement mental as well as physical disease, my letter must have been a strange and loathsome affliction. Or in writing that last page were you thinking, "Naculumacii, Fortius et melius Fusci plerumque secat res"—were you using the "naso adunco" at the Ixerebias of a certain constipated fancy? You ironical man!

My soul, Barker, is cumbered by the irksome fetters of a head affection with which solemn assertion I close.

                          Ever yours sincerely,

WRITE   G. D. Brown.

P.S. I am almost afraid to send you the accompanying verses but they're lying on the table—it was an amended copy that "flew to where ma lassie bides." As usual I thought them good once, but don't think so now: the perpetual alteration of the same rhyme is displeasing or otherwise according to the tone in which you read them. Murmured with a deep harmonious thrill in somebody's ear they might—they would then—be poetry, but what the critical Barker may think—!

To an absent sweetheart

Dear and only love o' mine,
Swear thou canna leave me,

If my lassie I should tine[1]
　　Ever would it grieve me;
A' she ever granted mine
　　Fortune may bereave me,
But my verra heart maun[2] *pine*
　　Should my lassie leave me.

If I saw that face o' thine,
　　Could I doubting grieve thee
Ae[3] *look o' they een divine*
　　And I beet[4] *believe thee;*
In the garland life shall twine
　　Bonniest flower I'll weave thee,
Then return, ae[5] *dear o' mine,*
　　—Lassie, dinna leave me!

G. D. B.

Brown found a measure of relief in writing to Barker during those dark and weary weeks of nursing, but it was soon plain that his mother's slight rally had but teased his hopes: the end was near, and he braced himself to face it.

She died, worn out, on the 13th of May 1895, and on that day his youth died with her.

He arranged for her burial in the kirkyard at Ayr, near a tree where he knew that the birds would always sing, and there she was laid in the brown earth.

To one of her friends of long standing he wrote on black-edged notepaper.

Crofthead,
Near Ayr.

Dear Agnes,

You will be sorry to learn that my mother died on Monday last. The immediate cause of death was disease of the heart.

There will be no formal memorial or notice of her death, but, as you were very kind to her and she liked you, I thought I would write you a short note to let you know and to thank you for your kindness. Believe me to be

Yours very sincerely,
G. Douglas Brown.

He turned him richt and roon aboot,
Said: "Scorn na at my mither,
Licht loves I may get mony a ane,
But minnie ne'er anither".

[1] tine: lose.
[2] maun: must.
[3] ae: one.

[4] beet: must needs, stronger than must.
[5] ae here: one and only.

79

There was nothing more to say. Those last four lines, which might have served as her epitaph, would have pleased the simple heart of Sarah Gemmell.

9

After his mother's funeral, Brown stayed with the Smiths until it was time to face Oxford, and as his letter to a college friend, J. D. Symon, clearly showed, he did not delude himself about his chances of success. Symon, a sentimental Aberdonian with journalistic interests, had suggested a piece of literary work to him.

"Here," replied Brown, "here is my difficulty. My mother died last week. I was her only living relative and had, naturally, a good deal of nursing and sitting up at nights. Even by heavy cramming for the last three months I could not have scored more than a second; as it is, I shall have to spurt for the three weeks remaining to get a third or a fourth. There is some of my work that I haven't seen yet. So that I shan't have much time for writing."

When he went up to Oxford, his grief raw within him, Brown was in the same fatalistic mood. On the morning of the examination he did not feel well enough to present himself, and at the back of his mind he argued that it did not matter. The Master, who had had Brown in his class in Moral Philosophy at Glasgow University, was not prepared to let the matter slide. He sent for Brown and pressed him to sit in the afternoon. Brown agreed—against his own judgment—and came down with the "dump" that he had prophesied to Barker: Third Class in the Final School of Literae Humaniores. "Had he sat for the whole exam," the Master still maintained, "he ought to have taken a good Second Class."

Brown wanted to be left alone to lick his wounds, but Emanuel and Maughan had other plans for him. Emanuel had often declared that, when Final Schools were over, they would walk to London, a feat which Hilaire Belloc and some of his friends had made popular, and Maughan now agreed that it would be a most romantic way to leave Oxford.

Intending to reach Emanuel's home in four stages of approximately thirteen miles each, they accordingly started off from Magdalen Bridge at five o'clock on a morning in mid-June, and although Brown ominously remarked that he had not been to bed, they made steady progress throughout the forenoon and early afternoon.

As they passed High Wycombe, however, the heat was oppressive, and at Beaconsfield, when Brown and Emanuel began to argue about some trifle, their tempers snapped like dry sticks. In an effort to restore peace, Maughan pointed to an old house.

"Look," he remarked. "That's where Disraeli used to live."
Brown turned towards him.

"Maughan," he said angrily, "you're a damned liar! You're
only trying to stop us arguing."

Not until a friendly meal at Uxbridge did they laugh over the
squabble and feel ready to tackle the last lap.

Brown thus entered London for the first time in gas-lit darkness.
Emanuel led the way to his parents' home at 67 Queensborough
Terrace, and Maughan, hearing the strokes of twelve o'clock as
they reached the front door, reflected that they had accomplished
what they set out to do.

Emanuel's father was a solicitor of few words and a sarcastic
tongue, but despite this he delighted to entertain and was an excellent host. It was typical of both him and his wife that hot baths,
good food and wine awaited the tired and dusty trio. Mrs. Emanuel,
a vivacious and very pretty woman, obviously loved to talk, but
Brown noted that she did not chatter. There was intelligence in
everything she said.

When he was shown to his bedroom Brown knew that he would
not sleep. It cut him to the quick to reflect that he had disappointed
John Smith and William Maybin. Why, he still treasured his exercise books from the Ayr Academy days. "You know I have great
hopes of you," Maybin had written in one of them. Brown winced.
He had flared up like a rocket, and, by God, he had fizzled out like
one. Apart from anything else, he had besmirched the record of the
Snell Exhibitioners. Adam Smith, the Master himself, W. P. Ker,
Andrew Lang and other able men had all belonged to the proud
company. And he, the odd man, had not upheld its great and
distinguished succession.

Yet unknown to him Oxford had left its indelible stamp upon his
mind. It did not show in ease of manner and refinement of speech,
but, when his hour came, it revealed itself in his work. Those four,
unhappy years had not been wasted, for if, as he believed, he had
failed Oxford, Oxford in the end did not fail him.

PART THREE

THE BRAVE YEARS

I

London in 1895, especially if you had golden sovereigns in your pockets, was a pleasant place in which to live. Since 1885 there had been a period of almost complete peace throughout the Empire. Gladstone had just passed from the parliamentary scene to the quiet of Hawarden, but, with Queen Victoria still on the throne, life was as solid and secure as it had ever been. In the literary world Kipling, Wells, Barrie, Shaw, Doyle, Grant Allen, Anthony Hope, Hall Caine, Marie Corelli and many others were established names, while Ian Maclarcn and Samuel Rutherford Crockett were delving with considerable success in their ain kailyard.

Being outside this prosperous circle, Brown shared rooms with his friend, Symon, in Westbourne Park, and he thus was within convenient distance of Monty Emanuel's home, where he invariably received a welcome that reminded him of the Coylton schoolhouse. He often went shopping with Mrs. Emanuel in the forenoons, when they usually became so absorbed in conversation that she forgot what her cook had required for lunch. Her eye for the idiosyncrasies of people whom she knew was as quick as Brown's own, and she took a mischievous delight in capping his stories of Scotland with those of mid-European folk-lore and the Talmud. She was a fine pianist, and though Brown did not understand music he liked to listen to her playing. She had, in fact, come into his life when he needed her friendship most.

When alone he carefully considered his position. Now that his mother was dead there was no need to worry about the future. Security and position, which he had wanted for her sake, could go to the devil. He would devote himself to literature, using journalism as a means to that end.

Through Symon, who was now on the *Illustrated London News*, David Meldrum, editor of the *Success*, invited him to submit "Scottish idylls of a more robust character than was the fashion at that moment."

"Of course," replied Brown, "I shall have to feel my way a bit. I daresay one might write what was possible, perhaps, from one point of view, but still not the sort of thing you require. I shall try, therefore, if possible to let you have various short pieces in different styles to see what is the most suitable. By 'Written in the Scots vernacular' I suppose you mean, of course, that the conversation only will be Scots, the connecting prose being English. Or did you mean otherwise? It is very difficult, I admit, to write Scots that is not fatuous and vulgar—I mean, to keep the racy twang of the native dialect, and yet make it fit to appear in a 'prent beuk'—as Scott, for example, and I think he only, could do supremely well. It is far easier to write Scots verse: at least it is easier not to be silly in verse; and for this and for other reasons much of the Scotch printed nowadays seems to be vulgar in its humour and maudlin in its pathos. It is much easier, of course, to criticize than to write, and I am very diffident of success where better men have failed; but I'll try."

The first example of Brown's work, an anonymous sketch entitled "On the Carrick Road," duly appeared in the *Success* on 14th September 1895, and the following extracts illustrate his passion and feeling for words.

About three o'clock on a market afternoon the High Street of Ayr is a jolly, bustling, curious spectacle. It is when the ostlers are putting horses to gigs and the guidwives are gathering their parcels that the cronies show themselves in all their glory. Here stands a group of 'sponsible men, weel-kenned from Essex to Aberdeen for excellence of stock—Osbornes, Lindsays, Murrays, Wilsons, Montgomeries. Some are already away rattling up the street. How jolly and masterful they look, sitting great-coated by their canty dames, "garrin' toon-bodies stand abeigh" as they whip the mettled roadsters! Maybe on the back seat are two braw blushing lassies, and maybe two lads, on their way back from market, will drop into the milking-shiel about "the time the kye come hame"—for this is courting night in Ayrshire. Maybe, too, if they give themselves airs, the lassies will "scoot" milk at them past the "luggie's" edge: such things happen at times. . . .

. . . With most of the men about, rearing prize cattle is a mania. Their advice on the subject is eagerly sought. An Ayr man was once asked by an American to describe the broad, "gaucie" head of a prize Ayrshire. He defined her as "a coo wi' an intelligent foreheid."

Though there is still plenty of joviality in Ayrshire, there is little of the "roarin' and rantin' and rampin'" that marked the homeward drive thirty years ago. On one occasion a cob galloped home with the shafts dangling, leaving its master seated amid the debris of the trap—"cowpit at his ain road-fit." As he was stottering up the road he met one of the servants. "Jock," he said, very drily, "tak' a poke wi' ye doon to the road-en' to fetch hame the gig wi'."

Away south of Maybole lies the country of Hew Ainslie. It was Hew who wrote:

> *Gie her sail, gie her sail, till she bury her 'wale,*
> *Gie her sail, lads, wile it may sit,*
> *She has roared through a heavier sea before,*
> *And she'll roar through a heavier yet.*

"There's a grand Scots 'gurr' there—a ringin' dirl in the words that gangs straucht to the heart o' a man."

So Tam Dulap said.

Tam is a cattle-dealer with a monstrous squint, "a grand heid,.and great po'er o' langwidge," who picked me up one day on the Girvan road.

"Ay, man, 'e're richt aboot Hew Ainslie. Few things gie the awsome loneliness o' an October nicht like that bit rhyme o' his,—

It's dowie in the hin' o' hairst,
At the 'wa-gang o' the swallow.

But an auld Eerishman owre here aince cam' oot wi' a thing that gangs clean ayont Ainslie. It says mair in fewer words; and to talk little and say muckle's the verra kernel o' expression.

"At the feck o' times he was a rantin', cheery buddy, this auld plooman, but ae nicht, I've mind, he was sittin' a' his lane, terrible waesome and wearyin'-like. 'What ails 'e, Pat?' quo' I. Man, I'll never forget the far-off tone his voice took—dowff and low; when he ca'ed himsel' 'lonely'; it soonded like the lonesome wind. 'Hach, hach, ananee,' he cried, 'it's the ould country I'm thinkin' of, and them that I've buried there, and I'm as lonely, lonely, lonely as a night in the hind-harvest.' Ay, man, and it is lonely when there's a cauld, yellow licht alang the bare stibbles, and the wind tak's an eerie sough aboot the gloamin'."

Another published sketch, which he wrote at this time, was about a boy called Buddly Rudds, but in the main he was only feeling his way, and underwent the experience of all free-lance writers.

"My offerings came back like boomerangs," he said. "Talk of casting your bread on the waters. I cast my manuscripts into the pillar at the corner, and the next morning at breakfast up they came with the *Daily Mail* and the morning roll."

Yet he had no cause for complaint; he was luckier (and better equipped) than most would-be writers. On the recommendation of Meldrum, he became literary adviser to the publishing house of John Macqueen, wrote regularly for the *Realm*, which was edited by W. Earl Hodgson, and contributed reviews and odd paragraphs to the *Illustrated London News*. For most of his first year, too, he did a certain amount of tutoring.

Even before he became associated with Macqueen, one of his letters to Barker, although written on black-edged notepaper, was far from funereal. And how Barker smiled over Brown's impulsive and romantic train journey, which was so typical of the man.

11, Cornwall Road,
Westbourne Park,
London, W.

My Dear Barker,

Just a line to let you knów my whereabouts. Yes, eliminate from existence and from memory the address you found.

I am here doing hack work for the *Realm* and an ephemeral new production called the *Success*.

Last Thursday night I went to St. Pancras and loud above the grinding, foolish turmoil emitted a clear, cooing whistle. A lady in grey came along the platform attended by a chaperon and many friends. She, unobserved of the others, indicated the West of Scotland train. They placed her in a first-class compartment and under the care of four guards; but I got out of my third-class at Kentish Town, three minutes later, and travelled with her to Bedford—ninety minutes of dear, sweet happiness. She has a heart of God's own gold—et moi, je ne l'aime pas? Yes, it was Heaven's own delight, but, bad cess to it, it cost me fifteen shillings and a night's sleep, for there wasn't a train back till next morning.

I'd like you to write to me occasionally. As you know I'm not the man to ask for friendship in a mawkish sort of way, but I have no relatives now and friends mean a lot to me. I am living with Symon, and he, pauvre sujet, is mawkish enough for twelve. "The drowsy, languorous warmth of the summer afternoon filled the quiet garden. There was a slumberous murmur in the air. From the ivy-muffled casement filtrated the soft, slow tones of a dulcet, rhythmic harmony." That's a favourable parody of his style—as easy and effusive as any other excretion of nature.

I meant to send a note and have written a letter. Send me epistles about anything—drink, women, books, criticism, emotions, animosities.

D'you know those lines?—

> Gie her sail, gie her sail, till she bury her wale,
> Gie her sail sae lang as it sit,
> She has roared thro' a heavier sea before,
> And she'll roar thro' a heavier yet.

There's a grand Scots "gurr" in these lines. They're by Hew Ainslie.

Yours ever,
G. D. Brown.

P.S. I get bad fits of the blues as usual, but London itself is not a bad tonic for a man.

P.P.S. I'm not so sure about that "je ne l'aime pas."

On another occasion Brown addressed Barker much more pointedly.

Why the hell don't you write to me?
Brown.

While he was ever ready to exchange views, to turn a subject inside out if need be, he was faced with difficulties.

"I have a lot of things to write about," he once declared, "but I'm too lazy at present. I couldn't write to any purpose without tumbling myself out on paper, and it costs a lot of exertion that. Like my big Highland friend Duncan, who failed repeatedly in some not very profound philosophical examination, 'I have tamned fine sheneral ideas, but it's the details that pother me, yess, by Golt, it iss the details.'"

Brown was tormented by the difficulty of expressing himself. He tried to explain his case by saying that the thought of the printer putting this that he was writing into type always stultified him in the moment of writing it. Consequently, he often experienced a wild impatience when, conscious of his own superior, though inarticulate ability, he watched the easy performances of smaller men.

Yet with the help of Shakespeare he always subdued this feeling. "When workmen strive to do better than well," he would quote from *King John*, "they do confound their skill in covetousness." And he would reach for his hat and go round to see Monty Emanuel.

2

Brown did not miss a single detail of his new environment. His lodgings being high in a house that overlooked a railway, his insomnia was punctuated by the clanking and banging of nightly shuntings. When he peered out of the window, he saw in the glare of powerful lights the gleam of metal, trucks of coal, sheds, and men at work. One evening, too, he watched an unusually fierce thunderstorm until, as he confessed to Symon, the nervous strain was no longer endurable. Although no coward, he was capable of being wrought up to an extraordinary pitch of imaginative sensibility, and the vivid horror with which he figured the possibility of his being "blasted to a cinder" by the lightning remained, like the noises of the goods yard, a permanent impression. He was morbidly sensitive to the uncleanliness of the streets and of humanity, and more than once he burst out, "London is a big wild beast of a place!" In less liverish mood he liked to watch dusk creeping over the city and then to watch the play of lights upon girlish faces. Soon, Symon noted, it was possible to anticipate his state of mind. If he had no evening papers when he came in, he was certain to be cheerful and talkative; with the newspapers under his arm, however, he was more likely to be in low spirits. He read them, so he pretended, "to keep himself from fierce visualizations that unstrung him."

With all his atrabilious vagaries, he wasted less time than people imagined, and he had already discussed with David Meldrum, who had gone over to the publishing house of Blackwood, the possibilities of a historical geography of the British Empire, "done with sweep and colour." For this project he did an enormous amount of reading, and bombarded Meldrum with detailed notes. Nothing came of it, but about the same period he gave much practical help to Meldrum in the editing of John Galt's novels for Blackwood. The scheme of the edition embraced notes, and for one of these to *The Entail*, on the state of agriculture in Scotland at the end of the eighteenth century, Brown made researches far beyond the immediate requirement. Subsequently it was decided to include a glossary in the edition, a task ready-made for Brown. When it was finished, Blackwood's literary adviser, Alexander Allardyce, did not agree with all of it; but he did not belong to the West of Scotland, and Brown and Galt were Ayrshire men. When he was later challenged about various words in his own use of dialect, Brown always referred his critics to the Galt Glossary for the best information on the Ayrshire tongue.

In a letter to Meldrum, written a considerable time after this work, he mentioned Galt in a manner that indicated how deep had been his reading.

"A man's memory by its very infirmity helps him greatly to achieve artistic values. The aim is to suggest, to get the distinctive word or phrase or thought, and just because it's this salient point only that abides in the memory, it's this point that gets on to the paper. Through hidden processes of cerebration the selection goes on in a man's mind. And Galt is strange in this connection. He had too good a memory; and yet it is because his memory was better than the average good that he attains universality. If a man gets all his world down he may bore you, but he will give a sense of totality: just by his marvellous reproduction of *everything* he is universal, he is big, he achieves the bigly-motived greatness. The man with a fair memory or observation who tries to do this falls between two stools. He neither selects the salient nor gives the whole. The more informed Shakespeare minds select the revealing point of light, they suggest. Note, too, that the Russians (*War and Peace*) are apt to get this secondary universality, and so Whitman. . . . And this insistence on the value of selection does not militate on the belief in the value of writing landscape with your eye on the spot. Because there, you mustn't, indeed, describe particular twigs, but you must get yourself into the feel of the thing, the temperamental mood, the dreamy state, the 'tid'. And this can best be done when you are there, or immediately after. You remember your own impressions; whereas if a time elapses you forget your own impressions and try to describe by the memory of the eye—by the physical memory—you know what I mean—not the mental."

Brown's work on Galt did not render him unfaithful to Burns. Having in mind the fact that the centenary of the poet's death was due in July 1896, he looked out his Oxford notes with a view to writing an article, for his estimate as a student did not differ from his judgment as a man. Day after day he conned his little, well-worn Globe edition of the poems until he covered it with so many annotations, references, and cross-references that its binding yielded to his fierce thumbing.

Symon said that "Brown seemed to feel peculiar keenness that he was of the same countryside as the Bard, and there were moments when he seemed to realize that the spirit of Ayrshire's most gifted son was alive within him, and that, if he chose, he could compel his fellows to yield him recognition."

Certainly Brown was steeped in his subject, and he believed quite seriously that, in the improbable event of the entire text being lost, he could restore it from memory. He extended his critical knowledge by an exhaustive study of Allan Cunningham's edition, which he called "a wilderness of a book, but a mine of Burns's material."

With so much matter to digest, the article did not come easily, and Brown turned from it to write to Barker.

Meldrum and I have an article in the June "Blackwood". I have wanted to rewrite my Burns thing for 8 weeks but I haven't had the spirit to attempt it.

11 Cornwall Road,
Westbourne Park, W.

Dear Barker,

When I saw your note on the table I reddened with shame at the thought that I'd never written to you. Believe me it was from no want of liking or respect for you. You're the man at Oxford to whom I cottoned with frankest unreserve, the man who understood me (so far as such a madman deserves understanding) with readiest sympathy. And in token of that I have for many months meant to write to you a most long and intimate letter—such a letter as I would write to no one but yourself. But again and again I've put it off, because to write of oneself with fulness and accuracy takes time and care—and, as you say, I'm always indolent—and, then again, the mood would change and I'd question the propriety of amusing or annoying Barker by shewing him my mind in its pyjamas. And so I've drifted on. But I could talk to you—and would like to talk to you or listen to you—my dear fellow, my dear friend, for hours on end together. Only I cannot come to Oxford this term, much as I would like to, much as I thank you for the invitation. (If I can come on May 9th I'll let you know.) I'm very tired and I've written very fast: however I *will* send you some kind of big epistle soon. Always yours most sincerely,

G. D. Brown.

Completed at last, the article on Burns was accepted by Blackwood, and Brown spoke of expanding it in a volume of literary essays—another scheme which never took shape. There was a suggestion, too, that he might edit the poet's works for Blackwood, but other editions were due on the market, and it was decided that the time was not propitious for another.

His article, which appeared anonymously in *Blackwood's Magazine* for August 1896 thus remained his first and last major pronouncement on Burns.

3

Anything else that Brown wrote about Burns was fragmentary. Yet his notes continued to be pregnant with meaning, especially as there was so much of himself between the lines.

It is a great thing to have the detachment, the self-mastery, that ignores insult; but if a man's nature responds to low insult, low insult must lower him. Burns squirmed, I have no doubt, at the sneers of people. To the individualistic mind, what Meredith says of the Welsh is true.[1] Doubtless Burns may have come from the field with the sound of the wind in his soul. Suddenly he remembers what that damned cad the cobbler said long ago; in a moment he is in the quick of the old injury, the beauty of the evening vanishes . . . result: a virulent, ugly, terrible epigram.

So in Burns's "Wearin' the day awa",—an inferior melancholy perhaps, but little so because in Burns's mind too there was the sense of man's poor effort, and sorrow for it. Burns felt all the pathos of the poor man's constant toil there.

Wi' claivers and haivers
Wearin' the day awa.

From over in the wooded trees comes the lonely soft note of a cushat, and "Man," says Burns musingly, "but that's a queer, queer, lonely cry." But Jeems, who is a respectable young prig, a mere acrid nonentity, a postule, a mere blotch on the face of the world, destined to end its days as Superintendent of a Sunday School,— Jeems looks at the speaker with furtive suspicion in his narrow eye, and asks his father in the gloaming "if he doesna think yon Burns daft?" "As for me," he says, "I canna mak' heid nor tail o' him." . . . Note the value of the *Still* in

Still shearin' and clearin'
The tither stookit raw.

[1] Evidently a reference to *The Amazing Marriage*. "Now to the Cymry and to the pure Kelt, the past is at their elbows continually. . . . Historically they still march with Cadwallader, with Lewellyn, with Glendower; sing with Aneurin, Taliesin, old Llywarch; individually they are back in the heart of the injury done them thirty years back; or thrilling to the glorious deed which strikes an empty buckler for most of the sons of time."

It gives the sense of unendingness of their toil, the monotony of it, which is brought out in "tither stookit raw." Row after row goes up, and one has a feeling, "Oh, will this field never be finished," while the women straighten their backs to get rid of that intolerable anguish which only the harvester knows.

Apart from his eternal note-taking, Brown was finding life irksome. Symon was getting on his nerves, and Macqueen's manuscripts were trite. There was seldom any sign of the stuff that Brown regarded as "essential." When he told Emanuel and Maughan that he could write better himself, they knew that he did not boast out of a royal arrogance of intellect. They were confident that he would make his mark.

Behind his impatience—and indeed deep within himself—Brown was equally as certain that, when he had overcome his difficulties, he would succeed. On his fleeting visits to Ayrshire, he told Isabella M'Lennan that he knew he would "arrive," and once, in roaring spirits, he bet her one hundred pounds that he would earn £5,000 a year by the time he was forty-five. Isabella laughed, but he set out the wager in black and white, they signed their names to it, and he entrusted the document to her cousin, Mary Smith.

And so far his only work of note had been an anonymous article on Burns! Acting on the principle of *omne ignotum pro magnifico*, each literary authority on the poet had been inclined to suspect some other of the authorship; but they had lost interest quickly enough when it had been disclosed that the writer was one George Douglas Brown of whom they had never heard. The door to literary London was not so easily opened.

In this same year—1896—David Maughan left for his native Australia, and as they shook hands Brown wondered when they would meet again. Then into London on a brief business visit came William Menzies, who, with insufficient funds to sustain him at Oxford, had returned north to make education his career. Brown was delighted to see him, and as Symon was out for the evening, they talked without interruption for a couple of hours. Then suddenly, with a guilty look at the clock, Brown sprang up.

"God, Menzies!" he cried. "I was to dine with Emanuel at seven-thirty, and it's after eight!"

They hurried round to Queensborough Terrace to apologize to Monty, and afterwards went off to visit Finch, another Oxford friend. Finch was out, and on Menzies' suggestion they made their way to a Piccadilly restaurant for supper. While they lingered over the meal, an important-looking gentleman recognized Menzies and came across to their table. Brown was introduced, but, following the advice that he had once given to his mother, he remained "quiet and reserved." The conversation lasted a bare minute or two, and after his acquaintance had gone Menzies cast a quizzical eye at Brown.

"He's one of the wealthiest and most influential men in educational circles today," he said. "What do you think of him?"

"Greasy bugger!" replied Brown.

When they returned to the crowded, noisy streets and walked towards Menzies' hotel, Brown spoke of Ayrshire, Oxford, London, and the future. He would have talked all night if his friend had not had an early train to catch. He was in good spirits when they parted; the Piccadilly supper had not quarrelled with his stomach; and he never dreamed that, as with Maughan a short while before, he had seen Menzies for the last time.

He was in no hurry to return to his lodgings. He had had enough of them and of Symon; for he and the Aberdonian were ill-matched. It was a mistake to share rooms. Besides, he wanted to think, and where could a man be more alone than here in the heart of London? He no longer felt that it was "a big wild beast of a place"; as he had told Barker, it was not a bad tonic for a man. Tonight, he had described some Ayrshire characters to Menzies, and now his brain was alive with the thought of them. He remembered what he had written in a letter to Meldrum; indeed, he had copied the particular passage from his own notes:

The great-hearted and valorous peasants of the South-West of Scotland have never appeared in literature; nor are they like to, for lack of the man to describe them. (I am forgetting, though, they have appeared, and to some purpose, in Burns.) Dandie Dinmont came near them, but he hadn't their brains. And they have all in greater or less degree something of Burns's terrible vividness. They not merely see what they say, they *say* it so that you see it also. The voice enlarges the word. When a peasant of the West says "birl" or "dirl", the word itself birls and dirls to the ring of the tongue. In the borrowstouns,[1] Scots has been bastardized by the Board School, but would you hear the patois spoken with the dignity of a classical tongue, would you hear it spoken as Scott and Galt alone ever wrote it, go up the glens and along the hillsides and spier for the wale o' the West. And there you will meet with peasants who know the power of great vocables. Above all you will find men who can plant a picture in the mind for every single terrible phrase. "I'll gar your brains jaup red to the heavens," said one to another in a quarrel, and a nervous bystander looked up to the far fleecy clouds in the peaceful blue to see if they were yet bedabbled by the spouting gore. The hero of the last story once made his way to Paris. On his return an anxious Protestant enquirer said, "Geordie, man, what's the incense like in Notre Dame?" "Burnin' stink," said Geordie. "Jock was a true fellow," said another, musing, of his great comrade dead. "The thoomb-mark o' his Maker was wet in the clay o' him."

[1] Royal burghs.

94

Once at a hill gathering I saw the lordly and leonine master of Esonquahm insulted by a with o' a fellow. Esonquahm's lip scarce curled, as he glanced down at his opponent, so assured was the pride of his arrogant manhood. "You, man," he said—and his eye shot but the one stab—"you, you waff, I could kill ye wi' the yae glower," and the fellow was withered before him. Finest of all was the remark of the godly old crippled Elder, sunning himself on his bench at the head of the long wall o' Ochiltree, watching the last of the black-coated worshippers disappear within the kirk-post half a mile off. By came a farmer, picking the hay-seed off his homespun. "Late as usual," said the Elder, more in sorrow than in anger. "At the Blessed Resurrection, when the hindmost of the Redeemed are gaun skelpin ower Corsoncan yonder, you'll just be rising sleepily frae the grave, and pu'in the mools oot o' your een to glower after that departin' glory in the sky."

But it is not only the outer and external phrase they can give the visual picture of; they can pierce behind the trappings and paint character by one dynamic word. Carlyle's "willowy man" has met with extravagant applause. Why, in stables of a wet day in harvest I have heard fifty telling things from men who sat about on the lids of corn-kists and chewed beans to the invariable accompaniment of that occupation. The fact is that the power to flash fierce intuition into a single phrase has been credited to Carlyle as a separate and individual glory, whereas it is as common to fifty per cent (at the very least) of his countrymen. One example—There was a silly fellow in Kyle once, only one and only once. He was a tall, thin, angular man, at once jerky and solemn, and always dressed in a rusty old black surtout, with a rusty silk hat atop the pate o' him. He had a habit of starting suddenly away from his acquaintances, with a flap of the black coat-tails behind him, "because he had a meeting to attend, a very important meeting you understand," and at that the white of his eyes went Heavenward. You have recognized the type—equally pompous and worthless—not uncommon I am given to understand in the Kingdom of Fife and the counties thereunto adjacent. Well, this fellow was lauded once "for a very decent man." "O'ts aye," said Geordie, the hero of the Parisian story above, "he's a decent man; but he's just a damned wullup." And "the Wullup" he remained from that till the day of his departure. You see, not merely a visual picture of those jerky and important coat-tails the word gives you; it pins down in a word the whole moral nature of the man, the flapping emptiness of the creature—*motus et praeterea nihil.*

Good stuff, that. It was a sin not to make use of it. But how? Brown had told Meldrum that such characters had never appeared in literature "for lack of the man to describe them." And yet what was he trying to do but describe them? Had he not the right to think that, after all, he might be the man?

95

4

Before the year ended Brown had a visit from Barker, who at Oxford was now reading Greats. Brown was at his old trick of making night into day and day into night, and he thought nothing of walking into Barker's room at four o'clock in the morning to wake him up for a talk. Afterwards he would drag his friend off to a workman's tavern for coffee and boiled ham, the briny savour of which Barker never forgot. Like the Walrus and the Carpenter, they talked of many things, and out of it all Barker became more firmly convinced that here, in this big-browed Scot, flamed the fire of genius.

In the spring Brown decided to get out of London. During the winter his throat had troubled him, and he had occasionally experienced that feeling of suffocation that had first assailed him at Oxford. He therefore parted on good terms with Symon—for he had still to rely on the *Illlustrated London News* for odd jobs—and went to live up-river at Camstraddon, Shepperton. There the air indulged his natural indolence and irregular habits of writing, and, declaring himself to be "unhappy in his stomach," he felt more disinclined to work than ever before. If, however, he was not giving out to any marked extent, he was, as Meldrum put it, "storing impressions for future use."

In this memorable year of Queen Victoria's Diamond Jubilee, when England was enjoying a full measure of peace and security, Brown was not infected by London's wild fever of rejoicing and display of Empire. He preferred the easy, sociable life of Shepperton. "He ran across curious people of all sorts and conditions," said Meldrum. "Men like Brown make these discoveries by a kind of instinct."

Meantime Brown had been thinking round a short story, *John Rockingham's Wife*, and at last, in spite of all distractions, he got it down on paper. It was ultimately offered to, and accepted by, the editor of *Chapman's Magazine* to whom Brown sent it under a pseudonym, William Douglas.

It was a straightforward, sombre story. As John Rockingham travelled home much earlier than expected from a business trip abroad, he looked forward to a happy reunion with his wife. He had given her no hint of his return, and his mind was full of the pleasures ahead. To his dismay, however, she was not at home, and in prowling around he found (rather too conveniently) a letter from her lover.

"Kate, my Beloved," it ran: "Rockingham won't be back from

Germany and Belgium for another fortnight. You have nothing to be afraid of, dear. We cannot make a home together yet; but that will come ere a twelvemonth is over. Meanwhile, we can easily have a holiday at Linton, a foretaste of happiness, without rousing suspicions. You will be back in London before his return, and I will be toiling to make a fortune for the woman I adore. Till death I am yours, WILL.

"I have taken rooms at Clifford's Hotel for Mrs. Rockingham and her brother."

After the initial shock, Rockingham saw himself as "a small being apart, to be studied with pitying coolness. . . .

"Nothing but death could atone, could restore a balance so terribly jarred. To his curious aloofness his individual wrong was as nothing; or, rather, it was far away in its proper place; it was not for a private vengeance he was thirsting, he was the vindicator of eternal laws. As he sat and brooded the whole night through, he was inspired with a kind of greatness; he was co-ordinate with the vast movement of the world—and equally pitiless."

Early next morning he took the train to Linton, but on reaching Clifford's Hotel he was informed that Mrs. Rockingham's brother had gone and that the lady herself was still in her bedroom. Explaining that he was her husband, Rockingham then went upstairs.

At that moment his wife was putting the house of her mind in order.

"She was not a woman of an evil nature or of coarse tastes, though absolutely untrammelled by convention or conscience. She would not wilfully do what was cruel. She was simple and natural, like an unthinking animal, and went her own way with an unimaginative blandness to results. . . .

"She had fallen in love with another man (as she fancied) and had spent a week with him down at Linton. Faugh! what a beast he had proved. Now she was lying in bed and watching the yellow smoke as it rose in the beautiful morning air, contentedly, with happy thoughts of her husband. She was glad he was a good man; she had learned that by a bitter contrast. Her conscience pricked her just a little. Oh! she had been very, very wicked! But she would make it up to him; and he would never know; and it wouldn't do him any harm. She would go back to him today, she resolved."

Then there was a knock at the door, and her husband entered.

"She half started from the pillow with a cry of 'John'; but when he came forward, tip-toeing, to the bed, she lay back and smiled in his face. 'Good morning,' she pouted, 'you have been travelling all night, naughty man.' Her black hair tossed down the white pillow to her shoulders; her bright, exquisite face was framed in it. Bending with a strange smile he put both his hands to her neck where it showed above the lace of her night-gown, and she, thinking

G   97

he meant to tilt up her chin for a kiss, smiled softly up at him. When he clutched her throat horror leapt in her eyes like a living thing. She stared madly, wildly, knowing that he knew. . . ."

After killing her, he drew the blinds and calmly walked out.

"He had no thought of escape, no settled plan. A lull seemed to have come into his life. Only he must walk forward, he felt; his mind was more equable when he walked swiftly.

"In the evening he stood on a beach where a brook slid glistening to the sea; on his right a great headland jutted darkly. Some open bivalves were lying round, little silts of sand at the bottom of the upturned, filmy-lined shells. The wave came lipping to a smooth margin, its surface crinkling in the tiniest ripples, without breaking the glossy skin of the water. A little blue stone stood out above the wash with a whitish dry round top on it. He watched the wavelets come again and again, creeping higher with every advance. Far away along the shore two men in dark clothes were making towards him rapidly; but he felt tied to the spot where he stood until the stone should be completely covered. After it was quite beneath the water he moved away and climbed to the headland. He was conscious of a delightful coolness in his brain, a feeling of pleasantness and ease. There was a great impulsion in his mind, steady and sure, but it did not hurry him. He thought of many things passively, and among them of the figure lying, with staring eyes, in the shaded room with the yellow blinds. On the verge of the horizon the sun touched the white edge of a cloud, rosily. He gazed on the growing splendour till the whole cloud flamed in the heavens. The air was still, with a beauty autumnal rather than spring-like; the sea lay beneath him, a flat blaze. A gull went past, gilt by the beams.

"A fisherman, rocking in his boat away below, looked up and saw him—his dress reddened by the glare, rustily, as the dark trunk of a pine is. Suddenly, as the man watched, the figure flung its arms in the air and shot downwards from the rock, falling solidly, like a plummet.

"The fisherman stared, horror-bound, open-mouthed, till a faint splash was heard across the water. Then, as if released by the sound, he rowed to the spot. There was nothing to be seen but the circling gulls and the waves washing on the sunset-flooded shore, and the two men in dark clothes suddenly coming round the corner into the little bay."

The editor of *Chapman's Magazine*, according to Brown, cut out some of the best phrases.

"Take a little example," he wrote to Meldrum. "'His mind was a dark flame.' I daresay he thought that an extravagant metaphor. But it's even medically correct. It's well known that under a violent shock the brain seems to lighten and darken in quick alternation. It's caused by the rush of the blood to the head—that's the bare fact below the phenomenon. Your mind seems a fire—and yet there's no light in it—you cannot think. You literally seem to have a dark flame inside your skull, instead of an intelligence."

Brown's work was still done fitfully, but lethargy alone did not discourage him from writing. His eyesight was weakening, and he began to be haunted by a terrible dread. Suppose he went blind! The horror of this possibility became so intense that in the end he knew that he must learn the truth. From Shepperton he paid a visit to the London Eye Hospital, was examined and reassured, and, out of the experience, wrote an article which was offered to, and turned down by, the *Pall Mall Gazette*. Yet rejection did not matter. His mind was free from fear, and, as he wrote in the article: "It was as if a whole world had been given back to me."

5

When Brown learned that his father had died on 28th September 1897, he did not relive the intimate grief that he had felt at his mother's death. His father was a name, a small dark figure in a gig, an aged man by the fireside at Drumsmudden; his mother a memory enshrined forever in his heart.

Since the verdict on his eyesight he had found it easier to work, and his theories about literature now began to take definite shape. His letters to Meldrum were full of the psychology of character in embryo, and in one about the neglect of it in novels he wrote:

The reason for the neglect is obvious. There is nothing sensational in boyhood, in early boyhood at any rate, before fifteen, say; no mental crisis, and not even a material crisis (despite the Henty's), no great combat of body or of mind. A boy "jist growes" and is more or less obedient; he never torments himself with thought. Childhood, in fact, is poetic not dramatic. Love, for example, sexuality—children know little of these; boy and girl are unreflecting animals developing on parallel lines, pretty much of a muchness, scarcely interacting opposites. But it's just there (at puberty, I mean) that the rattle and clash of life begins for the adult—a rattle and clash both of the outer incidents and of the minor thoughts guiding them, or guided by them; love's the crucial point for most humans; there you have fighting and interoperative within a single centre, feeling, imagination, honour, thought—and don't let us forget the animal—you have the matter, in short, of a composite psychology. Hence in literature you find that nearly all novels and dramas, being concerned with love or other passion of the mind matured, begin subsequent to childhood, because only then do they find their incident in plenty. But it is obvious, surely, that we begin to build the men we are to be long, very long, before the period of puberty; we do so indubitably; how we do so has not often (or at all) been considered; that is, there's a great phase of life not studied yet, but waiting to be studied. True, there is no clash or battle in the boyish mind, nothing "thrilling," and so your gay, hopping skippers of literature and life, gluttonous of silly incident and void of thought, neglect it, are even unaware of it, oblivious of the quiet growth that goes on in childhood, of the character patiently evolved.

With this theory in mind, Brown first sought to expound his ideas in a short story about a Yorkshire boy of quick and sensitive impressions.

JOHN VINCENT

By William Douglas

John Vincent stood in the doorway of his master's yard, and watched the postman coming up the hill. The old man waddled with bowed head, gripping the slanting road with his staff at arm's length in front of him.

The fields were lying reddened beneath the early dawn. The air came with a pure keenness to the nostrils. The only sound to be heard was the stamping of the cob, in the stable to the rear.

The lad watched in lazy enjoyment of the morning; glad to be out in the coolness, but stretching and yawning after the warm blankets. He was exquisitely conscious of his own body; it felt the bathing air. A bird darted on the road and cocked a sideward eye at him, beady and alert. He watched it with a kind of heedless curiosity.

The delight of the morning was his without an effort; he tied his mind to none of its beauties; they came of themselves and floated through his being. His mind flew vaguely to metaphor; and this feeling, he thought, is lucid and whole, a crystal pause rounded in from troubles of the day.

He had no personal interest in waiting for the letters (for they never came to him); so his mind flowed on, placid and clear, unruffled by expectation. There would be envelopes addressed to "Mark Willan, Auctioneer and Salesman"; for Mr. Willan's adopted son there would be nothing. As Willan told him, "he hadn't a friend in the world but his master." He thought of it contentedly, now, in a drowsy acquiescence.

The blackbird came nearer, hopping, its fine legs set shapely to the ground. Suddenly, with a whirring scream it flew away up. It continued to chatter and scold when hidden in the copse.

Deaf Simon had waddled to the gate, bow-legged and bent.

His blue trousers slouched above his boots in dusty corrugations; and the grey on the blue was remarked by Vincent with interest and curiosity. Today everything appealed to him.

"Marnin, mester!" yelled Simon, grinning and shewing his toothless gums.

"Good-morning!" said John, a quiet humour in his eye.

The old man swung the post-bag to his side and rummaged it, his spectacles, with their white and heavy rims, sliding forward on his nose. Fumbling a little he brought out a letter, and perked back his head to examine it at arm's length. As his head went back his mouth opened automatically.

"Mester . . . John . . . Vinshent," he read out slowly, and handed the letter to the boy, with a direct, satisfied look from under his shaggy brows. Then bawling another "Marnin," he shuffled up the hill, his splay feet scraping on the road.

At the sound of his own name the blood pricked Vincent through all his veins. Then he felt his heart stand for a second, and he was conscious of a momentary apathy; and the next minute it was galloping rapidly, irrationally, so that he was annoyed a little at his own fluttering. He went into the yard where the noise of the postman's step came faintly from the distance. A cock-pigeon was ruffling his gleaming breast and *rooketty-cooing* in the spring sunshine. Large clear drops fell slowly from the spout of a wooden pump and splashed on a flat stone. The place was very still.

He turned the envelope over and looked at it curiously, almost fearfully, without seeking to open it. He felt there was excitement before him and, scarcely knowing why, he paused to dally with, to enjoy, the thought of it. Meanwhile, he was intensely conscious of the pigeon swelling in its bravery, of the clean yard, the dripping pump, and the great stillness.

That was his own name in the strange delicate writing! "That's your own name," his mind repeated, but he was possessed by a vague wonderment and could scarcely realize the fact. At last he roused himself from a kind of dream and broke the seal.

But he had barely glanced at the note when a slithery step made him start. Turning, he saw his master.

Mr. Willan was just out of bed; he yawned and blinked as he came forward. His chin was covered with a dirty bristle. A loose pair of carpet slippers were trailing on his feet; his huge body was enveloped in a black frock; his shirt was without a collar. Above the shirt his neck lay over in a bulge,—white, as with disease, and repulsive.

"Hullo!" he growled; "a letter?"—and he held out his hand.

Vincent drew back. His glance at the note made him quick to guard it. He looked surprisingly resolute.

"It's for me," he said, simply.

"For you!" said the other, running up his brows. "O, indeed! And who's the correspondent?"

His hand was still out in expectation.

"A friend," said the boy, placing the letter in his breast-pocket.

Willan gaped like a man meeting an unforeseen impediment—some subtle, impalpable power that he cannot brush aside. For a moment there was a silent and steady wrestle of their wills. Willan blinked.

"A friend?" he repeated, staring between long pauses and staggered with surprise; "a friend . . . you!"

He was quite set aback. A gleam of suspicion shot to his narrowing eyes; he regarded the boy with a measuring look, and then:

"Get those advertisements in proper order," he commanded sullenly, trying to assert himself by going off to another subject. His jowl was a swollen purple. A turkey-cock that had strayed into the yard blustered back at him, waggling a gill like his own. The resemblance of Willan to the angry fowl was so obvious that a thin smile went over the boy's lips.

"Be off with you, now," cried Willan, lowering doggedly.

"Bubble-ubble-ubble," went the turkey-cock.

The auctioneer grew redder and redder. As John went off, Willan followed with his eyes, blinking rapidly. Then he stood for a long time, staring with a vacuous scowl at the corner where the boy had disappeared. The turkey-cock, leg in air, hung waiting for the next move on the part of his enemy. At last Willan shut his mouth with a vicious snap, and shuffled off to the parlour where his wife was getting breakfast.

The vainglorious bird spread himself abroad and "bubbled" after him derisively.

Mrs. Willan was a gaunt woman with jutting upper teeth. The tip of her long nose was so pinched, the skin of it so tightly drawn, that it wagged when she spoke. It seemed to glisten with unnatural tensity.

"That boy has got a letter from somew'ere," said Willan.

She flapped her apron with a slight gesture of despair.

"I al'ays knew," she said wearily. "I al'ays knew. It must come out someday. And, oh, Mark!" she said, "we ought-a do the right thing; we ought, sure."

"Get my breakfast, will ye?" said her husband.

Vincent was no sooner in the office than the letter was spread upon his desk. But he was uneasy. He was in a public place, liable to sudden interruption. Through the big, gaping windows, with their bare panes, he was visible to three corners of the yard. He had a sense of insecurity, of being overlooked and spied upon.

He ran up a narrow stair that led to his bedroom, the door of which he locked behind him.

This was his own den; inside it he was snug from the world. He was alone with a white patch of sky to companion him; the impertinent and peering earth was hidden from his view. Kneeling by the bed, he spread the letter on the warm and tumbled clothes. His heart was beating thickly.

The note was short; it seemed to have been written in great agitation.

The Grange,
Ellaton-on-Thames,
5th April 18—

To Mr. John Vincent,
    Blythwaite,
        Yorkshire.

Dear Sir,

My father, who is very ill, is anxious to see you. It is something about business. You are not to tell anyone of this; there are people who wish to prevent you from meeting my father. Be at the Grange boat-house, near the village of Ellaton, at 3 o'clock on the 6th, and I will come to meet you. The boat-house is a tumbling shed.

Yours truly,
Mary Vincent.

There the letter ended, but, below the signature, the words, "*Do come*", were dashed in impulsively and underlined.

Vincent started to his feet, and the note fluttered white to the rug.

He was more than "Willan's foundling", after all; he was of interest to someone in the great world! The name of the correspondent was his own! That fact hummed in his blood. And the words, "*Do come*", drew him out and on; they brought the writer near to him from the circle of mistiness around; they cried with a tender and intimate appeal. He had a vision of a girl, a kinswoman needing his aid. He picked up the letter from the rug and looked down on it with most curious interest; here in his hand was one end of a subtle chain, at the other end was—What? cried his mind and galloped away with him. His quick fancy saw her in a picture. She was beautiful (assuredly)! and she was writing to him; and the lustre of the lamp ringed her about. But there his fancy jibbed; the girl would not raise her head; only the light glistered on her hair and brows. Imagination is a wilful jade, and often refuses to work as we direct her. An eluding peep of beauty was all she allowed him.

His heart went out in answer to the message. Yet he was in no hurry to act; this was tidings to brood on musingly. He sat on a deal table, dangling his legs in a kind of dream. He looked round his room, vaguely, yet with a pleased interest in its familiar details and homely privacy.

Suddenly, a leap of impatience shot him from the table. He heard the voice of Willan in the yard, and his mood changed. The mean place seemed to stifle him. He eyed the squalid washstand and its chipped basin with a sudden disgust; he thirsted for the open world.

He had a few pounds of his own. He would answer a summons that must lead to something. With this resolve he went downstairs and found his master in the office.

"Is this how you do your work?" said the auctioneer, lowering in stolid anger.

"Yes," said the boy, inconsequently; "but I—I'm going away for a little; I'm sorry, but I have something to do."

"Damn the step will ye go," Willan exploded, thumping on the desk. His big face loomed, threatening and red, like a moon in the frosty harvest, over the edge of a stubble field.

Vincent had the braced look of the fighter. His lips were as tight as a drawn wire.

"Yes, I'll go," he said quietly, and left the room. Ten minutes later he walked out of the gateway.

At the little country-station he tasted for the first time the fresh thrill of his adventure. All was familiar, yet all was strange. He seemed to see things through a sunny veil of unreality. Well-known carts and gigs waited for the train, with horses munching in their nosebags. Milk-cans from the neighbouring farms were gleaming in the sun; the place was homely. But its pleasant bustle, its consequential morning air and expectancy a-tiptoe, proved it the entrance of a larger world. The rails stretched away in the distance, shining mercilessly, worn bright with much travelling of men. They were lost to sight in a cutting, and appeared again, like a flickering gleam, on the far horizon. Through Vincent darted a sinking sense of the foreign and adventurous.

By the middle of the day he was dull of heart. At first the quick motion had exhilarated, as the train rumbled on by green meadows where the brown cattle quietly grazed; he breathed freshness and freedom in the clear air. Later a clammy hand seemed to touch him, and his courage oozed. The day was overcast by a pall of smoke, that hung greasy and low, from the great manufacturing towns. The thunder and roar of traffic beneath that spewing fog frightened and bewildered him. In a pause at one of the stations a workman's train disgorged hundreds of grimy figures who tramped dully past him on the wooden footway. *Thud-thud-thud* went the feet, hastily clattering. The face of each man was intent and preoccupied; looking at them, thinking of the multifarious interests each of them represented, Vincent was suddenly made aware of his personal insignificance and felt himself a mere atom in their midst. An imaginative horror took hold of him; the world was too big to contend against. Men swarmed; they seemed to swamp by the sheer weight of their numbers. Here he was (he thought), adrift from his safe haven in the Yorkshire hills; the tossing uncertainties of life might engulf him. Suddenly his hand touched the letter in his pocket, and his mind leaned forward to Ellaton-on-Thames. He heaved a deep breath of comfort. After all, he, too, had a stake in the world, something to cling to.

He reached London in the afternoon, and went to a hotel which he had heard spoken of by Willan. As he walked to the Park after a hasty meal, the early lamps tossed in the clear air like great yellow flowers; they looked larger and more lustrous, or so the novice thought after his dull Northern day. He felt in pleasant unison with the jostling people on the pavement. He watched the last light fade on the Serpentine, a beautiful dying gloom. A thrush sang to the heart of darkness. The dusk grew among the trees; the peaceful roar of London sounded far away. Vincent sat on, forgetting where he was, and absorbed it all. A strange and subdued happiness possessed him; he felt the greatness of the world.

The second part of the story revealed a threadbare plot. Conducted by Mary to her father's bedside, John learned that the sick man was his uncle, Fred Vincent. Fred had had a half-brother, Harry, and unknown to their father, a wealthy, fiery-tempered squire, they had secretly married girls below their station. Harry's wife had died in giving birth to a baby, and when Harry himself, a soldier, had been posted to India, he had left his child, John, in the care of a nurse in Brighton. Later, by some mysterious means, the squire had found out about Fred's marriage and had cut him off with the proverbial shilling. No sooner had he done so than news of Harry's death in action had arrived—and the shock had promptly killed the squire. Amongst his father's papers Fred then had discovered a tell-tale letter: Harry had betrayed his half-brother's clandestine marriage. Accordingly the squire's will had been made out in favour of Harry and his heirs. In his fury at this treachery, Fred's dominating thought had been revenge. He alone had known of the existence of Harry's child, and he had made arrangements to have him brought up by the Willans in Yorkshire. In this way he had gained the family fortune; but now, at the approach of death, his one desire was to set matters aright. Thus John Vincent came into his inheritance, and to round off the story there was every indication that he would marry his cousin, Mary, in a future that promised to be happier than the past.

The story was never offered to a magazine editor, for Brown had no illusions about it. It was unsatisfactory from many angles, and the second part in particular was poor stuff. Perhaps it failed mainly because the structure of the plot creaked so abominably. No matter. The opening study of the boy was on the right lines, and, as an experiment, the story therefore had been worth while. Brown was content to let it go at that. He felt that he was on the verge of something bigger, something in keeping with what he preached to Meldrum, even though he did not realize at this stage that he had conceived the character who was to become the scion of the House of Gourlay.

6

In the following year Brown paid one of his periodic visits to John Macqueen, the publisher. After they had discussed business matters—for Brown could be practical when he wished—Macqueen took him to the Duke of York's Theatre to meet Francis Neilson, whose interests then lay in stage direction. Neilson, who was two years older than Brown, had travelled in Mexico, Canada, the States, and Europe, and had proved himself to be no mean journalist. Brown took to him almost at once: here, he felt, was a man of ideas, a man of the world, a man whose friendship might mean a great deal to him. For there now ran through Brown's complex personality a peculiar streak of opportunism. It was foreign to his sturdy independence of mind, but it nevertheless existed.

Behind it he was true to his purpose and his dream. He pictured himself a man of letters, with Isabella M'Lennan as his wife. They would have the great times in London, he the successful writer and she the lovely, witty hostess. But he could not afford to dally or, more plainly, to wait until he had achieved recognition. He knew that in Glasgow another man by the name of Russell was often in Isabella's company. Unfortunately, he identified Russell only as a rival for her hand; he did not recognize in him the man of her choice; and therein lay the irony of his mistake. It was a triangle in his own imagination.

Then Isabella and her sisters, suitably chaperoned, were sent off on a long holiday trip to the Continent, and from her gay, friendly letters Brown knew when they were due in Paris and even the name of the hotel at which they would be staying. With his flair for the dramatic, he thereupon formed his plan. Paris was the ideal city in which to meet the girl he loved: there he would ask her to be his wife.

With Meldrum he accordingly spent a few days abroad, and at the appropriate time they arrived in the French capital. Brown then wrote to Isabella and suggested a meeting-place. He did not doubt that she would honour the appointment, albeit he never dreamed that his letter would fill her with a sense of sadness. For she realized as never before that there was a serious intent in him that she could not possibly reciprocate. It was wrong to live on in a court of dreams: the daft days must end.

When they met she thus told him of her thoughts and of her feelings . . . and he knew then, with stark desolation in his heart, that he had lost. Yet there arose no angry words, no bitterness between them; for (Brown remembered Milton) who ever knew truth put to the worse in a free and open encounter? And when at last he went away—how might he have cried with Romeo, "Arms take your last embrace!"—he carried with him the heavy burden of his loneliness.

Back in Shepperton he tried to force himself to work until it became necessary to return to London. He moved to rooms in Bayswater, and gave no hint to Emanuel or his other friends that he had been struck a cruel blow. Happiness was, perchance, of secondary importance when a man was fated to follow the star of his unconquered will. Even to Tom Smith—at this moment, at any rate—he did not mention Isabella. He began by referring to a letter which he had received at Shepperton.

That letter you sent me was a godsend. I have got to be that I can live in absolute loneliness with tremendous satisfaction to myself—still there are times when one's own company is a monstrous bugbear—and the night I got your letter was one of them. I had been down watching a great mournful sunset burning itself out above the river—the sullen glory reflected in the broad stream. Bare trees stood up lonely against the yellow sky. A mist stole across the lower meadows like a white silent ghost. The frost nipped, and from somewhere near came the curious melancholy smell of potatoes beginning to decay.

You know the kind of eerie *yellow* gloaming. "I was as lonely as a night in the hind-harvest."

Through the open window of our cottage when I went home, below the lamp (which the servant had just lit) I saw a letter on the table.

"Damn it!" said I, "a bill."

I've become such a careless correspondent that a letter which is not a bill is a thing to be marked by a——[1] in the post.

Well I went in and loafed about a bit without looking at the envelope. Then I picked it up.

"Jing!" said I. "I should ken that hand o' write, tae, na!"

Then it flashed in on me who it was from, and I tore it open.

A sensible man must be reticent in the expression of his feelings, Tom, so I only say that I thank you from the bottom of my heart for that letter and for its warm welcome to the schoolhouse at Xmas. I'd have come like a shot, but it was impossible for many reasons. But the mere reading of the thing did me a power of good. "For ever welcome at the schoolhouse"—that was the expression that went into me.

The cottage at Shepperton is let for the winter, and I've come to dig here. I'll never go to live in the country again—*English* country, I mean. It's like *Paradise Regained* coming back to London—not that I care a rap for the London so dear to some folk—the London of mere glitter and slap-dash. I like to slouch about Kensington Gardens in the twilight listening to the encircling muffled roar of the mighty place coming from far away. There is something inexpressibly sublime to me in that sound—the perfect solitude near you in among the quiet evening-shrouded trees—the dull thunder in the distance. It is like the hoarse murmur of some gigantic sea.

It's near twelve o'clock, and I must hurry up to catch the midnight post. . . . By the bye I saw a most vivid phrase in a review today:

The linnet broken-winged
Dies in a bright-eyed silence 'neath the bough.

[1] This word, which is difficult to decipher, may be "hag", meaning—bungle.

"Bright-eyed silence" is good, isn't it?

Guid-nicht, Tam, and the wale o' best wishes to you and yours from

G. D. B.

Brown now found his material acceptable to *Sandow's Magazine* and he frequently met the editor, Howard Spicer, in the offices of this publication. During one visit he was introduced to Spicer's friend, Andrew Melrose, a Scot whose ambition and interests lay in publishing. Melrose was ready to discuss Scots literature, but Brown did not commit himself to any great extent. He was working on a long short story, and he had no intentions of saying anything about it . . . yet. It promised to be better than anything he had done. He had thought of a good name for one of the characters: Gourlay, John Gourlay. You could believe in a man with a name like that, even if it was too soon to see his story whole.

With Melrose and Spicer, as with friends of longer standing, Brown was unreasonable. Calling on them at all hours, he liked to know what they were doing—and thinking, but he never invited them to his own quarters, and he hated to be asked about *his* affairs. Now that he had lost Isabella M'Lennan, he required friendship and solitude, two impossible bed-fellows. Ill-fortune had trailed him since the cradle, so that even in the crush of London he never quite forgot his illegitimacy. It rankled in him when he was depressed and, in lighter moments, caught him unawares. He had got into the habit of dropping in on Neilson at the Duke of York's Theatre twice or thrice a week, and one evening he lighted his pipe and listened as his friend read part of a play to him. Neilson happened to stress a sentence in which the word, "bastard", was flung at a man, and Brown started and looked strangely shaken.

"What's wrong?" asked Neilson quickly.

Brown drew a deep breath.

"Man," he said, "I thought you threw that at me."

Painfully he explained why, and Neilson sat there, nodding now and then but making no comment. He had the good sense to know that Brown, in the bleakness of his lonely pride, did not want sympathy.

If, however, the disclosure did not ease Brown's soul, it strengthened the bond of friendship, and on Sundays he often found his way down to the other's home in Bedford Park. "Mr. Brown," without the bribery of sweets, thus became a favourite with the Neilson brood, and once, after lunch, he was found in the study teaching the seven-year-old daughter to read out verses in the Bible. Yet the pleasure that her presence brought to him was masochistic. She set him thinking of the child that might have been his some day . . . if Isabella M'Lennan had agreed to be his wife.

From those Sunday visits to the Neilsons, Brown returned to the drudgery of hack work. He knew that Melrose and Spicer were concerned about his mode of living, and he wished that they and everyone else would not interfere. He was not cut out for an office desk. Admittedly, when money did not come in regularly, he was hard up; but Emanuel could always be relied upon to help him out. Over a year he earned little more than three pounds a week: enough for his needs, even if his hand-to-mouth existence did make him rather touchy at times. If he had wished, of course, he could have become an able and successful journalist. He was aware of the trend of public feeling and knew what people wanted to read. The glories of the Diamond Jubilee being vivid still, Britain, with her Soldiers of the Queen, was the salt of the earth, and in consequence a mixter-maxter of red, white and blue was ready to be exploited in cheap fiction. The sterner side was driven in on Brown when he learned that an Oxford acquaintance, serving as a war correspondent, had been killed at Omdurman, and his tribute to him in verse appeared in the *Speaker*.

THE HON. HUBERT HOWARD

Killed at Omdurman, Sept. 2nd 1898

Rowing bow in the Balliol eight,
Hubert Howard!
Breasting a river in roaring spate,
With a laugh on your lips and your head elate—
Oh, you had the heart for a wrestle with fate,
Hubert Howard!

Death to a man is a thing of naught,
Hubert Howard!
And yet today, when the news was brought,
I dully stared at the blinding thought,
And my breath, i' the nick o' my throat, was caught,
Hubert Howard!

I can see the look on your face as you died,
Hubert Howard!
When your life gushed out in a crimson tide,
You stared at Death with a frowning pride,
Steadfast-mouthed and resolute-eyed,
Hubert Howard!

Sound be your sleep in the waste alone,
Hubert Howard!
Where the arch of night is a burning zone,
And the winds of the desert faintly moan,
And ghostly glimmers your grey death-stone,
Hubert Howard!

At this time Brown also considered a series which was to consist of chapters of a doctor's autobiography. As an experiment he jotted down an isolated incident.

I will set down a single picture which is sharp in my memory to show the kind of gossips I was plagued with. I was whisking up a close at the foot of the Smiddy brae to see a burnt child at Kitty Langstaffe's, when I heard the voice of Mr. Gilliper (the damned pomposity) about twenty yards higher up the slope.

"Doctor," said the authoritative man, "Doctor!"

"I hear you, Laird," said I.

Down he came, marching, groomed for his morning walk, with his well-scraped chin in the air, and a starched peak like the bow of a pinnace on each side of his collared jowl.

"Now, Doctor," he said, laying a solemn hand on my lapel, "you must tell me a-all about it; a-all about this Kelton a-afferr."

He murdered his vowel sounds, a thing which I loath, though to a Scotsman the slaughter should be natural.

I looked at him hard. "For God's sake, Laird," I cried, "let me see your tongue."

He went as green as an early jaundice.

"I—I have not got it, Doctor!" he stammered; "h-h-h-have I?"

"Got it!" said I. "Laird, this is something serious."

And I grappled for his pulse.

He went flabby as dough; his fat cheeks were trembling like white pork; I laid my ear to his heart—it was beating like a bird's.

"Laird," I said, "this is a thing that maun be seen to."

He hung on my words like a soul at the Day o' Judgment.

"Slip away cannily home," said I, "creep into your own warm bed, with a stiff jorum o' punch to comfort you—and I—oh, I'll be round in an hour or two."

Away he crawled up the hill, a broken man, and I whistled on my way, chuckling.

Brown decided to expand "this Kelton affair" into something more substantial—and sensational, albeit the opening picture of the village was drawn from his old notebooks.

It was two in the afternoon. . . . Three minutes earlier, the road had swarmed with a babel of children, jostling and shouting in the sun. Now it was absolutely still. The children had gone into school.

A smell of wallflower oozed in the hot air. A cat crept along in the ribbon of shade by the houses opposite, stealthily, her belly close to the ground. From the red and grimy door of the Smithy came, at times, the faint tinkle of an anvil.

Away down the street a white-capped crone hobbled across with a pail of water. For a moment the sun glinted on the tin, a bright and lonely motion that flickered in the great stillness. Then a door closed upon the aged disturber and the village dozed in the heat.

Brown then contrived a melodramatic feud between two young squires, but before he had written half a dozen chapters he abandoned the project. In explaining why, he gave a hint of those general speculations on the novelist's art to which he devoted more serious thought than he did to his own tentative and scattered efforts.

In a letter to Meldrum, he wrote: "A man ought to have an absolutely clear idea of the psychological situation before he starts a novel. I have known that this many and many a day, and I don't say that I haven't a clear idea in this case; only I began the little thing in a happy-go-lucky, go-as-you-please, unserious mood, and a story of that kind is apt to be a crack in a fissure leading to nowhere."

7

Francis Neilson began to notice a disturbing trait in Brown, a perverted tendency to play one friend against another, and he was at a loss to understand what it meant. Like many others, he regarded Brown as an invigorating companion, with an infectious zest and an original mind, but he knew that there was much more to him. The truth was that no one ever got near the real Brown. His loyalty, now that Isabella M'Lennan had chosen another man, was to himself alone.

He had innumerable discussions with Melrose and Spicer about books, and often enough his tongue was in his cheek. Quite suddenly he would spring up, pacing the floor as he had done when an Oxford student, and declare himself on literature with such passionate emphasis that the others had, perforce, to listen. They never realized that his statements did not necessarily arise out of their talk; as often as not, he would be quoting from one of his notebooks. He was always well prepared.

Then, for the time being, he sacrificed his ideals before economic necessity. John Macqueen invited him to try his hand at a book of adventure in which the Union Jack flew high, and although it went against the grain, this idea of turning out popular trash for money, he had no option. If he wanted freedom to write, he would have to be prepared occasionally to tackle ephemeral fiction for hard and ready cash. Besides, he could conceal his identity behind a pseudonym and thereby safeguard his future reputation.

In this frame of mind he began what was, strictly speaking, his first novel: *Love and a Sword*. Visualizing the hero, Lieutenant Roderick Gordon, as "a tall stripling on the verge of manhood, with grave eyes and a firm mouth", he opened with a lukewarm sketch of the scene that so often occupied his mind. Newhall, "a little old-fashioned town, or large village rather, close to the Scottish border," had been pricked out of its lethargy, and as the doctor and the parish clergyman walked towards the station, the doctor remarked, "What did I tell you? See the folk gathering already!"

"Prosperous-looking tradesmen, with white aprons girded over their fat paunches, stood in their doorways, and peered out curiously above the bright rims of their spectacles, as who would say, 'Who has a right to see what happens if we don't?' The farmers had not removed the glinting milk-cans yet, but chatted together, looking round them now and again as if waiting for something to happen. Several gentlemen were strolling on the platform. A group of schoolboys stared, open-mouthed, at the white little wooden gate where the tickets were collected."

A pile of luggage was labelled "Lieut. Roderick Gordon, Bombay, via Brindisi and Port Said"; and presently Sir James Gordon, "the aged General", arrived with his son. They shook hands with soldierly restraint, and after the train had gone Sir James retraced his steps along the platform.

"When he came to the bystanders, and saw the gaze of bucolic admiration, the smile went like a flash, and 'Losh!' as one of them said afterwards, 'he seemed ill-pleased, *and his e'e just bored us through.*'"

On the Calais boat, Roderick took stock of his position. "I'll go where the row's thickest," he decided. "I suppose that's the best way to please the General."

In the French train "a huge foreigner" shared Roderick's compartment. "The lower part of his face was hidden by his fur coat; nothing was seen but his high-peaked eyebrows and shut, lashless lids."

Farther on, where the countryside had been flooded by a deluge, the train was derailed. Roderick's carriage overturned, the foreigner was knocked unconscious, and water poured into the compartment. Roderick managed, of course, to extricate himself and the other. He took out the injured man's brandy flask, and a piece of paper fell to the ground. Thinking that it might give him a clue to his companion's identity, he picked it up, and "what he saw made the blood start through all his veins and prick his skin like a thousand needles."

"St. Petersburg,
"15th June, 1897.

"You will proceed as soon as you possibly can to India, via Brindisi. Several officers on leave in England have been ordered to join their regiments. Ingratiate yourself on the way out. Use your knowledge of English to learn all that you are able. Get to the front, work in conjunction with Mirkha Khan, learn and do everything possible, and report via Kabul to our side.

"Z. Z. Z."

With his eyes glued to this message, Roderick did not realize
that the foreigner had recovered consciousness until a bullet whizzed
past his ear. He spun round, and a desperate fight took place,
with Roderick eventually gripping his opponent by the throat.
"A little gurgling noise came from the throttled wind-pipe. The
Russian lay limp and still."

Just then the engine of the submerged locomotive exploded, and a
woman passenger was swept away by the resultant "great swashing
wave." Roderick rescued her, and when "a pair of pure grey eyes
opened upon him for a moment" it was obvious that she would
become, for him, the one woman in the world.

Meanwhile, the foreigner's body had disappeared, an indication
that he had not been strangled after all. He was, indeed, to become
Roderick's arch-enemy: Petroff, a Russian spy; and the fact that
he had been careless enough to carry his instructions on his person
was beside the point.

The girl whom Roderick had rescued was Jessica Martin. She
was travelling with her brother, Jack, who was on his way to
India to join his regiment, and Roderick soon became friendly
with them. He was badly shaken when he learned that Jessica
was going out to be married. She and Jack were orphans, and her
future husband, Arthur Raleigh, was an old family friend. When
her father was dying in straitened circumstances, he had promised
to marry her rather than let her "drudge as a governess." To pile
on the agony, Jessica had given a promise to her father that she
would marry Raleigh. All this was clumsy and contrived; but
Brown did not expect his readers to be very critical, and it was
one of the rules to make the course of true love as rough as possible.

After various adventures on the voyage and in Port Said, Roderick
and the Martins reached India and travelled north to Peshawar.
When they were met there by Arthur Raleigh, Roderick knew that
he and Jessica had come to the parting of the ways.

Before her wedding day, however, Jessica and a native groom
went out riding towards the hills. They did not return, and when
Roderick and his search party found the groom dead, they realized
that Jessica had been kidnapped as a hostage.

Apart altogether from Jessica's disappearance, the campaign
now gathered impetus, and the British arrived at the Gate of the
Afridi.

"The moon was shining down full and beautiful on the Kohat
Pass. Wild and precipitous mountains lay around on either side,
their deep flanks in shadow, their peaks and rounded slopes bathed
in soft, dreamy splendour. Not a sound broke the spell of silence
that seemed to hold the great, brooding hills and the deep, dim
valleys in a spiritual leash."

But Roderick saw beyond the grandeur of the scene. "His eyes were fixed far away, on the great frowning peak of Dargai, intently, as if to overlap it by a sheer effort of the mind. 'Perhaps she is there!' he spoke forth in silence."

The Battle of Dargai followed, strictly according to the rules and best traditions. "'God!' cried a Ghurka, with pride in his eyes, 'but these (the Gordons) are the comrades to fight with!'"

Out on patrol afterwards, Roderick fell over a cliff and was taken prisoner. In a Pathan encampment, while scarcely able to move, he was confronted by Petroff. Incredibly he got to his feet, snatched a burning brand from a convenient fire, and smote the Russian across the face. "Back went Petroff with a horrid yell, staggering, falling, blinded, his hair ablaze." Roderick swooned, and, on recovering, found himself in a tent, looking down on the Tirah Valley in the heart of the Afridi country.

With the British pushing on, he now had a battle of his own on hand. The Pathans had discussed the problem of Jessica, with Mirkha Khan presenting the case for Petroff and one, Azim-al-Mulk, arguing on behalf of Roderick, and they had decided that the two antagonists must fight it out, man to man. Petroff had been injured about the eyes by Roderick's blazing brand; they were therefore to be blindfolded and pitted against each other on a precipitous ledge; and the fate of the white woman was to depend upon the victor.

"The place was a natural amphitheatre, opening on the outer side upon a sheer precipice. It seemed to have been scooped out of the side of the mountain. All around the bowl-like enclosure were tiers of dark-faced Pathans, at least a thousand in number, assembled to witness the blind fight of the two white infidels."

Roderick and Petroff were then brought, like gladiators, to the spot.

In the desperate struggle that followed, Petroff fell awkwardly and broke his arm, while Roderick, all sense of direction gone, nearly toppled over the ledge. With the courage of a true villain, Petroff rose and returned to the attack, and they grappled this way and that until Roderick finally got his chance and flung the Russian to his death far below.

Roderick then learned that Jessica was a prisoner in a hut on the far side of the Black Nullah and that Alzakoff, Petroff's henchman, had already gone off in that direction.

Led part of the way by a native, Roderick went on alone in the darkness to the hut.

"Suddenly a woman's scream curdled the night!

"He dashed to the window. Jessica was there—in the middle of the room. The light fell full upon her face, ghastly-pale, beautiful, martyr-like. An uplifted dagger gleamed in her hand. Alzakoff stood before her with outstretched arms.

"Her eyes were set and staring. Her bloodless lips moved, and a low, agonized voice came out slowly—hers, and yet not hers.

"'If you come nearer I will kill myself.'

"Alzakoff moved.

"The dagger glittered.

"'JESSICA!'

"The cry would have brought her from the tomb. The bright steel rattled on the floor—and, oh, the wonder and joy that smiled in the sweet, pale face as she stood and listened, the childish gladness, the rapture of a lover, the bliss of a rescued soul!

"Alzakoff wheeled to the window, but saw no face there. In a moment Roderick was in and on him."

After a desperate struggle, he overpowered Alzakoff, and killed him—only to find that Jessica shrank away.

"He dimly realized what a terrible look must still be in his face —non-human, deadly, elemental. He had been lifted above humanity by Vengeance; man no longer, but a doom; and the awful glare of a supernatural necessity must still be in his eyes, it could ebb only slowly away. He saw it killing the heart of Jessica, like the dread face of a Gorgon.

"He gazed at her helplessly, wonderingly, pitifully.

"'Oh, it was for me you did it,' she cried suddenly with a great burst of tears; 'it was for me you did it!' and she flung herself in his slaughtering arms."

To the hut came a friendly Pathan to warn Roderick that the rear of the British Army was to be ambushed where, below Guli Khel, the River Bara flowed through a gorge.

Dressed as a Pathan, Roderick set out, warned the Army of its danger, and then, to tidy matters up, killed Ferreida, the last member of Petroff's gang.

On learning that Jessica was in love with Roderick, Arthur Raleigh retired with a sad little smile and a murmured "God bless you." A month later Roderick and Jessica walked beneath a spring sunset where "the beauty and silence joined them like a spiritual sacrament."

"'Jessica,' he said at last, 'will you be my wife?'

"And Jessica said, 'Yes, Roderick.'"

Brown did not deceive himself. He knew that any writer of mediocre talent could have written *Love and a Sword*, and he accordingly selected the nom de plume, Kennedy King, under which some of his short stories appeared in *Sandow's Magazine*. Macqueen did not care for the subtitle, *A Tale of the Indian Frontier*, and when the book appeared in September the title page read:

LOVE AND A SWORD:
A Tale of the Afridi War
by
Kennedy King
"Avaunt Topographer!"
—The Magician.
With Illustrations by R. C. Woodville, P. Bell,
W. B. Wollen, H. C. S. Wright and John Williamson.
London
John Macqueen
Hastings House
Norfolk Street
Strand
1899

"Some of it," Brown wrote to a friend, "is raw enough in all conscience; and the plot is a torn piece of melodrama; but on reading the proofs I was myself surprised to see how vivid and real it seemed in places. I can say this to you without fear of being thought conceited; for you know that I'm diffident about my own work usually; besides I don't set any surprising value on mere physical vividness unless it's joined to better qualities. And how could there be 'better qualities' in a 'pot-boiler' for boys—even if it had been mine to compass them? I had a kind of fierce resentment at the job, and some of it I did at a canter, three or four thousand words a day; other days I did not do more than two hundred; not that I laboured to perfect them, but I sat and scrawled, and swore and ate the end of my pen, and thought about other things! I'm a grand man to think about other things whenever I have work to do. I can be positively brilliant (I assure ye) in all manner of useless side-directions. And all the time the blank white page lies in front of me, crying 'Work!' like a slogan, but my gaily-gambolling mind won't be tethered to the job in hand. If I knew another man like myself I'd be apt to call him 'a damned fool'. But I have a tenderness for my own infirmities."

Brown sent a copy to Meldrum with a note which read: "Herewith the pot-boiler. I would have inscribed the flyleaf, only I was ashamed of the offering . . . the book's very slack in the middle —like hungry Jock Robinson."

And a month later he sent a copy to Tom Smith with the following letter.

3, Bark Place,
Bayswater,
London, W.

My Dear Tom,
I have put off writing to you all this time because I meant, when I did write, to let you have a devil of a screed—to let myself go, in

fact, as I might if we forgathered some nicht at e'en in Kyle, in a snug room, with a due supply of drink—and before a fire that roared its defiance to the roaring storm. Many such meetings be ours! Well (as Downie says when he begins a story) with a view of achieving some such monstrous epistle I began a screed to you more than three weeks ago, and wrote several pages, meaning to add to them until they were something worth sending. But, damn it, I've mislaid them somewhere, so when I wanted them to-night, I couldn't find them, and, as you see, I had to begin afresh. Here goes then.

And first let me send you a book I have written under the pseudonym of "Kennedy King". It has been lying in my rooms with your name on it for the last month—waiting the completion of that letter I lost. I sent some books to the schoolhouse to-day; that yours was not included in the parcel is due to the fact that it was here. I don't set much value on the thing myself—it was written rapidly for Macqueen who wanted a boy's story and was willing to plank down some ready cash—but I had an idea you'd rather have it than another novel—for the sake of the fellow who wrote it[1]. . . .

8

Between the completion and publication of *Love and a Sword* Brown planned to write a sufficient number of short stories to make a volume under the title *Scots Chronicles*. He, however, only wrote two, *The Wooing of Sibby Douglas*, which never pleased him, and *When Janet Goudie Came Home*, which appeared in the *Speaker* for 15th July 1899.

Except for the interest that Brown's friends took in this story, it did not attract attention, and two months later *Love and a Sword* fell into the silences. The Boer War began on 11th October, and as readers showed more interest in the Transvaal than the Indian Frontier, Brown at once adapted himself to the new demand, turning out stories like *In the Boer's Grip*, which appeared in the Christmas number of *Sandow's Magazine*.

For a man who professed to be handicapped by laziness, he did a tremendous amount of writing that year, and, in addition, he never neglected his reading for Macqueen or his paragraphs for Symon. But, unknown to him, the real significance of those months lay in their effect upon his character. His disappointment over Isabella M'Lennan had not embittered him. It had brought rather a wider sense of sympathy and deeper understanding. After her marriage, one of his letters to Tom Smith revealed how immeasurably greater he had become in stature.

[1] Unfortunately, part of this letter is missing. The existing page ends with these words: "The identity was meant to be a secret (for I think it somewhat *infra dig*, you know, to go in for. . . .""

I think (he wrote) Isabella did right in marrying Russell. My future (though I may believe in it myself) was much too precarious for a delicate and wealthily-brought-up woman to share in it. She's a damned fine girl, Tom. She met me in Paris last year and told me, with tears, how lonely she was, and how Russell was always at hand, and how she was being chaffed because her sister was married before her and—well, one could see that she wanted (very rightly) to fulfil her destiny and be a wife and mother. So I kissed her and said "good-bye." Thus do our dreams fade.

My head's thick to-night, and I'm in no vein for tumbling ideas out upon the page. But send me a screed soon, Tom, and you may be sure I'll answer it. And remember you're coming to London in summer as my guest. We'll have great cracks. Give my best regards to Mrs. Smith, and tell Downie when you see him—that I should like to see him.

Yours ever the same,
Geordie.

Ay, dreams faded. Here he was, still struggling on in London, while Tom Smith had become a teacher—and a respectable married man to boot. At the thought Brown recalled how he had been forced after the wedding to send an apologetic letter to his friend.

3, Bark Place,
Bayswater,
W.

My Dear Tom,

I write in a deuce of a hurry, so you must overlook the deficiencies of this screed. I was horrified to find when I looked at the card of invitation yesterday that your wedding was in April instead of May —I'm damned careless, to tell the truth, always overlooking dates and getting into scrapes in consequence. But you and your wife are not stuck-up folks, so I know you'll forgive me. You'll believe me when I tell you that I wish you both all the happiness marriage can bestow. I daresay you had a pretty good spree—I would have liked fine to be there.

Buy the good-wife something with the enclosed, Tam, and make my peace with her for not writing sooner. Send us a screed whiles.

Yours ever and always,
G. D. Brown.

Brown continually hankered after news from his friends up north. He realized that they were finding what they wanted out of life, and in moments of depression he sometimes experienced a curious foreboding that he would never join their ranks. Even so, his belief that he would "arrive" held firm.

With Melrose and Spicer he was now engaged in a spare time publishing venture which they had agreed to run under the names, Hood, Douglas, and Howard. Hood, as Brown later explained to Tom Smith, was Melrose's middle name. All three pretended to be amused by the partnership, but each one was aware of its possibilities, and Brown especially was prepared to work hard for its success. As soon as an idea occurred to him, he dashed off a letter to Melrose.

3, Bark Place,
Bayswater.
Wednesday Night.

On the Service
of the Three.   Secret.
Watchword: See that ye tell it unto no man.

I see that "In Scotland guide-books must be reckoned with as forming a large part of the summer's business."

Now I've thought before that a "Guide to the Burns Country", not dry and catalogue-like as most guides are but written with a literary flavour, with reminiscences of interesting literary figures who've been in Burns country (Keats, Wordsworth, etc., quoting their verses and poems on places), *full above all of local anecdote*— I've thought a book or booklet could be made of all this. Perhaps we might stick in the Border too, and perhaps in any case we would get the egregious Crockett to write a foreword.

I don't press the point, as W. Whitman says, I but fling it out (the whole suggestion) as a hint.

The point is that in this book, as in most of the books we publish, there must be innumerable saliencies. The damning fault in most of the books I read is that nothing in them leaps at you from out the page. They are talky-talky, vapid; there's an article in next *Sandow's* in which a man has talked round about his subject for nine aimless pages. Now easy, sleepy writing may have a charm in a very few places; but most books, and certainly all books of the kind we want, should be pregnant and packed. For this particular book I suggest this kind of thing: "It was at this scaur that Black Jock Macmichael killed six of Claverhouse's troopers, and it is still known among the country folk as the Covenanter's Scaur. (Give the story of the fight.) Farther on the coach passes the quarry whence Burns carted the stones for the building of Ellisland. At the top of the hill Keats saw Ailsa Craig lowering from the distant sea, and addressed it in the well-known sonnet (quote). At the old coaching inn half a mile away lived So and So, a man known all over Ayrshire fifty years ago for his extraordinary gift of epigram. Innumerable stories are told of him. And here give the stories. For we should fling a very wide net to get vivid stories, work them in upon every page; they will add greatly to the popular interest of the book and will be of sincere value as giving the proper atmosphere.

Do you know that there are more Americans visit Alloway-on-Doon than Stratford-on-Avon? I have seen it stated as a fact.

I write with a bad pen and in a great hurry. But think it over.

Yours ever,
G. D. B.

Other letters to Melrose, whom he often addressed as "Centurion," were signed by various boyish nicknames; but the suggestions that he propounded were always sound. For instance:

Hood, Douglas & Howard
Literary Agents

Falcon Court,
Fleet Street.
Tuesday Evening.

My Dear Centurion,

Why shouldn't we republish "Lamb's Tales from Shakespeare?" It ought to be a very acceptable book in the modern cheap yet prettier style; and I don't think it has been done. This for the future, I mean.

It struck me today very forcibly that whatever reprints we do should have very distinctive and illuminating introductions. They needn't be long; one packed and pregnant paragraph would do the trick. I'm convinced that it's that kind of thing that makes the reprint sell—that, and not the "name" of an editor, like Shorter or Lang, who writes some facile gossip but never sends a light wide as the world flooding over his author. Facile gossip is of no use, but a wise word said about a writer will make what you reprint of him talked about. And a whole series prefaced by wise words (if you only get 'em!) would, I am sure, be very serviceable both to publisher and public. It would grip on.

Goggles.

Brown did more than offer ideas. He again attempted to cash in on the prevailing mood by writing in patriotic vein *Famous Fighting Regiments*, and this book, published at a shilling, was one of his most slipshod efforts. According to the title page the author was George Hood, while the rest of the responsibility lay with

London
Hood, Douglas, and Howard
1 Falcon Court
Andrew Melrose
16 Pilgrim Street, E. C.,
1900

A prefatory note stated that "To the proprietors of the *English Illustrated Magazine* the thanks of the writer are due for permission to republish three of the following articles"; while the articles themselves, which occupied 121 pages, were brief histories of the Buffs, the Norfolks, the "Death or Glory Boys", the Black Watch, the Scots Greys, Royal Welsh Fusiliers, the Royal Scots, Gordons, Fighting Fifth, and Carabiniers, the Dublin Fusiliers, and Five Great Regiments.

Brown's description of the part that the Dublin Fusiliers played in the capture of Nundy Droog was typical of the whole book.

First, he dealt with the name of this fortress, which was perched on a precipitous rock over two thousand feet high.

"Though lucky in everything else, the 'Blue-Caps' are certainly unfortunate in the names of their victories. It needs a very strong regiment to bear up against the burden of names so comical as Nundy Droog and Beni Boo Ally,—just as you don't expect a man to be a poet if he's christened Jeremiah Swigglesbig! Nundy Droog! —why, it's a ridiculous name, appropriate to nothing so much as a bandy-legged Hindoo water-carrier. But if the name is ridiculous, the place is terrible."

Then Brown drew a deep breath and really let himself go.

"So high was the fortress above the British position that the bugle-calls of the enemy seemed to come floating down from an infinite distance. At last the assault was sounded, and the Fusiliers dashed at the steep. Hell opened above them. Cannon-shot ploughed through them, musketry raked them, rockets blasted them, great boulders rolled down from above and carried them away. But they never stopped. They walked up the face of that cliff—and then they dropped the enemy over it."

Despite its mediocrity Brown sent a copy of the book to Tom Smith.

> 10, Queen's Road,
> St. John's Wood,
> London.

My Dear Tom,

I send you a copy of a book I wrote the other day. I never put my name on any piece of hack-work that I do for the money and nothing else; so I put "George Hood" on the title-page of this. Hood is the middle name of Melrose, who is a partner with another fellow and myself in a little publishing business, "Hood, Douglas, and Howard". (I don't expect there will be much money in the said publishing house, but it's good fun.) That explains how "George Hood" happens to be synonymous with "Geordie Broon."

Write us a screed, man, and tell us how you are.

> Yrs. ever,
> G. D. Brown.

A study of Kruger was another of Brown's tasks. He expected Melrose and Spicer to collaborate in it, but when the *Morning Herald* purchased the serial rights his partners suggested that, having most time on hand, he alone should undertake the work. Brown raised no objections, but when the instalments began to appear in print he complained about the sub-editing.

My Dear Centurion, (he wrote to Melrose),

The *Morning Herald* people are castrating our stuff damnably; there is no other word for it.

They run paragraphs together that ought, for clearness, to be separate.

Then when an ironic aside has been written in a separate paragraph (as it ought to give it salience) they jam it in with a big paragraph preceding, where it passes unnoticed in the crowd.

Their more particular blunders are exasperating in the highest degree. They have a right to cut our stuff, but they have no right to insert it under our names. . . .

I had written that Potgieter found "spiked babes, mothers stabbed between the breasts, and men that stared with awful eyes at the smiling heavens."

They omit "between the breasts", spoiling the literary value of the thing entirely. In the first place "stabbed" by itself is fatuous; you can't talk of "a stabbed man"; in the second place the words "between the breasts" emphasized the horror of *mothers* being stabbed. They had been suckling their babes, perhaps, when the Matabele fell upon them, and, poor women! they were stabbed in the tenderest and benignest of their being. The words "between the breasts" were meant to make the horror of the thing *visible to the eye*. But, as these crocks put it, while you can see the dead men staring up with awful eyes, you can't see the women; they pass unnoticed in a vague generalization.

I had written, "Henceforth there was black Hell between the Matabele and the Boer." They have a right to change that, of course, although I don't think the language a bit too strong for the situation. But they write, "Henceforth it was trouble between the Matabele and the Boer." "It was trouble"—appropriate to nothing more serious than a row between Brown and his landlady. Besides, it isn't English. No man says "it was trouble"; he says "there was trouble."

There are lots of other things that madden. I shall address a remonstrance to Cooke.

Yours ever,
G. D. B.

Brown's anger had increased by the time he saw Melrose and Spicer in person, and his voice was shrill as he paced up and down before them.

"I wrote, 'When the first Mrs. Kruger died, which she soon did'; and do you know what some damned fool on the staff has done? Changed it to 'When the first Mrs. Kruger died after a brief wedded life'."

And he called upon his friends to picture some smug hypocrite, with uplifted eyes, proclaiming, "After a brief wedded life, my dear brethren . . ."

He did not pretend that his study of Kruger was better than his other hack work; but it infuriated him to think that such phrases purported to come from his pen.

There was, in fact, an underlying seriousness in everything that

Brown did, and with financial backing he might have established the firm of Hood, Douglas, and Howard on a sound basis. Some of his schemes would have been successful—if there had been enough money to carry them through.

My dear Melrose (he wrote on one occasion from 17, Woburn Square),

Overlook the demerits of this hasty scrawl; I am literally in the muddle of Macqueen's Manuscripts—they're to the right and left of me and all round about me.

I went to the British Museum after leaving your office yesterday; they hadn't *Lettres d'un Innocent* there, but I ordered it at Dulan's in Soho Square, and it will be here on Monday. It was sold at a franc in Paris; so there'll be stuff enough for a sixpenny book at least. The translation will be easy enough. Each of the three might do a bit to get it done quickly. And then there can be a general revision of the whole.

But what I want to say is this. If we had the money and an agent of sufficient address to approach Madame Dreyfus—if he had tact and diplomacy there mightn't be very much money required—we might, by getting all the Dreyfus Letters to and from the Devil's Island, secure a book of extraordinary human interest. Dreyfus is a man of very strong family affection—did you see his telegram of yesterday addressed to his wife? "I await with joy the moment of kissing you." What a moment it will be to the two! He used to write to his little boy to be sure and teach his baby sister how to build "those card-castles which you and I built together, and which used to come tumbling down so gloriously." That in itself is enough to shew that the fellow has a kind and simple heart. Again his letters are full of passionate reiterations of his innocence. His wife, on her part, never wavered for a moment in her expressions of loyalty and faith. So the thing, you see, is human drama of the profoundest. And his letters have, further, an intimate bearing on the material aspects of l'affaire, for the scoundrelly Generals grabbed them in transit to suit their own purposes. My dear fellow, if we could only get these letters in our hands, we should possess one of the most extraordinary human documents ever given to the world.

What do you say to our drafting a letter to Madame Dreyfus to the effect that a collection of her husband's letters (and, incidentally, her own also) would be the best answer to the generals and others who tried to make him out a heartless and immoral ruffian? We should do it carefully and suavely, of course. And even my friend, Miss Jacobs, a clever girl who is one of the Royal Society secretaries for French and German, would put it into good Parisian for us. She's safe, and we can give her a present if the thing comes off.

If it doesn't there's always the secondary plan—to publish such letters as have appeared in the Press and *Lettres d'un Innocent*—provided always the latter hasn't been bagged by a previous publisher.

I'll call tomorrow at 12, but write meanwhile to give you my rough idea of things.

Yours always,

G. D. B.

P.S. Immediately we get the book from Paris we ought to buy the rights at once, to make sure of that at anyrate.

Brown certainly knew what he was talking about when he later observed that "the Scot . . . has the forecasting leap of the mind which sees what to make of things—more, sees them made and in vivid operation." In this instance, however, imagination was not enough, and Brown's hope of presenting "a book of extraordinary human interest" to the world never came to fruition.

If the little publishing business had been his main interest, he would have been greatly discouraged; but it was only a sideline with possibilities—and even they were diminishing. When he was alone in his rooms after midnight, he thus closed his mind to the irritations of the day, and, as the great city outside faded from his thoughts, he lived again in the village of Barbie with John Gourlay and a malignant individual called the Deacon. They were not mere creatures of fantasy; they were truly and terribly alive; and their story was taking definite shape. Here—at last—was no pot-boiler.

9

On a Saturday evening in June 1900, Ernest Barker and his wife had just come from the Zoo in Regent's Park when they happened to meet Brown and Emanuel. Brown accompanied them to their hotel—his companion having a dinner date elsewhere—and in the lounge he talked about the work he had done and was doing. He told Barker about Gourlay, merely as a character he had imagined, "and so," Barker recalled, "I recognized Gourlay when I read the novel afterwards, and have ever since been fond of him as an old friend."

Brown invited the Barkers to lunch next day, and they found him in "pretty rooms" at 10, Queen's Road, St. John's Wood. They thought that he looked "sleek and comfortable", and without doubt he was in excellent spirits. "I remember," said Barker, "his reading to us in his wonderful voice from a book called *Patrins*, which he lent to me afterwards. During lunch my wife remarked on the beauty of one of the roses on the table; whereupon Brown would give it to me."[1]

[1] This incident had a touching sequel. "A fortnight or so after we heard of his death," said Barker, "feeling something in the inner pocket of an old jacket, my wife took it out and lo! the dry petals of the rose, concealed there these two years and more."

Shortly after this week-end Brown finished his story about Gourlay. It was an awkward length, between 20,000 and 25,000 words, and was therefore too long for a short story and too short for a novel. It then occurred to him that it might be worth while to let some of his friends read it. Their opinions and reactions would be interesting, although he did not care what any of them thought about it. He *knew* it was good, and he wondered if he ought to reconsider it as a full-length novel.

He gave the manuscript to Francis Neilson and his wife, and they were enthusiastic. When they urged him to extend it, however, he did not commit himself; he allowed them to think that he was uncertain what to do. His next move was to read the story to Melrose and Spicer, and, as he expected, they also advised him to develop the theme. He seemed so genuinely impressed that they never dreamed that others had already given him similar advice.

Here in full play was that peculiarity which Neilson had already noted: a tendency in Brown to pit one friend against another. Out of it there arose a suspicion that he was not always loyal; but Neilson became convinced that it was a twisted form of leg-pulling and that Brown got "a great deal of amusement out of this Iago-business." One evening, when challenged about it, he laughed and said, "Man, Neilson, when you get them on properly, it's perfectly astonishing to know how they swell their chests." Yet it was, as he discovered, a ticklish sport. Melrose and Spicer were not in the same camp as Meldrum and Neilson, and, with the opportunist in Brown striving to remain sweet with all parties, tension often resulted. Ere this, there had been a storm in a tea-cup, or rather a flare-up in a lobby, over a play which the firm of Hood, Douglas, and Howard, as agents had offered to Neilson, and to smooth matters out at the time Brown had sent a long letter to Melrose.

28, St. Petersburg Place,
Bayswater, W.

My dear Centurion,
I perfectly accept and agree with all you say about the Triumvirate speaking with one voice, and as one man, against all outsiders, even if these outsiders be personal friends of one or other member of the Triumvirate. The words I used in the lobby at the Garrick may have seemed to indicate that I was standing up for Neilson against my own side; but they were really meant quite otherwise—they were based on the knowledge that we had the right to go over the text of the play, and they were, at worst, a hasty assertion that Neilson himself had expressly confessed and admitted that right, only the night before, in asking us to blue-pencil objectionable passages. "Oh, yes, my dear Centurion, but Neilson himself has already asked us"—or something to that effect.

Well, if that be so in that particular case—and that it *was* so you will believe me when I say it—much more do I admit the fact that we three should speak and act as one man against outsiders. I answer thus expressly, and even formally, because you said truly that if I held other views (which I do not) it would lead to the weakening of our partnership.

To come to matters much more personal and intimate and much less formal.

All I said on Thursday—and I only said it because we were mutually trying to explain how we had come to misunderstand each other at the Garrick—was that I sometimes thought you betrayed a quick impatience and irritation in voice and eye because you failed to grasp what I was, no doubt imperfectly and blunderingly, trying to express. I confessed that this apparent irritation (as I thought it) on your part irritated me. But it seems I was mistaken—that the irritation was only in appearance and not in reality. But, my dear Melrose (and this is the point) even if the irritation had been real on your side, even if you had railed at and scolded and hurt me, it would have made no difference to the love and affection I have for you. For the accidents of a man's nature make no difference in my regard for him when I know what he is essentially—when I feel myself in sympathy with all the inner greatness of his nature. There can never be any essential difference between you and me. Even if we parted in anger (which God forbid) and never spoke to each other again—our souls would still be friends.

I come to the third point mentioned in your letter, and as to that I think I owe you an apology—as I do for violence of manner or anything else that caused you pain. I had no right to mention Spicer in this matter. Mind you I did think honestly that you spoke to him with just the same quick impatience, shewn in eye and voice, as you spoke to me—and that not always owing to his fault but because you sometimes failed to understand him. You understand, of course, that I'm referring to the *manner* of your speech, and not to the *matter*—I would not suggest and never meant to suggest, that you ever tried to exercise undue influence either over Spicer or myself. And certainly he never said or hinted to me that you tried to domineer him—his loyalty to you is far too great to permit of his going behind your back with a complaint of that kind. For a like reason I cannot broach the subject to him. But, as he has never shewn any resentment, I do not see that an apology from you to him is either necessary or desirable. It is I who ought to apologize to both of you—I had rather you had never known me than look on me as a mischief-maker.

My dear "Jhonie", I have features in my character which I know you can't altogether approve of, and yet you love me in spite of them. And so I love you in spite of all your faults were they a thousand times worse than my too-hot temper ever made them out to be.

Yours always,
"Gaudie."

Now, however, Brown was not thinking in terms of any triumvirate. He had found, as he had always known he would find, his true purpose. For long absorbed by the theory and practice of the art of letters, he was ready to apply the results of his speculations.

In the London parks, where the trees were tinted by autumnal frost, he brooded for hours on the fall of the House of Gourlay. He had always maintained that love-interest was not absolutely necessary in a novel. Here was a chance to prove his argument: Gourlay's business would serve as a substitute. It would be necessary, too, to develop the character of the son—and that also would be in keeping with what he preached. "It is obvious, surely," he had written to Meldrum, "that we begin to build the men we are to be long, very long, before the period of puberty . . . how we do so has not often (or at all) been considered; that is, there's a great phase of life not studied yet, but waiting to be studied." As the jigsaw in his mind thus fitted into place, he grew impatient of advice. Melrose and Neilson (unknown to each other) tried to tell him what to do and what not to do; but the time for discussion was past, and he needed help from no man.

Later, when he made notes for a new novel which he planned to call *The Novelist*, he wrote:

"Perhaps I ought to get into *Novelist* all the obstructions I myself have found in writing. All I would have to do would be to think them over—I've certainly got plenty of them. . . .

"Get in where all kinds of silly advisers try to turn the Novelist from his bent. Get in there, too, all your theories about advice being immoral. . . .

"It's almost as indelicate to ask an author when his book will be published as to ask a woman when she expects her lying in.

"'It shews weakness in a man when he displays irritation at another's interference,' said (a friend of the Nov.).

"'I don't see that,' said Nov.

"'If he were conscious of strength he would toss the interference aside without bothering too much.'

"'Yes, but he might be determined on his own way, yet maddened at the presumption of others in trying to divert him.'

"'Madness of that kind's a waste of strength. A man should go right for his goal and never heed the brambles that tug at him.'

"'That's so. Still it's ill to be philosophic when a bramble tears open the back of your hand.'"

By late autumn Brown was in an opposite mood to the one in which, on returning from Shepperton, he had vowed to Tom Smith: "I'll never go to live in the country again—*English* country,

I mean." That was precisely where he wanted to go now; for solitude and escape from well-meaning friends were essential.

He got fixed up at Briar Cottage, Haslemere, Surrey, and there, under the care of a Mrs. Boyes, he made arrangements to stay all winter. Being within convenient distance of London, he knew that his routine work for Macqueen and Symon would not be interrupted and that, now if ever, he was ready to match his hour. He had brought a plentiful supply of large, black-covered exercise books, and one night, when he had settled in his new environment, he at last penned the words:

THE HOUSE WITH THE GREEN SHUTTERS

I

The frowsy chamber-maid of the "Red Lion" had just finished washing the front door steps. She rose from her stooping posture, and, being of slovenly habit, flung the water from her pail straight out, without moving from where she stood. The smooth round arch of the falling water glistened for a moment in mid-air. John Gourlay, standing in front of his new house at the head of the brae, could hear the swash of it when it fell. The morning was of perfect stillness.

10

Although the long period of gestation was over, Brown found that he could not work easily for any length of time. When the glow was upon him he wrote well; but he was at the mercy of his stomach and liver, and much of his day's output depended upon how he felt when he got up in the morning. In a letter to Melrose he declared:

"I myself am suffering from appalling lethargy of mind and body (it's liver not laziness); I could idle away existence in a gross and heavy dream. I'm going to walk and physic it off before to-morrow. At present I've got to pinch myself angrily in order to do things."

Then his restless brain began to work, and he went on:

"I think some day I'll make a study of the lethargic character; an incidental sketch rather. There is a distinct place for incidental psychologic sketches in a novel; sometimes you are very familiar with significant traits which, nevertheless, are hardly big enough to make the framework of a whole novel; but if you work them in features of your minor characters these impress by their truth and (if well handled) add to the full conviction of the whole. Balzac has done that with character of La Fosseuse in *The Country Doctor*."[1]

[1] In his Memoir of Brown in *Scottish Art and Letters* (November 1902—January 1903), Arnold Fraser-Lovat pointed out: " In *Le Médecin de Campagne* there occurs

Because of his erratic temperament, Brown, who had desired solitude, now craved occasional companionship. Yet when Francis Neilson and his family spent a long week-end with him, he left them for the most part to their own designs.

"We were there four days," said Neilson. "We did not see him until dinner-time at night, and, after the meal, he read from penny copy-books the work he had done during the day."

Brown then listened attentively—especially to Mrs. Neilson who represented the feminine point of view—but he had not altered his opinion about advisers. As time went on, in fact, he became so sensitive that he left no one in doubt about his attitude. "He could not stand criticism at all," Melrose was ultimately forced to admit. "'I don't care a damn,' he would say. He was not willing to have anything he wrote unfavourably criticized."

What Brown's friends did not realize was that he not only recognized his faults in style and technique but very often wrote in defiance of them. For example, he had insisted that characters should explain themselves by their actions; now he analysed young Gourlay almost at every turn.[1] He had made the exciting discovery that as soon as he got inside his characters he could also watch them *from the outside*.

In his notes for *The Novelist* he said: "He (the Novelist) got into that non-moral state in which he could watch himself commit a fault with a certain amount of pleasure at seeing the issue of the struggle. In most men there is good and evil; in some writers there are three Principles; Good, and Evil, and a Third—an artistic watching sense which is keen to see whether Good or Evil will conquer, not morally concerned for the result (as every man ought to be) but interested in the issue of the dramatic contest, as if the field in which it was fought was not his own personality.

"Apart from any personal concern as to how it shall turn out for him—is not that Artistic Interest coupled with, indeed, derived from, his perception of Law, Remorseless Law in Human Life? Being, by the condition of his function as an Observer, outside Human Life, he sees that his evil quality of Loafer, say, comes from his pursuit of Wise Philosophic Indolence; he is satisfied to explain the evil, to link it back, without seeking to amend it.

"That is the Point. As the Observer of Humanity *from the outside* he is satisfied with watching the operation of the law. To himself he

---

a significant passage, to which I have not hitherto seen attention called. The doctor is describing to Genestas ' the transformation of the *cretin*-haunted desert into a happy valley.'

"'And when I saw *the* newly-built *House with the Green-painted Shutters*, the vine beside the door, and the bench, and bundle of osiers before it . . .'

"This is hardly one of those many and not unnatural coincidences that are certain to exist amidst the mass of overlapping human achievement. The sequence of words which constitutes the phrase is, like the completed phrase itself, unusual."

[1] Brown defends this inconsistency in his letter to Barker on Page 165.

is but another instance. And so individual passion for his own improvement is lost in his general studying. Qua artistic and philosophic observer, he is non-human."

In this reasoning lay Brown's theory of "the implicit idea." He revealed that, on the last Sunday of the 19th century, it came to him—"obscurely but very vividly in the moment of its coming"—that a book could only be elevated "by showing a big spiritual intention behind it," and he concluded that, if this purpose was carried to fulfilment, a sense of greatness was bound to result.

This knowledge spurred him on in a manner which he subsequently described in *The Novelist* notes.

"He jotted down apercu after apercu. Some days he lived in a whirl of mental excitement. Points, appreciations of life's dilemmas, wise generalizations (or what seemed such!) streamed in upon his mind. He ran from note-book to note-book—he left notes half finished in the hurry of inserting others. His mind seemed to tower, to achieve; he was abundantly content; he felt himself working in the line of some progressive idea which he felt to be working through his life."

And again: "He was impressed by the power of his own mental impressions to conquer fatigue. Often he had taken notes, in his mind or on his cuff, and when his conscience jogged him to go and write them out he often pleaded laziness and lost them. For if he kept them till the week after he generally forgot them. But if he went to his papers, however tired, he found that his own interest in getting down the things of his own mind drove tiredness away—he would write unconscious of the passing hours, of his dead fire, of everything but the glad feeling that he was conquering a new perception of a new truth."

Brown then noted the nervous and almost inevitable reaction.

"Now that he began to write successfully, in full and fluent vein, he was beset by a new fear—and a laughable. Men of the world will set it down to the ridiculous vanity of scribblers. He never laid down his pen at night without a fear that he might die ere morning and leave unfinished the great work in which he was engaged. He used to think it a pity that humanity should lose the benefit of his great ideas and many observations! Poor fool! As if it mattered a pin to the world. But he could not rid himself of a sense of impending calamity which should cut him short in his career. He was all nerves and brain when he wrote; he lost control of his mind and it worked of itself, so that he could never get a rest. 'I'll take a walk and think of something else,' he would say; but the moment he quickened his step, he was with his characters, talking to them, and laughing at their answers. And the moment he got back he flew to his desk lest he should lose a word of it. That the brain-driven flesh resented this galling task-work, there is not a doubt; and the morbid condition of his nerves had something to do with his fears. For the rest, they were not the result of vanity but an honest desire to leave his work complete. 'I don't care, if I can only live to finish this one,' he would say to himself, trying, in subconscious desire, to make a bargain with the Deity. The worldling will laugh less, no doubt ('tis no less laughable, but the worldling is frightened by big names) he will snigger less, perhaps, when he learns that Zola and Keats had the same fear of death cutting short their work 'before high-pilèd books, in charactery,' should 'hold like rich garners the full-ripen'd grain.'"

Despite his nerves and dyspepsia, his seething emotions and dark moments of fear, Brown felt the surge of his greatness and worked in the full sweep and rush of his power. Fifty years earlier Charlotte Brontë had said that "the writer who possesses the creative gift owns something of which he is not always master—something that, at times, strangely wills and works for itself." So now with Brown. He had laid down rules and expounded theories; but John Gourlay walked in the shadow of a terrible doom, and Brown had no choice but to follow in his wake.

II

In a commonplace opening—a man standing before his new house on a fresh, sunny morning—Brown achieves the very essence of tragedy. John Gourlay, saturnine and rough-hewn, sees the hands of the clock across "the Square" pointing to eight o'clock. They are yellow in the sun. He hears the silly *tee-hee* of the chamber-maid of the "Red Lion", then the sound of her door-mat being pounded against the end of the house. It is a peaceful morning in Barbie, with the smoke rising thin and far above the red chimneys and sunshine glistering on the roofs and gables. The railway has not yet reached this part of the country, and Gourlay is the town's only carrier.

He smoked in silent enjoyment because on a morning such as this, everything he saw was a delicate flattery to his pride. At the beginning of a new day to look down on the petty burgh in which he was the greatest man, filled all his being with a consciousness of importance. His sense of prosperity was soothing and pervasive; he felt it all round him like the pleasant air, as real as that and as subtle; bathing him, caressing. It was the most secret and intimate joy of his life to go out and smoke on summer mornings by his big gate, musing over Barbie ere he possessed it with his merchandise. He had growled at the quarry carters for being late in setting out this morning (for like most resolute dullards he was sternly methodical), but in his heart he was secretly pleased. The needs of his business were so various that his men could rarely start at the same hour, and in the same direction. To-day, however, because of the delay, all his carts would go streaming through the town together, and that brave pomp would be a slap in the face to his enemies. "I'll shew them," he thought, proudly. "Them" was the town-folk, and what he would shew them was what a big man he was.

For, like most scorners of the world's opinion, Gourlay was its slave, and shewed his subjection to the popular estimate by his anxiety to flout it. He was not great enough for the carelessness of perfect scorn.

When Gourlay's carts go down the brae, we know in our hearts that every turn of the wheels is carrying him nearer to destruction. Even now he does not have his sorrows to seek: his wife is a slattern, his son, John, a shrinking, lubberly boy, and his daughter, Janet, a poor, consumptive creature. Already the malicious gossips—the Scots "bodies"—are watching like vultures.

"He's getting a big boy, that son o' Gourlay's," said the Provost; "how oald will he be?"

"He's approaching twelve," said Johnny Coe, who made a point of being able to supply such news because it gained him considera-tion where he was otherwise unheeded. "He was born the day the brig on the Fleckie Road gaed down, in the year o' the great flood; and since the great flood it's twelve year come Lammas. . . . Ye mind what an awful day it was; the thunder roared as if the heavens were tumbling on the world, and the lichtnin sent the trees daudin on the roads, and folk hid below their beds and prayed—they thocht it was the Judgment! But Gourlay rammed his black stepper in the shafts, and drave like the devil o' hell to Skeighan Drone, where there was a young doctor. The lad was feared to come, but Gourlay swore by God that he should, and he garred him. In a' the countryside driving like his that day was never kenned or heard tell o'; they were back within the hour! I saw them gallop up Main Street; lichtnin struck the ground before them; the young doctor covered his face wi' his hands, and the horse nichered wi' fear and tried to wheel, but Gourlay stood up in the gig and lashed him on through the fire. It was thocht for lang that Mrs. Gourlay would die; and she was never the same woman after."

The bodies, silent at this presentment of Gourlay's courage on the day that had scared them all, are vital and alive: Provost Connal, full of self-importance, lisping Deacon Allardyce, Tam Brodie, "the most brutal among them", Sandy Toddle, Johnny Coe, Tam Wylie and the kindlier baker.

Little escapes them, although, to be sure, they are not in evidence on one of the days that young Gourlay sneaks away from school.

The street was lonely in the sudden stillness. The joiner slanted across the road, brushing shavings and sawdust from his white

132

apron. There was no other sign of life in the sunshine. Only from the smiddy, far away, came at times the tink of an anvil.

John crept up the street, keeping close to the wall. It seemed unnatural being there at that hour; everything had a quiet, unfamiliar look. The white walls of the houses reproached the truant with their silent faces. A strong smell of wallflowers oozed through the hot air. John thought it a lonely smell, and ran to get away.

There at last! A *lonely* smell. It had taken years to achieve this finished, perfect description.

With the coming of the railway and the arrival, from Aberdeen, of James Wilson, a native of Barbie, the seal is set on Gourlay's downfall. But Wilson is only the son of a mole-catcher, and it angers Gourlay when this upstart dares to inquire how business is.

. . . . it was the assumption of equality implied by Wilson's manner that offended Gourlay—as if mole-catcher's son and monopolist were discussing, on equal terms, matters of interest to them both.

"Business!" he said gravely. "Well, I'm not well acquainted with your line, but I believe mole traps are cheap—if you have any idea of taking up the oald trade."

A week later Wilson announces to the inhabitants of Barbie and surrounding neighbourhood that he has taken "these commodious premises, No. 1 The Cross, which he intends to open shortly as a Grocery, Ironmongery, and General Provision Store." He is careful to add that he "will deliver goods at your own doors, distributing them with his own carts either in the town of Barbie or at any convenient distance from the same."

While the nippy Wilson is working up his business and establishing his own delivery service, Gourlay loses his lease of a stone quarry owned by Templandmuir, a local laird. Templandmuir breaks the news as they are walking home from a public meeting which had been convened to discuss the new railway. The rebuff goes deep—it takes Gourlay so completely by surprise—and he is left, a cauldron of wrath in the darkness.

He walked blindly to the kitchen door, never knowing how he reached it. It was locked—at this early hour!—and the simple inconvenience let loose the fury of his wrath. He struck the door with his clenched fist till the blood streamed on his knuckles.

It was Mrs. Gourlay who opened the door to him. She started back before his awful eyes.

"John!" she cried, "what's wrong wi' ye?"

The sight of the she-tatterdemalion there before him, whom he had endured so long and must endure for ever, was the crowning burden of his night. Damn her, why didn't she get out of the way? why did she stand there in her dirt and ask silly questions? He

133

struck her on the bosom with his great fist, and sent her spinning on the dirty table.

She rose from among the broken dishes and came towards him, with slack lips and great startled eyes. "John," she panted, like a pitiful frightened child, "what have I been doing? . . . Man, what did ye hit me for?"

He gaped at her with hanging jaw. He knew he was a brute—knew that she had done nothing to-night more than she had ever done—knew he had vented on her a wrath that should have burst on others. But his mind was at a stick; how could he explain—to *her*? He gaped and glowered for a speechless moment, then turned on his heel and went into the parlour, slamming the door till the windows rattled in their frames.

A sharp piece of business, engineered by Wilson and "Cunning Johnny" Gibson, the builder, then results in Gourlay losing a large, well-paid contract, his hands being tied by a poorer contract which, unknown to him when the agreement was signed, compels him to do some carting for Wilson. When he discovers how he has been tricked, Gourlay is as dangerous as a bull tormented by gad-flies.

"I'll see Wil-son . . . and Gib-son . . . and every other man's son . . . frying in hell," he said slowly, "ere a horse o' mine draws a stane o' Wilson's property. Be damned to ye, but there's your answer!"

Gibson's cunning deserted him for once. He put his hand on Gourlay's shoulder in pretended friendly remonstrance.

"Take your hand off my shouther!" said Gourlay, in a voice the intense quietness of which should have warned Gibson to forbear.

But he actually shook Gourlay with a feigned playfulness.

Next instant he was high in the air; for a moment the hobnails in the soles of his boots gleamed vivid to the sun; then Gourlay sent him flying through the big window of the Red Lion, right on to the middle of the great table where the market-folk were drinking.

When Gibson screams and threatens to fight him through all the law courts in Britain to make him implement his bond, Gourlay nearly goes at him through the window. Gibson quails at his look.

"To hell wi' your law-wers!" cried Gourlay. "I'd throttle ye like the dog you are on the floor o' the House o' Lords."

But that day was to cost him dear. Ere six months passed he was cast in damages and costs for a breach of contract aggravated by assault. He appealed, of course. He was not to be done; he would show the dogs what he thought of them.

He sends his son to the High School of Skeighan, and later on, when he learns that young Wilson is going to the university, he makes up his mind to send his son there, too. It is the most disastrous decision of his life.

"Get yourself ready for the College in October," he ordered his son that evening.

"The College!" cried John aghast.

"Yes! Is there ainything in that to gape at?" snapped his father, in sudden irritation at the boy's amaze.

"But I don't want to gang!" John whimpered as before.

"Want! what does it matter what *you* want? You should be damned glad of the chance! I mean to make ye a minister; they have plenty of money and little to do—a grand, easy life o't. MacCandlish tells me you're a stupid ass, but have some little gift of words. You have every qualification!"

"It's against *my* will," John bawled angrily.

"*Your* will!" sneered his father.

The move at first seems justified. Young Gourlay wins the Raeburn, a prize of a few books for an "essay in the picturesque." This small success goes to his head, convivial company completes his ruin, and he is sent down from the university for drunkenness and insolence towards one of the professors.

Now Gourlay's men have been slipping away, one by one—the scene in which he discharges Peter Riney is touched by true pathos —and the bodies watch and wait in unholy fascination.

Simple expectation held them. It was a dramatic interest—of suspense, yet certainty—that had them in its grip. "He's *bound* to come down," said Certainty. "Yes; but *when* though?" cried Curiosity, all the more eager because of its instinct for the coming crash. And so they waited for the great catastrophe which they felt to be so near.

Gourlay, who receives word from Edinburgh about his son, is aware that total ruin stares him in the face. His money has gone, and, with interest due on a mortgage, he knows that he must swallow his pride and try to borrow from someone in Barbie.

He had a triple wrath to his son. He had not only ruined his own life; he had destroyed his father's hope that by entering the ministry he might restore the Gourlay reputation. Above all, he had disgraced the House with the Green Shutters. That was the crown of his offending. Gourlay felt for the house of his pride even more than for himself—rather the house was himself; there was no division between them. He had built it bluff to represent him to the world. It was his character in stone and lime. He clung to it, as the dull, fierce mind, unable to live in thought, clings to a material source of pride. And John had disgraced it. Even if

135

out the jar. For we mean to make a night of it, this gentleman and me . . . A night that Barbie'll remember loang!" John "takes off his dram", and his father, in mock admiration, invites him to stand up.

He turned his son round with a finger and thumb on his shoulder, in insolent inspection, as you turn an urchin round to see him in his new suit of clothes. Then he crouched before him, his face thrust close to the other, and peered into his eyes, his mouth distent with an infernal smile. "My boy, Johnny," he said sweetly, "my boy, Johnny," and patted him gently on the cheek.

John raised dull eyes and looked into his father's. Far within him a great wrath was gathering through his fear. Another voice, another self, seemed to whimper, with dull iteration, "I'll *kill* him; I'll *kill* him; by God, I'll *kill* him—if he doesna stop this—if he keeps on like this at me!" But his present and material self was paralysed with fear.

When the iniquity in Gourlay has almost spent itself, the scene moves to its climax.

. . . he came crouching and quivering across the floor slowly, a gleaming devilry in the eyes that devoured his son. His hands were like outstretched claws, and shivered with each shiver of the voice that moaned, through set teeth, "What do ye think I mean to do wi' ye now? . . . What do ye think I mean to do wi' ye now? . . . Ye damned sorrow and disgrace that ye are, what do ye think I mean to do wi' ye now?"

"Run, John!" screamed Mrs. Gourlay, leaping to her feet. With a hunted cry young Gourlay sprang to the door. So great had been the fixity of Gourlay's wrath, so tense had he been in one direction, as he moved slowly on his prey, that he could not leap to prevent him. As John plunged into the cool, soft darkness, his mother's "Thank God!" rang past him on the night.

At the Red Lion John gulps down several drinks. Then Deacon Allardyce comes in, ready to make the most of his opportunity. "Ith it Dyohn?" he cries. "It *ith* Dyohn!" And he toddles forward with outstretched hand. "Man Dyohn!" But sport for the Deacon is spoilt by the blunt-edged Brodie whose insults so infuriate young Gourlay that he throws his glass at his tormentor. Brodie sends him flying.

"That's a game of your father's, you damned dog," he roared. "But there's mair than him can play the game!"

"Canny, my freendth, canny!" piped Allardyce, who was vexed at a fine chance for his peculiar craft being spoiled by mere brutality of handling. All this was most inartistic. Brodie never had the fine touch.

138

John plunges out into the night, and now that whisky has deadened his fear he returns home: he is ready for his father. While awaiting this moment, Gourlay, in order to fix steel rests in place of wooden pegs on the rafters, is sitting on top of a step-ladder in the kitchen. Even now he has the instinct to embellish his house. From this height Gourlay gloats over, and taunts, his victim; but John, who has gone across to sit by the fireside, picks up the poker. "It was so huge, owing to Gourlay's whim, that when it slid through his fingers it came down on the muffled hearthstone with a thud like a paviour's hammer." In the end John can endure his father's gibes no longer.

"By God, I'll kill ye," screamed John, springing to his feet, with the poker in his hand. . . . As Gourlay leapt, John brought the huge poke with a crash on the descending brow. The fiercest joy of his life was the dirl that went up his arm, as the steel thrilled to its own hard impact on the bone. Gourlay thudded on the fender, his brow crashing on the rim.

A footstep is heard, and Mrs. Gourlay snatches the poker from her son and thrusts it in the fire.

"Run, John; run for the doctor," she screamed.—"Oh, Mrs. Webster, Mrs. Webster, I'm glad to see ye. Mr. Gourlay fell from the top o' the ladder, and smashed his brow on the muckle fender."

After the funeral—for, with the doctor declaring that it would have killed any man to fall from such a height on to the sharp edge of the fender, there was nothing to delay it—John is haunted by his father's eyes. He saturates himself in drink and locks himself in the stable.

An hour later he woke from a terrible dream, flinging his arms up, to ward off a face that had been pressing on his own. Were the eyes that had burned his brain still glaring above him? He looked about him in drunken wonder. From a sky-window a shaft of golden light came slanting into the loose-box, living with yellow motes in the dimness. The world seemed dead; he was alone in the silent building, and from without there was no sound. Then a panic terror flashed on his mind, that those eyes had actually been here—and were here with him still—where he was locked up with them alone. He strained his eyeballs in a horrified stare at vacancy. Then he shut them in terror, for why did he look? If he looked, the eyes might burn on him out of nothingness. The innocent air had become his enemy—pregnant with unseen terrors to glare at him. To breathe it stifled him; each draught of it was full of menace. With a shrill cry he dashed at the door, and felt in the clutch of his ghostly enemy when he failed to open it at once, breaking his nails

Inexorable as Time itself the story draws to its sombre conclusion. The morning postman runs down to the Square with the news that the Gourlays "have a' killed themselves," and the unshaven bodies turn to stare.

. . . No man dared to speak. They gazed with blanched faces at the House with the Green Shutters, sitting dark there and terrible beneath the radiant arch of the dawn.

When Brown opened the door of *The House with the Green Shutters* he opened it from the inside. He had lived with an idea, and its driving power forced him to tell the truth, the whole truth, and nothing but the truth. Yet it is important to note that the novel is *not* autobiographical in the narrow sense that Brown makes use of young Gourlay alone as a study in self-revelation. When the boy curls up with books in the garret, Brown is picturing himself in the hayloft at Duchray; when John, in his Edinburgh lodgings, hears the train shunting and the *clank, clank, clank* of wagons, Brown is thinking of the goods yard below his first rooms in London; but when old Gourlay suspiciously wonders if people are talking about *him*, he, too, is Brown; and the unforgettable scene in the brake, when Gourlay is baited by the bodies, arises out of the incident in that waggonette where Brown was referred to as "'Smudden's bastard." Most serious writers are, in fact, moulded and directed by past experiences, circumstances and surroundings, and the key to the revelational side of Brown's novel is found in his Notes for *The Novelist*. "To get something down," he makes the writer say, "I fall back on my morbid gift of seeing and remembering and visualizing physical things, and I stick them down, blocking up my page with unessentials." But *The House with the Green Shutters* is big enough to rise far above its faults. Unlike Emily Brontë in *Wuthering Heights*, Brown never allowed himself to become divorced from reality, and while by pure fancy she obtained her reality, he by reality reached his apex of imagination.

PART FOUR

THE LAST YEARS

Howard, and Brown was delighted when it was accepted by an American house: M'Clure, Phillips & Co. From 10, Queen's Road, St. John's Wood, he sent this letter to Melrose.

My Dear Centurion,

M'Clure has taken *Green Shutters* for America. I am rather pleased. Macqueen might have fobbed it off on Lippincott's man (whom he dines and wines when he meets him in London) but M'Clure took it on its merits. It was read by Charles Whibley (one of the Henley school) and M'Clure told me his report was "commendatory throughout." I tell you this because you will be even more pleased than I am. To tell the truth, I'm not very bright to-night—I feel as sluggish as the weather.

Yours always,
G. D. B.

P.S. M'Clure is keen to postpone publishing till September. He says that books by new authors in the States must be out in the very forefront of the season, or else be crushed by other productions. I agreed.

G. D. B.

Meanwhile, Brown was forced to continue his hack work. Sometimes he threatened to settle down on a farm in Scotland—he even drew up a plan for an improved cow-shed—but on a brief visit to Coylton he spoke more about books than dairying. Besides, Lizzie M'Lennan happened to be there. From a rather gauche schoolgirl she had grown into an attractive young woman, and Brown quickly responded to her charm. They recalled the occasion that he had induced her tears after news of the murder of a family friend in Africa. "I hated you for it," said Lizzie . . . but Brown saw that she was smiling now.

After his return to London, he wrote to her with a regularity that, for him, was unusual. Yet to what end? He was so hard put to it to support himself that a wife was out of the question. He winced at the thought. He had lost the optimism that had carried him to Paris to propose to Isabella. He knew, of course, that if he accepted one of those lucrative posts that his friends occasionally urged him to consider, all his financial worries would be at an end. But he refused to weaken: fundamentally his true union remained with letters.

He began to plan far ahead. In addition to notes for *The Novelist* and another novel, *The Incompatibles*, he began to work upon *Hamlet: A Study in Essential Criticism*. With this venture into belles-lettres he connected many of his own experiences; indeed his impressions grew more pregnant because he brooded upon them, and he worked them up in vividness and detail until they far transcended the originals. An example of this literary instinct at work found its way into his Notes (as a comment on the Ghost) to *Hamlet*.

At best your allegory is only a plausible lie: teach a child to read it and you teach him to lie plausibly. Consider that, Mr. Moralist! I am firm in my opinion that the crowded condition of our gaols and poorhouses is largely due to the allegorizing tendency of Sunday School literature. The hatred and disgust instilled into young and gentle souls who are deluded into swallowing moral jelly that conceals a pill is (I am assured of it) a main cause of later perversities of character. I feelingly speak from a bitter experience. While "books with a moral tendency" did yet my green awakening youth engage, I was once presented by my Sunday School teacher (for I too had a Sunday School teacher) with a Valuable Work. There was a significance in his manner as he made the gift, a kind of loaded meaning in his eye, which seemed to indicate that the work was exactly suited to the needs of the recipient. And at first I agreed with him entirely. I could not sufficiently admire his nice and subtle perception of my literary tastes. 'Twas a tale about the Ogre! A monstrous beast that devoured and devoured and yet was never satiate! How I tip-toed with held breath to the mouth of the cavern he abode in: with what awed fascination I stared at those two red awful eyes, glowing steadily from a vista of farther gloom, twin lights of bale. Sometimes they turned suddenly to green! And then my heart thudded against the cold rock I lay flat upon, to hide myself. How I trembled at his bellowings and regurgitations! And I loathed the foul monster, thrilled to every vicissitude of his innocent victims. And then, O hapless and deluded child, thinking no evil, I turned the page and read—and the Ogre's name was Selfishness. The foundation of the earth seemed to be loosened under my feet—the moral order was subverted—the arching heavens were a lie! Surely such things could not be allowed. I read desperately on to oust the monstrous suspicion. 'Twas no use. Not only was the Ogre's name Selfishness, it was Selfishness as Personified in a Little Boy who, having Pilfered Apples from an Orchard, added to the Enormity of his Crime by refusing to share the ill-gotten Gains with his Starving Comrades. Now, not to mention a closeness of application in the moral which I considered nothing short of a personal insult, I was conscious, over and above that, of a feeling of ludicrous outrage, of appalling and incredible deception. I had been hoaxed! I had been tricked into reading a story that was no story, but a sermon, and to swallow what was no jelly but a pill. I had been taught to loathe for a foul monster that which was really a fine brave quality of my own nature, making for true strength of character. And his great big green tail did NOT wallop from the far end of the cavern! THERE WAS NO CAVERN!

In spite of his various projects, Brown regarded the summer of 1901 as a waiting period. He spent a great deal of time at Emanuel's home, and at week-ends he often drifted down to the Neilsons' house in Bedford Park. At the suggestion of Neilson he made an attempt to turn out a one-act farce, but he never considered it as more than an experiment. Later on, he promised his friend, he would study stage technique and write serious, full-length plays.

At present he could think of little but the fate of *The House with the Green Shutters*, and when the publication date was altered from September to October, he remembered what M'Clure had said and feared that it might be swamped by the flood of Christmas books. Yet the novel itself, under his favourite pen-name, George Douglas, and dedicated to William Maybin, was attractively produced. It was priced at six shillings, contained 329 pages, and was printed for Macqueen by the Riverside Press Limited, Edinburgh.

When the first reviews appeared, Brown had no reason to exult. On 21st October the *Scotsman* summed up: "There is something of the strength and much of the coarseness of a Gottfried Keller in the manner in which this gruesome story is told; something in the headlong downfall of human beings which it describes, reminding us of Keller's *Romeo und Julia auf dem Dorfe*, without its softer sentiment; for there is no Juliet here. Barbie is unemotional if alcoholic. And there is something also of the coarse bitterness of the old English satirist, John Skelton. In its literary workmanship—as a work of art—this novel is in a hundred ways open to censure; from beginning to end it is coarse; and there are many passages almost brutal in their naked ugliness. But it may be said there is nothing so ugly as drunkenness; and if this story brings home to the reading public that may not know or think what it means every time that a young life comes under the curse of drink and how easy it is for a Scottish lad to become 'just a mouth' at which 'you could set fire to his braith', so that a match to it would 'set him in a lowe'—then its coarseness may perhaps be forgiven for its morose purpose; and something more than literary success may be achieved by the writer of *The House with the Green Shutters*."

Four days earlier the *Glasgow Herald* had delivered its judgment, and Brown now wrote to Melrose.

10 Queen's Road,
St. John's Wood,
N.W.

My Dear Centurion,

Smith's people have re-ordered again—that is, twice since the original subscription.

Rather idiotic review in the *Scotsman*, but they put it first in their list of fiction, give it the longest notice of any book, and vote it "Disagreeably powerful." Goodish review in the *Glasgow Herald*; "true to the verge of being merciless;" "if we smile, it is at the cruel point of some stinging jest;" "brilliant vigour and undeniable power;" "shows—with a vengeance, too—the reverse of the

Drumtochty shield;" "overdrawn, but grimly true and full of promise."

So far nobody but the *Glasgow Herald* even has seen that I'm shewing up the Scot malignant—which you and I thought, in a way, the *raison d'etre* of the book. *Scotsman* fellow says, it is brutally coarse. Coarse!

Thine
Giglamps.

Shortly afterwards he posted another letter to Melrose.

10 Queen's Road,
St. John's Wood,
N.W.

My Dear Centurion,
You are working a great deal more for the success of the book than I am—in fact more than anybody else is. And you know that I am not ungrateful. If it doesn't go, it won't be for want of backing from my friends.

I saw Meldrum last night, and he thinks it very likely to go, in spite of its ferocity, because of its forthrightness, the public wanting not elusive stuff, but stuff hard on the nail. He professed to be greatly struck by it, and said he envied me some of it.

There's some truth in what Neil Munro says; still Barbie's a great deal truer to life than a piece of damned sentimental filigree like *Doom Castle*.

I was very seedy last week (liver and stomach bothers), but I have walked and dieted myself well, and am now swotting all day long. I've got a fit of industry on, which I'm going to woo to continue. So don't look to see me for at least a fortnight.

Thine gratefully,
The Budding Author.

Brown was never too busy, however, to forget his friends in Scotland. To Tom Smith, now teaching in Kirkcudbrightshire, he wrote:

10 Queen's Road,
St. John's Wood,
London, N.W.
Monday.

My Dear Tom,
Of course I am very pleased to send you a copy of *The House with the Green Shutters*, with your name and my name together on the fly-leaf. I was very glad to have your letter, and to know that you were settled down at Crocketford. If I should happen to break my journey at Dumfries, ever, I shall come and see you—that is, unless your father's death in the meantime—which God forbid—shall have transferred you to Coylton. But when he does die, Tom, you must go back to the old parish; the place wouldn't be the same (to me, at least) without a Smith in the Schoolhouse.

I'm glad to know there's a chance of your coming to London next summer. You stay with me, of course. I may not be actually living in London then, for I get tired of it at times—I know too many people in it—and I like to go off and bury myself in the country to do a little work. I lived alone in a cottage all last winter at Haslemere, and wrote that book. But we can always make descents on the capital.

I'm not sure that you'll like the book. There's too much black for the white in it. However the "malignants" of rural life in Scotland had never been studied, and I wished to shew them up as they deserved.

With best wishes to you and Mrs. Smith for Christmas and New's day,[1]

> Yours, as ever,
> G. D. Brown.

And later, in answer to a letter of congratulation from the old dominie himself, Brown sent the following:

> 10 Queen's Road,
> St. John's Wood,
> London, N.W.
> Friday.

Dear Mr. Smith,

I was glad to have your kindly letter. I have not sent you a copy of a certain notorious novel, because I thought you might prefer an example of the American edition, which was published simultaneously with the English. Bound copies have not yet come over from America; when they do, I will send you one.

I enclose a cutting from the *Bookman*, which was sent into me to-night by Romeike and Curtice in a vain hope that I would subscribe to their press-cutting agency. In the same number of the *Bookman* there was a very fine specimen of the work of Robert Bryden.

> Yours vy. truly,
> G. D. Brown.

The specimen of work to which Brown referred was a reproduction of a woodcut of Arthur C. Benson, one of thirty-three portraits from Bryden's woodcuts in *Poets of the Younger Generation* by William Archer. This was in the November issue of the *Bookman*, and the cutting which Brown enclosed in his letter to John Smith was, of course, a review of *The House with the Green Shutters*.

"Mr. Douglas," said the critic, "has written a strong and impressive piece of fiction. It is very quietly done; not till the story nears its close does the tragedy move quickly. When it does move, however, it moves to some purpose; we realize the force which has been accumulating from the outset; and the end is gruesome.

[1] New Year's Day.

The book is not gloomy; indeed, it is the reverse; there is humour in plenty. There are also clever, incisive writing, good phrasing, fine characterization, and true insight. Surely only a Scot would dare to draw such a picture of a Scottish village; it is entertaining, and it is apt in its witticisms, but it is remorselessly cruel . . . Mr. Douglas shows that he can handle strong situations, and his book proves that he is able to write with power and originality."

It seemed to Brown at this stage that the English critics understood the novel better than the Scots reviewers. The *Pall Mall Gazette* had declared it to be "one of the most penetrating studies of human nature that we remember to have encountered for many years . . . Without attempting to glorify it as a work of genius, we certainly feel disposed to place it among the first dozen of the year." And the *Manchester Guardian* had stated: "For a thoroughly surprising book which breaks with every sentimental tradition of the British novel, we have no hesitation in recommending this book. Here, while we have the usual Scotch village, with whose every detail the writers of the 'kailyard school' had presumably made us acquainted, we find at once what is virtually a wholly new setting . . . Rarely have the passions of rage and hate been so powerfully described."

All the same Brown had been a critic long enough to know that favourable notices did not necessarily constitute success, and he was beginning to wonder if, after all, his novel was doomed to fade out when—unexpectedly—he received a brief but important letter.

My Dear Centurion, (he hastened to tell Melrose)
I have just had a very pleasant letter from Andrew Lang, congratulating me on *The House with the Green Shutters*. This is very generous conduct on his part, as he doesn't know me from Adam, and writes as to a total stranger.
He says, "if this book is not excellent, I am much in error."
This mustn't get into print, of course, for Lang's a fastidious beggar who would squirm if he saw his opinion bandied about as matter of advertisement.
                                            Yours always,
                                            G. D. Brown.

Fortunately, Lang did not let his opinion rest there. He held a royal prerogative at the court of critics, and on this occasion he used it to the full. He praised Brown's novel in *Longman's Magazine* —"the style is so good that one does not think about it"—and went on to discuss it in *The Times*. He claimed it to be "the kind of novel which Balzac or Flaubert might have written, had either been a Scot, with a bitter sense of humour. . . . The veracity of the picture as far as it goes, the wonderfully keen and humorous observations, the rare hints that the author can see and take pleasure in better things, and the brilliance of vision, as in the case of the younger Gourlay, make the book *empoignant*, mark it as apart from the throng of novels. There is nothing of the novice, nothing of the amateur. Gourlay himself is worthy of the hand that drew Weir of Hermiston."

Other reviews appeared in line with Lang's example. The *Outlook* thought the novel "a notable and, in a sense, tremendous book," and the *Spectator* said, "Mr. Douglas, like the Ancient Mariner, is a narrator whom one cannot choose but hear . . . His masters are Galt and Balzac, but there are few traces of the novice, and none of the imitator." The *Morning Post, Illustrated London News, Vanity Fair, Black and White, Punch*, the *Academy*—in short, every journal and magazine of note—joined in the chorus of commendation.

In America the novel was also well received; columns were devoted to it, and the *New York Evening Sun* concluded a long résumé with a summing-up which was typical of similar publications.

"*The House with the Green Shutters* is like the tragedy of the Greeks, human woe in every accent and the heavens lowering black. There is no laugh of woman or prattle of child, no sweet thing, indeed, in this dark study of George Douglas, but it is undeniably powerful and written in round, strong, pregnant prose. If this is the author's first effort, we may look for a masterpiece some day."

More important (to a hard-up writer) was the fact that, as the public demanded the book in libraries and shops, edition followed edition; for Brown realized that without royalties flattery would have meant an empty triumph. Yet those people who assumed that he had achieved fame overnight were wrong. As *The House with the Green Shutters* had been the climax, so now this emergence from Spartan obscurity was the anti-climax to a life of harsh experience, deep thought and preparation. He had "arrived"— at tremendous cost.

2

When his novel was first published Brown sent a postcard to his friend Barker. On the back was printed an announcement of *The House with the Green Shutters* by George Douglas to which he added "alias Brown." Barker got the book and replied at once, and towards the end of the month Brown wrote again, this letter rather surprisingly bearing a date.

24th October 1901.   10, Queen's Road,
                                            St. John's Wood,
                                            London, N.W.
My Dear Barker,
    I'm a skunk not to have written before this to thank you for your
kind invitation to Oxford. It is very good of you, but for various
reasons I can't come. For one thing I'm trying to write an "Essay
in Essential Criticism" (ambitious Brown!), and it has been led
hitherto by a hundred obstructions and bedevilments. I don't want
to imply that I'm infernally busy, but what with my own indolence
and the necessity to earn the daily scrag of mutton, I seem to get
very little done. The fact is that when I want to work at what
really interests myself, I ought to get out of London and bury
myself. (Don't make the obvious joke, and hint at a possible
putrescence.) I wrote the greater part of *The House with the Green
Shutters* when I was living all alone in a little cottage at Haslemere.
In London there are a hundred distractions to throw me off the
scent, but I mean to stick this till I go to Scotland at Christmas.
    However, if you ask me down for a day next summer I shall
come most gladly.
    Well, I suppose you have read the *Green Shutters* by this time.
'Tis a brutal and a bloody work; too sinister, I should think, for a
man of your kindlier disposition. There is too much black for the
white in it. Even so it is more complimentary to Scotland, I think,
than the sentimental slop of Barrie, and Crockett, and Maclaren.
It was antagonism to their method that made me embitter the
blackness; like old Gourlay I was going "to show the dogs what I
thought of them." Which was a gross blunder, of course. A
novelist should never have an axe of his own to grind. If he allows
a personal animus to obtrude ever so slightly it knocks his work out
of balance. He should be an aloof individual, if possible, stating all
sides and taking none.
    I have taken to reading Virgil of late with great appreciation.
The fourth book of the Aeneid was always my favourite, even when
Latin to me was a mere thing to be crammed, and I've read so
much of it of late that I know screeds of it by heart. Virgil's no
good at a fight, but there's one passage, I think, which goes to show
that he might have made a fine emotional dramatist. You know it,
no doubt. Dido is addressing Aeneas—that unctious prig. (If
pious Aeneas were alive now, he'd be a Nonconformist parson of
the baser sort, a very Chadband. Perhaps he is a Doctor Parker.)
    "*Te propter Libycae gentes Nomadumque tyranni Odere, infensi Tyrii; te
propter eundem Exstinctus pudor, et, qua sola sidera adibam, Fama prior.
Cui me moribundam deseris, hospes? Hoc solum nomen quoniam de conjuge
restat. Quid moror? an mea Pygmalion dum moenia frater Destruat, aut
captam ducat Gaetulus Iarbas? Saltem si qua mihi de te suscepta fuisset Ante
fugam suboles, si quis mihi parvulus aula Luderet Aeneas, qui te tamen ore
referret, Non equidem omnino capta ac deserta viderer.*"
    That, I think, would be A1 upon the stage. I could gas about it
more than you would have patience to listen to. Not only every

153

line, but almost every syllable, has a dramatic value, is a cunning and artistic dodge. Note the bitter and emphatic "*Te*" flung in the very forefront of the line and its angry repetition in "*te propter eundem*"—the very manner of a woman wronged, and loving fiercely still. That emphatic "*te*" is repeated in "*de te suscepta fuisset*", and "*te tamen ore referret*"—Dido's mood of mingled anger and love is all one of "*You, you, you.*" And then "*fama prior*" flung again in the forefront of the line, salient to the very eye, to show all she has lost because of him; the pathos of "*moribundam*", the bitter irony of "*hospes*", and the pathos of the line that follows it. If that quick cry of the heart, "*Cui me moribundam deseris, hospes?*" is not dramatic, nothing is. And how profoundly true to human nature is her wish, immodest though it be. I like Virgil for that "*parvulus*". I can see the little chap playing about Dido's halls, and the following benediction of his mother's eyes.

Why do you pedagogues in high places not teach the classics as instinct with supernal beauty and significance, and not as mere composts of gerunds and absolute ablatives? Why, Oxford might have made something of me even, if the hook had been baited properly. But I'm willing to admit that it was less the fault of the angler than the fish.

Give my best regards to Mrs. Barker,

Yours always,
G. D. Brown.

Later on Brown fulfilled a long-standing promise and sent a copy of his novel to David Maughan in Australia.

10, Queen's Road,
St. John's Wood,
London, N.W.

My Dear Davie, (he wrote at the time)

You must think me an incorrigible skunk for not writing to you all those years. The fact is that the arrears of correspondence I was owing you accumulated to such an enormous amount that I got afraid of them. "Lord!" I thought, "when I *do* write to Maughan, I'll have to send him a volume", and the thought of such a task often deterred me when I thought of attempting it. "Damn it!" said Conscience, "you can't think of sending an ordinary little skiddling note when you owe him so much." "Yes," squirmed Self-Justification, "but Maughan knows I've a regard for him without my telling him, and if I begin to tell him all I ought to have told him, I'll need to write a book as big as Johnson's Dictionary." Thus, you see, it's really because I have a higher ideal of correspondence than Britton[1] and Emanuel that they beat me at the game. My epitaph will be: "Here lies a man whose ideals were so high that he never tried to realise them."

However, herewith a volume of sorts, if not of correspondence.

[1] A. E. Britton, a London solicitor, who had been at Oxford with Brown and Maughan.

You remember you made me promise to send you my first novel. Here it is. I wrote a boy's story (as hackwork) a couple of years ago, but I didn't consider it good enough to acknowledge and hid myself under an egregious pseudonym. So that didn't count. I hope this will: it has gone into three editions, and has been rather well reviewed, though a few Scotch papers damn me as a renegade.

I daresay you get all the news from Britton and Emanuel so I won't bother you much with home happenings. Emanuel is still plugging away at the law, in which I don't suppose he'll ever do much good. But Emanuel too, I should think, has chances in other directions. He seems to me a much cleverer fellow than he used to be. You and I always knew he had a wonderful imagination and a great deal of bizarre ability, but he has broken out in quite new directions since you left England. He reads much more and knows a great deal about books and painting. I suppose it was while idling in his chambers waiting for briefs that he began to read Ruskin and some other chaps, and his brain seemed to expand all of a sudden. He was always a good perceiver, he's now a good thinker. Only for God's sake don't tell him I said so, or he'll feel sick.

As for me, my dear Maughan, (whatever my sins of correspondence) I am always

Yours

G. D. Brown.

P. S. This is a copy of the first edition.

As he became known, Brown had to deal with increasing correspondence. Many people wrote either to abuse or to congratulate him, but he occasionally received letters which required more than passing consideration. One—from a critic—was sent to Macqueen in acknowledgement of a copy of the novel, whereupon the publisher immediately forwarded it to Brown.

I am, (said the critic) much obliged to you for sending me *The House with the Green Shutters*. I have read it with the greatest interest: it is certainly strong and original, and subtle in analysis. Barbie I take to be a kind of counterblast to Thrums, or a black purge for the Scottish sentimentalist. In this regard it may have its value, though I should be inclined to say that of the two extremes Barbie is the further from reality. The Scot, it appears, is part devil, part rat; the village is a little hell broth of meanness; the most amiable character in the book is a weary slattern made up of silliness and animal patience. It is all true in a way, but where is the rest of the truth? I hate sentimentalism; but here is life robbed of all its redeeming and denial elements which even Crabbe allowed for. The author misses tragedy (if he intended it) for tragedy is impossible without humanity. For whom are our sympathies bespoken? I closed the book with a sense of dull discomfort, due, I think, to the fact that only four of the inhabitants of Barbie had been put out of harm's way. The appearance of a sanitary officer with rat poison for the rest would have brought a certain relief. Nevertheless I enjoyed the book, and I admire it. The meannesses, suspicions, jealousies, and false genialities are most admirably dissected. The axe is laid to the roots of the Bonnie Brier Bush: may it cumber the ground no longer! Perhaps, some day, humanity may again take up its abode in the Kailyard.

In his reply, as "a mild protest against some of the strictures," Brown made several points.

1. Every clachan of Scotland *is* a hot-bed of scandal and malevolence. I had a letter the other day from a Scot previously unknown to me, in which he says that the picture of Barbie is absolutely true to the petty burgh where himself resides. He asks me whether I know Tennyson's remark that "if God made the country and man made the town, then it was the devil himself that made the small town." I didn't know it before, but I appreciate its truth. And if it be true of the English Tattle-cum-Clash, it's a thousandfold truer of the Scotch. For in democratic Scotland there's a keener hunt for prizes among all classes, and, by consequence, a keener envy.

2. Few critics have taken into account the power a character like old Gourlay has, to poison the mind of a community. I knew *of* a Gourlay (though I didn't know him personally), and I saw the exultation that greeted his downfall. It was hellish.

3. Mrs. Gourlay is not the only likeable character in the book— to me she is pitiable only, not likeable at all. But the baker and his wife, Tam Wylie and his son, Johnny Coe and Peter Riney, the old professor and Tarmillan—even Logan and Jock Allen—all these are made of the stuff of our common humanity. Whether the Gourlays are "human" or not is a matter of opinion. Some folk we know of think they are.

In those days literary schools were a lusty, full-blooded lot, and battle waged between the rival admirers of Barbie and Drumtochty. Yet Brown was aware that the fracas gave a wrong slant to *The House with the Green Shutters*.

"I've always said myself," he stated, "that there's too much black for the white in it. But those who hint that I've deliberately set myself to say 'black,' whenever Barrie and Maclaren say 'white', are talking burble. It was not for its own sake that I painted Barbie so, but because of its effect on the Gourlays. It was the elder and younger Gourlay I was trying to get inside the heads of."

Success began to mellow Brown. "The book's a brute," he often remarked with a smile, "but it's an honest brute, like its author." When he met with sincerity in other people, he therefore respected their opinions—and yet remained faithful to his particular point of view. He received a letter from a Scots authoress, Janet Milne Rae, whose novel, *Morag, a Tale of Highland Life*, first attracted attention in 1873. In this story, according to one reviewer, Mrs. Rae revealed "a faith in the Unseen but ever-present Friend"; and now, from the standpoint of her simple faith, she challenged Brown's treatment of Mrs. Gourlay and Janet.

Sir, (she wrote)
Having read your *House with the Green Shutters*, and been strongly moved by its genius, I venture to address you. Your strong and vivid portrayal of Scots character holds me. Your knowledge of the human heart . . . (some words indecipherable) . . . is wonderful and valuable. No doubt, as the Psalmist says, 'Whoso is wise shall observe these things,' and in John Gourlay's history you have given the sad results of a life lived on the low level of selfishness, vanity and brutality, and in his son's, the fate of the reprobate. You sent both to their own place, with justice, probably. But surely not so the mother and daughter who were seekers after God. I cannot believe that He Whom they trusted would have left them to perish. Pardon me if I suggest that a different ending would have been, if not more artistic, at least more fair. I do not take exception to the troubles you pile on the poor woman herself. Alas! such a record is true to experience in this troublous world, but the final act could never have happened to one who lifted up her heart to the Merciful One as this poor soul did. Could you not, for instance, have made some unseen, pitying spectator, say a creditor of nobler mind from another town, hear the last talk of mother and daughter and be God's instrument to save them, arranging, perhaps, that the poor woman should have kind and effective treatment from a good doctor, and that Janet should go to the Davos Platz, recover, and live to help others, as she had not been able to help her father and brother.
You will consider these very optimistic suggestions, perhaps. But I trust you will forgive them from one who has lived to see many proofs of the goodness of God in the land of the living. Truly, you have been wise and strong in your observing, but I think you have lost a chance in thus giving the loving kindness of the Lord its proper place, and I cannot think that such an impressive tale would have lost any artistic merit had you done so. Forgive this intrusion.

Yours faithfully,
Janet Milne Rae.

To this Brown replied:

67, Queensborough-terrace,
Hyde Park, London, W.
28th January 1902.

Dear Madam,
I am gratified that you should have been sufficiently impressed by *The House with the Green Shutters* to wish to write to its author. And, believe me, I appreciate your kindness in doing so. I'm afraid you are right, and that the book is somewhat too ferocious. At the same time I am not sure that in this world, as we see it, the innocent are not very often involved in the ruin of the guilty. In another world that injustice will doubtless be done away with. But the Gourlays

being what they were, I saw no end for them here but the one I brought them to—their doom was implicit in themselves—they suffered the results of their own characters. We all do that, of course, for if there is an inevitable law on earth it is the old Greek law which means that we must all bear the consequences of our own action or want of action. That may not be a comfortable doctrine, but it is a bracing and true belief.

Yours faithfully,
George Douglas.

Some discerning readers had already recognized this doctrine as one of the fundamental purposes of the novel; but those members of the literati who were squabbling in the Kailyard and on the Brae of Barbie did not consider it. A pity, perhaps. If they had remembered the wisdom of Aeschylus in the *Choephoroe*, they would have realized that from the windows of *The House with the Green Shutters* Brown surveyed horizons far beyond the *Bonnie Brier Bush*.

3

During the summer of 1901 Monty Emanuel had invited Brown to spend an evening with several Oxford men at a West End Club (where the company had included a stern-faced young man, John Buchan, who had since gone with Lord Milner to South Africa). The talk had got round to Brown's forthcoming book, and one member of the party had lightly described how, at the very least, its publication would make a celebrity of the author at home: there would be a welcome by the provost, a blast from the local silver band, and the presentation of an illuminated address. Brown had laughed and said that that was not what would happen at all. If he went back, no one would pay the slightest attention to him. He would put up at a drab hotel and, after a stodgy tea, slouch out to the street. There, in desperation, he would be forced to introduce himself to one of the greybeards.

"Eh, na," would come the reply, "Geordie Broon, ye sa. Weel, weel. Geordie Broon, eh? Was it no' you that gaed awa' to a college or something o' the kind?"

"I live in London now."

"London, eh? That's a lang road awa'. What are ye daein' there?"

"I'm a writer."

"A writer?"

"Yes . . . I write books."

"Ye write books, eh? Dee-e-ar me! Oscar Wilde was a writer, too, but, unless I'm mista'en, he feenished up in the jile!"

If Brown really expected such treatment from Ochiltree, he was proved wrong even before his novel was fully acclaimed. True, parochial reaction was not altogether in his favour. Although the Ayrshire weeklies dealt very fairly with him, a minority of readers resented his book, and one woman forbade her daughters to read it, an order which was naturally, if covertly, disobeyed. Others were convinced that Brown had been motivated by vindictiveness and spite, and they were furious when Ochiltree was referred to in print as "the Barbie of the story." On the other hand level-headed people realized that Barbie was a composite picture of more than one small town, and they believed that Brown deserved local recognition. As a result, he was invited to act as Chairman at the fortieth annual reunion of Ochiltree Schoolfellows on Hogmanay night.

Brown was pleasantly surprised. While the Chairmanship had always been regarded as a distinction, he felt that in his case it was more: it was a proof of his acceptance. He was no longer the despised illegitimate he had so often thought himself; he was a man who had proved his worth before the world; and Ochiltree, his birth-place, wanted to honour him for his achievement. His mother would have been a proud woman.

He gave a great amount of thought to the reunion, and by the time he travelled north in December he had himself well primed. He stayed for a week or two in Glasgow and, in the novel role of a man with prospects, discussed the future with Lizzie M'Lennan. He found an opportunity, too, to visit the Russells, who welcomed him and watched him, smilingly, as he held their baby in his arms. "Thus do our dreams fade," he had written to Tom Smith; but here, in Isabella's lovely home, he betrayed no hint of what was in his mind.

When he went to Ayrshire he stayed with a sheep-farming friend, Robert Wilson of Auchencloigh, whom he always called Cloigh; and on the last night of the year they made their royal way to the Schoolhouse in Ochiltree. "As usual," reported the *Kilmarnock Standard*, "there was a crowded attendance of parishioners and natives from a distance"; and as Brown marched to the platform he caught glimpses of many familiar faces.

While his impression was still vivid, one man wrote: "I had an opportunity of surveying his physiognomy. It is strong. The powerful jaw, the square, projecting chin, the high cheek-bones, the well-formed slightly retroussé nose, the towering forehead, the firmly set mouth and the flashing eye, all suggest the 'man o' wecht'. A friend of mine remarked to me that his face and pose reminded him of Nasmyth's well-known portrait of Burns."

Brown's first remark was calculated to go straight to the hearts of his listeners. "Steek that door," he called out. "I canna talk

wi' an open door." He went on to recite lines that he had composed
for the occasion.

Auld Ochiltree's the core o' Kyle,
    And deila man may bang her,
Since Burns in high-poetic style
    Sweet lilted her and sang her;
Her verra waters wait a while
    And want to taigle langer,
But or they run another mile
    They're roarin' lood wi' anger
                To lea't that day.

The men upon the upland hills
    They question our two rivers,
And ask them why they run sae bauld
    And ding the dams to shivers;
And Burnock, Lugar, answer back,
    "We run wi' siccan glee, sirs,
Because we've made a merry pac'
    To meet at Ochiltree, sirs,
                By licht o' mune."

Her men are loyal as her streams,
    And hardy as her rock, sirs,
And woe to him that fondly deems
    Auld Ochiltree to mock, sirs.
If ony outland Jock or Jeems
    Should turn her to a joke, sirs,
We've men to clod him ower the beams
    And dunt him wi' a shock, sirs,
                Fu' hard the nicht.

Wha has a heartier lauch than Cloich,
    That wale o' worthy fellows
If ye've a better man to show,
    Come forrit, sirs, and tell us.
A better man ye couldna find,
    Ye're noathing but a bellows;
Gae 'way, ye sumph, and hide your heid
    Below auld wives' umbrrellas,
                For shame this nicht.

Where could ye meet wi' finer folk
    Than honest Reidston Lindsays'
Their men folk dearly like a joke,
    Their queys have never quinseys,
For Bob first scrapes their bonnie horns,
    The muckle lugs he rinses,
And then when comes the cattle show
    He canters in and wins his
                "Ferst prize for queys."

What muse, what power, could fitly sing
   The wiles o' Wullie Wylie
If Ochiltree had had her richts
   He woulda been a b'ilie,
And, hirplin' to the Council ha',
   Would sorted matters geyly,
And brawly worn afore them a'
   A sonsie muckle tilie
           On's pow, by Jing!

I mind a gey camsteerie chiel—
   His name was Geordie Miller—
They tell me Doddie's doin' weel,
   And heapin' up the siller.
And then there was a blythe wee deil,
   Whase name was Whustlin' Davie;
Oh, he could gar the tunes out-squeal,
   He whustled like a mavie
           Fu' sweet by nicht.

But I maun pu' my pownie in
   Ere Pegasus be wabbit.
For if I garred him further spin
   His shouthers would be scabbit,
He's at the best a spavined beast
   And has a drouthy habit,
He never sees a drink like this
   But he maun up and gab it—
           Like some we ken.

Then here's to Ochiltree, brave lads!
   The Queen o' rocky toons;
Here's to her lasses and her lads—
   And here's to a' the Broons;
I fear they're whiles an unco lot
   And gey camsteerie loons,
And some, I doot, maun gang to pot
   And sup at Auld Cohoun's
           Some awsome nicht!

May Ochiltronians range afar.
   And win the prize o' valour;
They'll never meet 'neath ony star
   Men hardier and baller.
May Lugar sing them to their rest
   When they hae done and bye wi't,
And then to Haven wi' the best
   May they eternal fly wi't
           On yon Great Day!

After giving an account of an imaginary talk with the Burnock Water, Brown drew to a close on a more serious note.

"I thank the committee," he said, "for the very high honour they have done me in asking me to preside on this occasion. It is, as far as I know, an absolutely unique thing that the schoolfellows of the parish should meet annually for forty consecutive years in the same place at the same time to renew their recollections of the past and bid each other God-speed. This is a record of which you have every reason to be proud, and which, I feel assured, no other parish can equal. I congratulate you on what Ochiltree has proved itself to be in the past, and I want to express a warm wish for the happiness and prosperity of all connected with the ancient place."

Following a musical programme, the reunion ended with customary formalities, and in proposing a vote of thanks to the Chairman, Mr. Alexander M'Lennan, a solicitor, sketched Brown's career, and concluded: "He has given evidence of his powers by the production of a novel which has caused quite a flutter in the literary world and has received highest praise from men who are best able to judge its merits. While we ought to congratulate Mr. Brown on the attainment of such a success, we ought also to express the hope that he may still further distinguish himself and be enrolled among the most eminent literary men whom Scotland has produced."

To this, Brown made a short reply. "One thing I have never forgotten in the course of my career," he said, "is that I am a son of Ochiltree. Some literary men say that I have attacked Scotland, or disowned my country, but this I emphatically deny. I am proud of being a Scotsman, and I am still prouder of being a native of Ochiltree." It was the sort of sentiment that the people wanted to hear, and by their cheers Brown knew that he had said the right thing.

Yet his verses and his fanciful talk with the Burnock Water did not please everyone. Maggie Stevens's father waited until he got home before declaring that never in his life had he heard such a damned lot o' nonsense; but one of the other dissentients preferred to give Brown a direct thrust. "I'm no' sure," he said, "whether ye made a fool o' Ochiltree or a fool o' yoursel'." For all the notice he took, Brown might not have heard . . . but he never spoke to the man again.

With his cronies he afterwards stood at the gateway of the new year. He was warm with whisky and the lingering glow of the reunion. Tonight was more than an annual event; it was the end of an old song; and as twelve o' clock struck Brown raised his glass to Cloigh and the future. It was noticed, carelessly enough, that he was drinking hard. . . .

In the next few days he called on the Smiths and the Maybins, and visited his mother's grave. Then, with a collie puppy which had been gifted to him by his host, he returned to Glasgow.

Quite suddenly (or so it seemed) he and Lizzie M'Lennan announced their engagement. "The idyllic circumstances in which the novelist now finds himself," wrote a journalist in the style that Brown deplored, "will presumably find a counterpart in those future productions for which his admirers are waiting, and of which his single work now before the public has given such convincing promise. That the tender relationship now announced may soon lead to the happy union it foretells must be the wish of everyone." Over the tea-cups, however, the gossips opined that there was nothing romantic about it and that Lizzie had only been drawn to Brown by his sudden rise to fame. Their tattle came, of course, to Lizzie herself, but she dismissed it with a shrug. "How little they know me," she said.

One afternoon she and Brown went out to Renfrewshire to see Neil Munro. He had been a friend of her father (now deceased), and she was not a stranger to him. Munro, who had never met Brown before, was left with the feeling that he "was not entirely a happy man." This realization was shrewd enough in its way; but at bottom Munro failed to understand Brown. "In what could only have been the impulse of a reckless mood," he actually believed, "he had written a prose *Song of Hate* about his native village." A pity, perhaps, that Munro did not see a letter which Brown sent to an Ochiltree lady. Writing from Glasgow on 18th January, he confessed to a fear that she would be sadly disappointed by *The House with the Green Shutters*.

"It is," he said, "anything but a kindly book, yet it was written with a kind enough intention. I hate scandal, malevolence, and all manner of cruelty, and in this book I tried to hold them up to scorn and loathing. Hence the unpleasantness of the characters. But, believe me, not one of the characters was drawn from Ochiltree. Ochiltree has always treated me well, and never better than on my last visit."

With his young collie, which he had named Cloigh, Brown soon afterwards left for the south. Although he promised to have a holiday with Lizzie in the spring, he quailed at the thought of the work ahead. Somehow he would have to write a novel for the autumn, and he wanted to complete his *Hamlet* study. The trouble was that he had his old feeling of suffocation, and it filled him with a strange dread: he was, in mind and body, desperately tired.

4

Instead of lingering in London, Brown took up residence in a cottage at Penn, Bucks. One of his first acts—on 4th February— was to buy a dog licence, after which he and Cloigh made daily explorations of the surrounding woods and by-ways. The fact that he was the author of the year did not inspire his mind. He had no inclination to work, and even whisky failed to coax him. He supposed his liver was at fault—it had often caused lassitude in the past—but his feeling of suffocation at least had gone.

He received all the latest reviews about *The House with the Green Shutters*, and one in particular on the front page of a weekly Temperance newspaper, the *Scottish Reformer*, caused him considerable amusement. The writer, Charlotte Smith, declared the novel to be of exceptional value to Temperance workers. "Tense with interest, thrilling, electrical, it is yet such a delicate study of the mental development of the drunkard that it positively rises to the rank of a scientific text-book. The most learned University Professor might learn much from this novel as well as we who are interested in Temperance matters. For although many novels have been written showing us more or less imperfectly the horrors of drink, none (so far as I know) have exhibited to us with such a wealth of psychological analysis the horrors of the making of the drunkard." Brown scribbled a verse in the margin and sent the newspaper to Lizzie.

> *By mony a name have I been kent*
> *Since first to life my thochts I lent,*
> *But now on marriage I am bent*
> *I'm like to go till 'er,*
> *According to this paper sent,*
> *A damn'd teetotaller!*

A letter from Ernest Barker then enlivened Brown's mind, and he revealed much of himself in his reply.

Beacon Hill Cottage,
Penn,
Bucks.

My Dear Barker,

I was delighted to have your letter. You are one of the men I can always talk to—whether to your benefit I greatly doubt, but certainly to mine. And the men one can talk to are not so common. I was in Scotland for about five weeks at the New Year (in a very irresponsive circle, I admit), and I was sadly gravelled for topics of conversation. If you flung out an idea above the level of food, liquor, and local politics, you were met by a blank stare of unintelligence. Its difficult to knock sparks out of mud.—But you're the finest beater-up of intellectual game I ever came across, and (if I had the time) I could write pages in answer to your letter.

You are perfectly right about my style; it is too tense. I envy the mellow fulness and ease of a writer like Thackeray. I think a man might put himself in the way of it (not that he would acquire it, indeed) by writing with a wise unconcern. Very often in writing, as in other things, effort makes its own defeat. If you try to write too hard you tie your brain in a knot. I disagree with the general opinion that what is written with ease is read with difficulty; it's often the other way about. You can divide writers into two distinct classes, the intuitive and reflective. The intuitive boggle at a thing for a while—then get it out with a jerk, which gives a kind of epigrammatic snap to their writing. The reflective lead you gently onward from point to point with an easy curving sequence of language and idea. Now I'm intuitive, if anything; not much of a sequential thinker. Hence a certain abruptness in my writing. That was one of the many things that used to gravel me in essay-writing at Oxford. I was not devoid of ideas, but I could express them better singly than in continuity.

I have a cowardice of the public, too; I'm afraid of boring them with verbiage. As I write I hear something saying to me: "Get it short and quick, man; get it short and quick!" In his fine little essay on "Aphorisms" John Morley quotes a Frenchman who said: "If ever a man suffered from the desire to put a chapter in a paragraph and a paragraph in a single sentence, I am the man." I know that desire.

As to ultimate style, the style of great poetry, I mean, that is a Platonic mystery, and can only be talked of in the language of mysticism. Even then you can only show it to a man who knows it already. In the greatest poetry, the wedding of language and idea, the merging of two in a diviner one, the utter impossibility of divorcing the thought from the expression—to all that, a happily-wedded symbolist like you can doubtless find a parallel.

I am glad you liked old Gourlay. I had such an impression of the strength of the man that I used to feel him in the room with me as I wrote of him. If he strikes the reader more forcibly than the son (in my portraiture of the two, I mean) that's partly, I think, because strength always attracts more than weakness. Perhaps it's also because he's presented more objectively, while young Gourlay is subjected to too much analysis. As to analysis in fiction, I am drawn in two different ways. I believe in the dramatic in fiction, and have always preached that the characters should explain themselves, and not be explained by the author. At the same time the temptation to analysis is often irresistible. Suppose you make a character say or do a thing which the reader feels to be true to human nature, intuitively feels it, without the need of further explanation. Nothing more is required for the conduct of the tale. But suppose you can convince your reader that this speech or act of the character is due to certain deep-seated traits of human nature which you forthwith proceed to shew him. It seems to me you give him the pleasure of a fresh perception, you convince him that what you have written is not only emotionally true, but philosophically true. Still there are two great dangers in analysis. If long-windedly done, it bores the reader; and in any case is apt to make a character look like a bundle of motives rather than a live human being.

I "maun to my Day's Darg". I am wretchedly indolent, and have loafed about for weeks among the woods here without doing a stroke of work.

Yours always,
G. D. Brown.

The literary contents of this letter did not occur to Brown on the spur of the moment. From time to time he had made notes on the novelist's art, and towards the end of 1901 he had collected them under the title, *Rules for Writing*. He hoped eventually to publish a textbook on the subject, but beyond the following fragments nothing was ever accomplished.

RULES FOR WRITING

The artist must feel intensely the situation of each one of his characters, so as to give it with the full value of truth and emotion. *But he must not hold a brief for any one of them:* not only because by doing so he'd become prosy and didactic, but, more especially, because he would be false to true art. He should present his characters having their explanation in themselves, as Nature does. He must visit violations of the right line of human progress with the ruthless impartiality of Nature herself. He may be as emotional as is consistent with good sense in the vivid presentation of a suffering character, say, but he must never be overbalanced by his sympathy: *Saeva necessitas* must be in him. In his whole scheme he must be somewhat callous in short—'tis the weakling-artist who invites his lachrymose readers to a petty whine over the merited sorrows of the human race. Like Nature's own so his work must move to its appointed end by the immutable law of its own being, calm, majestic, awe-inspiring. And there may be a great calm joy all through this apparently hard elemental work—as there is a great calm joy all through the great steady march of Nature herself.

In humorous writing, if you view your characters humorously, you are betraying your own point of view—you're taking a side against your characters, to a certain extent. Of course if your humour in viewing them comes from a sense of the bigness of life compared with their deficient, and therefore comical, little lives, then you have a sense secured of greatness, of inevitableness; it's nature makes them ridiculous and not you, the author; you're merely the glass through which they're seen: it's *sub specie aeternitatis* that they are ridiculous, not *sub specie* of you.

I should think that a power of metaphor and a discursive way of seeing round things should keep one from that stodginess which is to be feared so much in narrative. For the avoidance of stodge is really the result of that quickness of nerve that is the protoplasm of literature.

·   ·   ·   ·   ·

A situation, especially a dramatic situation, I think, should be presented clear, single, complete in itself, detached. I mean by situation here the whole ethical situation which is the gist of a play. It should not be blurred. The reader should be able to grasp it: not, indeed, to see the strings by which the thing is worked, but to *feel* that this is and must be so. . . . Things may be introduced subsidiary to the main action, certainly, illustrating, helping it on; but a situation which is outside it, however ethical, however good in itself, should not be introduced within that play because it will spoil the oneness, the unity, the reality of it. . . . Everything should be contributory to the tendency of the story (a) inner, idea'd ethical; and (b) contributory also to the external action; i.e. every incident should have three values (1) vivid in itself and exciting, (2) elucidating the mechanic plot; (3) elucidating the vital idea.

. . . . .

The value of The Chorus. (1) It gives the moral environment. (2) In its composite character it is an actor contributing to the final result. The gossips in *The House with the Green Shutters* act directly on the two Gourlays. (3) It adds a convincing reality to the central characters. When you see these characters acting on the bystanders' minds and producing certain results, you begin to believe in their reality; and when the chorus comments on, and is moved by the action, it makes you believe in the reality of the action. (4) To shew the mind of an essential character through the mind of a secondary character is a convincing way of doing your psychology.

. . . . .

When characters are first brought on they must be seen at once with the good or evil qualities that shall make or mar them. The action begins simultaneously too to present the development of their qualities to the seeing mind. They must be shown at once to have these qualities so that the seeing mind may be gripped and become part-wonderer with the author as to whither the qualities will bring them. In a very real sense every character in life and letters is justified of itself. You must bar out accidents in either—so that the purblind may see the justification—although, in reality, character works itself out no matter what *material* good fortune comes in to prevent a man meeting the *material* reward of his qualities. His Heaven or Hell is in himself.

. . . . .

Τῷ δράσαντι παθεῖν is as great a maxim in letters as in life. Τῷ δράσαντι παθεῖν: it should always be in the writer's mind; it should always be in his book; the great, clean, wholesome sanity of that maxim, that philosophy. It means to be what you are, to eventuate as you are, to have your Heaven and Hell here and now—the reward of the act inherent in itself. So that in fiction, all you have to do is to create, to put upon the stage of imagination, characters, people with the characters, which will necessarily lead

167

them to certain acts, then to shew the commission of these acts, and the inevitable punishment of these acts—or reward if the acts are good.

. . . . .

'Tis the same great centrality of truth that's to be expressed in all forms of art. Just as the ethic-metaphysician, sitting at the centre of thought, sees all the ways of life converging into one point, one heart, one total centre of illumination, so the artist metaphysical— and the greatest artists must be so—sees all the ways of art centring in one truth.

Hence, I think, the folly of niggling and worrying about the mere way of expression. It seems to me that fretting over form will blotch a man's mind and blind it to the central truth he would fain express—nay more, that the real and only way to get the highest expression is to be careless of it, to have your mind's eye on the inner essence of what your conveying, and not at all (or if it all then subconsciously) on the manner of conveying, to be so possessed by your Idea that it expresses Itself, and, doing so, expresses Itself inevitably, adequately, beautifully, with the Greatness in it.

. . . . .

If you come to think of it this is what is meant by "The Great Style". The great style has no fierce mean particular excellence, begotten by much contraction of the fretted brows, it has no violence that blinds to the superior greatness, it is formed from beyond and one feels its influence; *whenever it will it rises to majestic heights having majesty ever present within itself.* . . . Poetry depends on the quick mind seizing and getting all a subject "on the impulse of the moment", with the "feel" of it on one, not by exercitation which spoils everything in life and in other kinds of writing. So what to do isn't to distrust yourself and say, "Oh, I'll wait and polish that— the idea'll come back and I'll use the *labor limae* at a more convenient season." When you go to it the soul of the thing, the life, will have fled. Get it out with the glow on. It is thus you have the whole picture salient, not in disjointed *apercus*, but with its totality of atmosphere in your mind.

. . . . .

Scenery ought always to be described in inti mate relation to mind.
This rule should be kept always with constant closeness. Five lines, even, of description, without the suggestion that the scene is thus because thus it appealed to me or to Jack or to Julia—five lines even are too many. . . . Why does Whitman do scenery so sympathetically? Because he always gives his own mood with it. "I went down to see the creek and stood on the shore and listened to the sighing wind" or whatever it may be.

. . . . .

How to get the mood in which ideas seem to flow into us easily. Can we superinduce it? I think so. By dreaming inwardly and conversing with our own minds. . . .

A novel should be not only sequential in its inner action, one thing inevitably coming from the bosom of the other, and sequential in its outer action, letting the reader see this; but it ought also to be sequential in its writing—i.e. it should be written with sympathetic fluency, the mind following on from point to point easily. And that will make for easy and clear and sympathetic apprehension on the reader's part. For the writer wrote it as it came easily to his mind, not breaking the clear rush of his thought to worry. If he does break the continuity of his inner idea, it becomes involved, leaving the reader with an uncomfortable mist on his mind, instead of the easy clarity—and the satisfaction of understanding which we all desire. If a reader understands, he is satisfied.

    .   .   .   .   .

The mind should never descend upon a subject like a labouring and murky cloud, enveloping the theme in the darkness it brings to it. It should wait and see. It should hover and glide above the subject till the salient points emerge, and then it should dart on them surely.

The mind is not expected to explain *all* the subject, only to suggest explanations. So, in Criticism, there are more things true than are worth pointing out.

The Carlylean mind, as we know, did come down on a subject like labouring murk, and from its gigantic throes sent lurid flashes to illuminate a monstrous world. Valuable intuitions. But the snarling tempest of the Carlylean mind is to be deprecated. Lucid ease, an atmosphere of sweet persuasion—these are the qualities we want in writing. And that is got—not by burying your head in a subject and plunging ahead like a bull through a briar bush, but by looking around you to find the right issue. There is no such thing as an intellectual *impasse*; there is always a way out if you wait for it.

    .   .   .   .   .

On critical writing. A man may write, so plethoric of ideas, that he stultifies himself—like a mob rushing through a narrow door. Balzac's sister was right when she said he had a "congestion of ideas"—right in her opinion that such a thing was possible, I mean. This is another kind of "tightness" ("tightness" save the mark!) from the "tightness" of writing hard in the physical fact. A discursive all-round-seeing mind, if it unhappily strains to get out its thought, confuses itself, sticks, loses its catch on sequence, and connection, the whole concatenation of the subject doesn't float in on it luminously and whole. Just as in the other "tight-writing", straining on one point of the landscape spoils the general sweet effect of it all; so here straining on one phase of thought spoils the general satisfying effect of the whole concatenation of thought. . . .

169

The moral is that in reasoning writing, as in life, landscape, drama, fiction, you should stand back from your work and view it with a big easiness, seeing it all in due order and proportion.

5

Leaving his dog in the care of his housekeeper, Brown spent several days in London. He stayed with the Emanuels, discussed business matters with Macqueen, and attended various social functions. London hostesses had come to regard him as a prize, and he responded to their adulation and publicity. In Melrose's private opinion, "he suffered for a time from the attentions of Lady Jeune and other tuft-hunters, and, unconventional though he was, there seemed to be a risk of his suffering from swelled head." Scarcely a day passed without some reference to him in newspapers and magazines. Leading publishers offered to publish his next book, and literary agents competed for the management of his affairs. But Brown was not hoodwinked. In *The Novelist* notes he wrote: "Get in author's relations with publishers, etc.: the false bonhomie in dining and wining him."

Back at Beacon Hill Cottage he felt sufficiently energetic to attend to his arrears of correspondence, one letter, with characteristic flashes of Doric, being addressed to Wilson of Auchencloigh.

My dear Cloigh,
You must think me an ungrateful dog for not writing to you sooner, after all your kindness to me at the New Year. But there's no correspondent in the world so bad as the man who is a writer by profession. He whiles gets a kind o' scunner at pen and ink. He's fair stawed with them. That's no excuse, but it's an explanation. Since I passed through London on my way south, I've only been once there for a few days, and had no time to get the jug for the cattle show. So I enclose an order for £3 (which is the sum we fixed on, I think), and leave it to you to get the proper article. I would like fine if you won it yoursel'. The other Cloigh is turning out a fine gawsey fellow, worthy of his namesake. He is verra browdened on his new maister. He comes scartin' at my door every morning before I'm up and bowghs, 'Hey, are ye waukin, Geordie?' My old Housekeeper says, 'Why, sir, 'e be wise enough to be a Christian.' I was near telling her that some Christians I kenned werena fit to be dawgs; but I didna want to hurt her feelin's.

                    Best regairds to a' at Cloigh frae
                        Baith the dowgs,
                                                    Geordie.

Brown now began work on his new novel, which was to be a love story with a Cromwellian background. In it he intended to prove his ability to deal with romance and to show, as he explained to his friends, the other side of his nature. Yet it did not enthral him as *The House with the Green Shutters* had done. He felt that he was merely turning out a novel because of public demand; "the implicit idea" and the "big spiritual intention" were lacking.

He was more interested in *The Novelist*. He intended it to be the story of David Allen, a sensitive, imaginative writer, "faulty, even in his perception of the truth", and his wife, Elsie, who believed that they "would always be alone . . . sufficient to themselves." David needed money, and he got a loan from an elderly business man, Harold Stokes, "the Philistine in every sense of the term." David became so eaten up by his work—"which defect," noted Brown, "will lead to his punishment"—he did not realize that Elsie's soul was being starved. When Stokes eventually seduced her, Allen was more engrossed in his work than before—one of his books had attracted attention—so that "now", noted Brown, "now comes the man losing his soul as the artist gains his art." Allen, however, failed to make money, and Stokes, who was growing tired of Elsie, now reminded him about the loan. In the heat of the ensuing quarrel Allen learned that Elsie had been unfaithful.

Brown never shaped the story into a cohesive whole. He knew how it would develop, and drafted a rough synopsis of eighteen chapters. For the last scene of all he wrote:

"Allen realized that he did not care. She had gone out of his life. He stood and looked at her without speaking. His mind was busy inside his head on the value of the situation.

"Stokes stood lumpishly. . . . Crestfallen, sweating visibly.

"Elsie felt the situation poignantly—the absence of feeling in it shamed her. Was she so little worth? . . . The inefficiency of it all, the casual way it evolved, like the slipping of a knotless thread, gave her a feeling of emptiness . . ."

The Novelist, which would have offended some of Brown's literary friends, would have been his third novel, while *The Incompatibles*, which was less advanced, would have followed later.

Although *The Incompatibles* was a provisional title, Brown had the theme fairly clear in mind. Alec Ramsey and his wife, Bella, were ill-matched. "In this chapter," wrote Brown, "you can indicate without comment, or suggesting the effect of repulsion it is yet to have in him, her manner, her too-much laughing, her too-muchness altogether, her habit of showing her white teeth when she flings back her head to laugh at a silly joke, her managing of him—which he submits to as yet and which is later to develop into nagging interference."

They moved in a Glasgow circle whose "vulgar snobbishness"

Brown was determined to flay. "Chapter V—a dinner of Glasgow bodies," he wrote. "Make it as bitter a satire as you know how. Get in (1) their scandalous talk of other folk and (2) their lowness of ideal—material estimates of things and people."

When Bella's baby was born Ramsey was full of plans for its upbringing and future; his wife listened to him "with bland acceptance, as if she understood his talk when she did not understand it at all." After the death of their child, he "felt far away from her, a creature apart." He took to drink and found himself a harlot. He experienced no remorse, becoming, in fact, maddened to excess by Bella's failings. In his outline of Chapter IX Brown wrote:

"You must get in these failings enormously, i.e., small aberrations in themselves but with an enormous effect on his weak character. And do them without talkie-talkie, briefly, vividly, in admirable suggestion, so that man and woman while seeing her good points will say, 'Oh, that awful woman, she would have maddened me, too.' She would be a fine wife to the man who could put up with her . . . But you must show how Ramsey became atrophied in soul."

When life could no longer be endured—his heavy drinking having wrecked his business—Ramsey left his wife and sailed to Australia, where he met Fay, "a sensible little woman, yet gentle, loving and understanding."

"Get that thing that has come to you in London," wrote Brown, "that thing you know yourself so well, the power to forget, to let the past slide, the dislike to open communication with it when once you have entered on a new world. Get this very vividly from your own relation to Ayr in particular and Scotland in general since you have been up here in London. It is most natural to a man of complex character disgraced in the old scene and coming to the new. The complexity makes him catch on to the new and so forget the past, and the sense of shame in the past also induces the desire to forget—shew how it all becomes a dream to him."

Under Fay's influence Ramsey ultimately regained his self-respect, and he told her the truth about his degradation and ruin. Fay was too much in love with him to care about his past: she was concerned only with what he had become. From this point Brown never made it clear how the story was to finish. Disjointed paragraphs indicated that Ramsey, Fay, and Bella were to come together in a strong scene in a church, and that Fay alone was to be with Ramsey when he died.

Afterwards, when she was alone, she was to find happiness in the knowledge that she was to bear his child.

All this, however, was vague and incomplete. What Brown wanted to do was to show the hidden tensions of domestic life, the

172

unceasing conflict of emotions between man and woman. He knew that he did not need an elaborate plot, but what he failed to realize was that he had too many irons in the fire of his mind. It was impossible to do justice to them all at the same time.

6

Having failed to do any consistent work, Brown journeyed to Scotland for his holiday with Lizzie, and accompanied by Doctor John Adam Boyd, Glasgow police surgeon, and his wife, a sister of Lizzie, and Quintin M'Lennan, a tall, lanky brother, they stayed in a white-washed cottage at Aberfoyle from 7th to 20th May. When the weather was dull and cold, Brown wore a close-fitting tweed cap and long gaberdine raincoat; on milder days he appeared in black jacket, waistcoat, striped trousers, and a bowler hat. He smoked a pipe or cigarettes according to his whim of the moment, and at picnics and on boating expeditions a bottle of whisky was always at hand. He and Lizzie were photographed at the cottage door, on a wooden bridge over a stream, in a rowing boat, and on the shores of Loch Ard, Lake Menteith, and Loch Katrine. It was all very idyllic, although Brown had a premonition, which he never divulged to Lizzie, that they would never be man and wife. True, she was already making plans for their wedding on 16th October; but in a letter to a woman friend in Ochiltree he had added a curious postscript: "God knows I may never be married."

On his return south he remained in London for several weeks. With the fifth edition of his novel, 12,000 copies had been sold, and the demand was still steady. A review in an Italian journal, *La Cultura*, greatly pleased him—partly because he knew enough of the language to read it for himself.

Meanwhile Brown tried to concentrate upon *Hamlet*. He submitted an article, *Some Notes on Hamlet*, to the *Academy*, but in spite of his reputation it was rejected. Disappointed but not discouraged, he continued to work on his major study, which he prefaced by a rather remarkable disclosure.

"I have to confess that I have never been lucky enough to see *Hamlet* put upon the stage. And so, alas! I have not been assisted by the genius of our great actors (Wilson Barrett and the rest) in forming a conception of the Prince's character. When I think of this, I sit astonished at my own audacity in venturing to describe this paper as 'an essay in essential criticism.' However, to those who remember that 'essay' means not 'performance' but 'attempt,' there will, I hope, appear nothing arrogant in that description."

173

To be sure, Brown had very little interest in the stage interpretations of *Hamlet*. For years he had studied Shakespeare's mind and thought, and he now wrote with a distinct note of authority.

When a dramatist of this kind turns to tragedy, to speculate on man's folly and decay, he displays an excellent cruelty. He sits throned and quiet in the midst of agitation; he sees men around him (busily engaged, for the most part, in working out their own damnation), and his mind is as that of their Creator applying the remorseless laws. He needs no Novalis to tell him that "Character is Fate"; that is the instinctive secret he works by; and he presents his characters, as Nature does, having their dooms implicit in themselves.

Hence his work has inevitable movement. For the tragedy that is founded in the idea of character is sequential in its own nature. It writes itself. It moves to its climax by the inherent law of its own being. Even the author himself will change the ending at his peril for it is necessary, not arbitrary. All the way through, the inevitable climax is latent in the *tragic flaw*.

The central figure in a tragedy of character (as opposed to a tragedy of blind Fate) exhibits a flaw that works his inevitable doom. There may be several flaws, of course, but, if so, they must work together to a single issue. This tragic flaw determines from beginning to end, the architectonics of the play. There can be nothing in the tragedy that is not referable to the tragic flaw, for the presence of an alien element would be irrational, would have no meaning in the piece. On the other hand, all the essentials referable to the tragic flaw must be there, unless the author is to ruin his work. For to neglect any necessary consequence is to present an incomplete picture; that is, a false one.

If the tragic flaw is so important, then, as explaining all the matter and movement of a play, it follows that if we can discover the tragic flaw in *Hamlet*, the whole drama will be clear. If it is not clear, and if there are many things which we cannot relate to a central germ and motive of the play, we must be pretty sure that our tragic flaw is the wrong one. The right tragic flaw in *Hamlet*, then, is the game we are after. May Heaven help us to find it!

Brown did not allow himself to be side-tracked by a loose belief in Hamlet's "weakness."

For one thing, it is too obvious. It needs no Goethe to tell us that Hamlet's soul was "unfit for the performance," and "sank beneath the burden." The fact stares us in the face from every second page. If that be the prop the play rests on, the prop is a little too plain.

More important still: if "weakness" be the primary tragic flaw, many things in the play are irrational and have no meaning in the piece. For mere weakness does not explain the Prince's peculiar

174

treatment of Ophelia, his peculiar violence, his callousness, his marvellous literary gift, his manner at the grave-side.

Above all to say that Hamlet is weak is no explanation of his weakness. "A soul unfit for the performance," says Goethe. One is inclined to move the previous question, and ask why the soul was unfit for the performance. Weakness, then, is not the primordial germ and protoplasm of the play; it is only a result; and, therefore though in turn an important secondary cause, fails to cover all the issues.

Besides, Hamlet in many ways was anything but weak. He *tackles the Ghost* the others are afraid of—though even the sturdy Horatio had been harrowed with wonder and with fear. He is physically brave, a trained master of arms; he has the soldier's sword no less than the courtier's eye and tongue; he is the expectancy and rose of the fair state. When he does act, he is swift and terrible in deed. . . .

If weak, then, he was weak with a difference. In fact—speaking generally and without derogation to Weimarian Joves—to say that a man is weak is always a poor explanation of his failure. 'Tis an absolute judgment, and absolute judgments are the curse of the world . . . Shakespeare, we may be sure, had a deeper insight. He meant us to go behind the general weakness and find the tragic flaw that occasioned it.

Above all—and this is the great objection to Goethe's theory—Shakespeare has given us a very plain indication from the mouth of Hamlet himself that a particular fault, and not a general weakness, is the cause of Hamlet's incompetence. That hint comes at a joint and nexus of the play which, for dramatic and profound significance, has no parallel in letters.

It is in the fourth scene of the first act that the Ghost first appears to Hamlet, to lay upon his soul the burden that shall find him wanting.

While he is waiting with Horatio and Marcellus on the lonely battlement, Hamlet—"the great mind, the all-too-teeming brain, quick on the instant to each side-issue and avenue of thought"—thus deeply muses:

> "*So oft it chances in particular men,*
> *That, for some vicious mole of nature in them,*
> *As in their birth,—wherein they are not guilty,*
> *Since nature cannot choose his origin,——*
> *By the o'ergrowth of some complexion,*
> *Oft breaking down the pales and forts of reason;*
> *Or by some habit, that too much o'er-leavens*
> *The form of plausive manners;—that these men,——*
> *Carrying, I say, the stamp of one defect,*
> *Being nature's livery or fortune's star,——*
> *Their virtues else,—be they as pure as grace,*
> *As infinite as man may undergo,——*

175

> Shall in the general censure take corruption
> From that particular fault: the dram of eale
> Doth all the noble substance of a doubt
> To his own scandal."

And, even as Hamlet speaks, the Ghost enters!

That speculation by Hamlet about the causes of failure in particular men (argued Brown) does not come in its particular place merely by haphazard. No doubt it was so familiar to his mind that he might have uttered it anywhere throughout the play. But Shakespeare knew what he was doing. He put it just where he did with most profound intention. . . . First, it is a clue to the meaning and movement of the play. Second, being that, it adds enormously to the dramatic significance of the instant apparition—for it is with the instant apparition that the meaning and movement of the play really begins. Third, the musing analysis, by Hamlet himself, of particular causes of failure—coming, as that analysis does, immediately before the supernatural command—is full of profound dramatic irony if it shall be seen that the speaker fails to fulfil this command, owing to a particular flaw within his own character, to which he has just made unconscious reference. There is tragic irony, as everybody knows, when a man's words refer to his own doom, himself unconscious the while. . . .

The very length and deliberate manner of the speech itself arrests our attention, gives us pause, compels our curious enquiry and thus makes us see the hint which it conveys. Shakespeare is not here musing upon life, as he sometimes does, because his myriad ideas escape from his dramatic governance, because as a thinker he was too rich—his full mind always running over and spilling bright thoughts upon the random air. Not from brimming and luxuriant thought this so minute investigation of particular faults, but because Shakespeare wishes thereby to heighten the tragic irony, intensify the dramatic significance, of those words on the lips of the very man who is himself even now to be doomed through a fault particular. Note the elaborate differentiation; the almost painful analysis, the iteration of point; the insistence on every variety of phase. It often happens to particular men, says Hamlet, that through some natural flaw, which comes to them by birth perhaps—and for that they are not responsible, since men are born even as they are; or through some twist in the brain that develops in their later years—and, developing, breaks down the continents of reason; or, it may be, through some habit that leads them too much to deprecate and yield: the stamp of a single defect, he repeats, whatever be its origin, whether it be natural or contingent, shall make their other virtues, though pure as grace and infinite as man may carry, to be corrupted, or to appear corrupted, in the popular opinion. And all from that particular fault: for the slight insinuation of ill ruins the whole noble substance, makes it perverted in itself and uncomprehended of the world. Why this painful particularity in the analysis of particular flaws if Shakespeare was not thinking of a particular flaw in the speaker's own character?

Brown identified himself with Hamlet. When he discussed the natural flaw which comes to men by birth and the "twist in the brain that develops in their later years", he was thinking of his own life. "My illegitimacy has been my curse," he once confided to an Ayrshire friend; and yet he now saw that it need not have been so. "A man ought to take long views of his own character," he noted. "It prevents despair."

Continuing his exposition of *Hamlet*, he considered that a man with "Time-Sense"—a "Universal-Visualist" who saw everything *sub specie aeternitatis*—perceived the over-arching bigness of the world in relation to his own appalling insignificance. More, Brown was convinced Hamlet was such a man and that, seeing all in terms of Change and Time, he was blighted by this "particular flaw." Consequently, Brown showed how, all through the play, "the plain proof of the Time-Sense in Hamlet" accounted for "his astonishing treatment of Ophelia, his callousness towards Polonius, his peculiar exhibitions of violence, his marvellous literary gift, and, above all, his failure to *act*."

Time-Sense destroying a man's action of will—that is the big, bold, bare conception which Shakespeare had in *Hamlet*. Such a bare conception, however, big and bold as it is, will no more make drama than the bare idea of eternity will make literature. It must be joined to complexity of character and circumstances on which to operate and make fecundity. . . . We see, I think, in the weak drift of Hamlet's character, how easily he might have been content to remain the glass of fashion and the mould of form, had all gone well: lapped round with the pleasantness of life, he might have been blind to its emptiness. Always the metaphysician, it needed the clash with the harsh world to fling him back upon a perception that the world is worthless. The essential drama in Hamlet's case would have been as great, doubtless, had he dreamed himself away at the Danish Court until the age of sixty; but to make the tragedy salient to the general mind, a strenuous necessity is required. And see what Shakespeare has done to fling it into salience. He invents a plexus of the most arresting, un-Hamlet kind. His father is murdered, his mother an adulteress—or nearly, his throne usurped, his Uncle the murderous adulterer and usurper,— "Remorseless, treacherous, lecherous, kindless villain": and lest these should be insufficient to stir him up to battle with his character, the Ghost of his murdered father comes to impose this duty on his soul.

Dissecting passage after passage, Brown laboured his point until, as he himself realized, he almost blunted it. Yet he could not avoid this minute analysis because he maintained that "in every line of Shakespeare there is a hidden clue to its dramatic meaning." Consequently, every character was placed under the microscope.

I am told by readers of Shakesperian criticism that the manly and sagacious speech which Polonius addresses to Laertes when that gallant ruffler will away to France, is generally held to be grossly inconsistent with Poloney's character. With all deference to erudite commentators I do not think it is. I have heard it remarked, moreover, that the speech of Polonius has no "dramatic" value whatsoever—that Shakespeare had a fine piece of incidental "copy", and stuck it into Poloney's mouth, irrespective of the old man's character and the general structure of the play. Shakespeare wasn't such an ass. The speech of Polonius is of manifold dramatic excellence. It is not inconsistent with Polonius's character. It is not merely good in itself, it is good in relation to the whole. And the special point for us at present is that, though spoken to Laertes, and not by him, it points us to his character and his subsequent action in the play.

'Tis a stroke of right cunning drama that makes Laertes, when he is sailing to the distant country whence he shall not return till he comes to avenge his father's death, be inspired by that same father with the precepts that shall then regulate his action. Consider what juncture of the play it is. 'Tis a juncture when, in Shakespeare's language, a necessary "question" must needs be considered. Of all the subsidiary characters Laertes, next to Ophelia, is the most important. It is he who slays Hamlet in the end. It is his act produces the climax. Yet, after this casual appearance, he is passing out of the action for practically three Acts. Shakespeare must direct our attention to his character before he disappears, must shew him equipped for the deed that awaits his return. And he does it by Poloney's speech. It is the very perfection of worldly counsel for a man who must mingle with the world of men, and it shows the training that bred him what he was. Both Hamlet and Laertes had a father to avenge. Hamlet, with all the chances on his side, cannot will himself to act. Laertes, with no opportunities, makes them. "And for my means," he cries, "I'll husband them so well, they shall go far with little." In fine, he follows to the letter the advice his father gave him when he was setting out for France. The counsel of Polonius has bred the effective instrument to avenge his own death.

All the same, Brown did not admire Polonius.

Of easy *savoir faire* and some irony, he is a rank materialist and his vanity is vast. . . . He is a consequential pedant and a conceited babbler, fond of spinning empty phrases, affecting literary knowledge. Unable to understand Hamlet in the least, he is proud of his reading of him.

178

> "*. . . or else this brain of mine*
> *Hunts not the trail of policy so sure*
> *As it hath used to do, that I have found*
> *The very cause of Hamlet's lunacy*".

"This is the very ecstasy of love" he says, and will not be persuaded that it is not this alone that ails the great soul of Hamlet the Dane. The pragmatic old fool must even give all the steps of Hamlet's malady, though he knows nothing about it:

> "*Fell into a sadness, then into a fast,*
> *Thence to a watch, thence into a weakness,*
> *Thence to a lightness; and by this declension*
> *Into the madness wherein now he raves.*"

To the very end he persists that this is so. Further, Polonius deals in cunning, and is proud of it. He is always the plotting, spying diplomatist. He sets Reynaldo to watch Laertes; at his bidding Ophelia is a decoy that he and the King may spy on Hamlet; and he makes the Queen a second decoy while himself is hidden behind the arras. And his senile conceit in his own cunning,—this and his materialism—leads to Ophelia's weakness and to Hamlet's disgust and cruelty towards her. In the end it leads to Polonius's own death: the engineer is hoist with his own petard.

Brown was no less emphatic when he came to deal with Hamlet's treatment of Ophelia.

Hamlet's alternations of love and neglect of Ophelia are in keeping with his nature, as I read it. A mind like his will cling most fondly to a particular love; and at the same time, whether moved thereto by its own inner great thought or by stress of circumstance, may stand apart and appear callous of it. For Hamlet was a man of genius, with an understanding of both sexes. If I say that he was a kind of mental hermaphrodite, fools will misunderstand me and think I am hinting at morbidities. It is not so; but the great genius, though the manliest of men, has in him a certain womanliness which enables him to understand the character of woman, as if he himself was inside the skin of her. And hence Hamlet's power to read Ophelia; and reading her nature, and contrasting it with the over-arching greatness, he feels its appalling insignificance; and he turns away from her, still loving her. It is a mistake to say that it was the burden of sorrow and duty upon him that led him to flout Ophelia. The knowledge of his mother's conduct and the acquiescence of Ophelia to act as a decoy soured him, it is true. But there was more than that. There was the general malady of the Time-Sense mind, leading him to regard all human and earthly things as little *sub specie aeternitatis*, and so to his scorn of Ophelia.

To the end, then, Brown was certain that the Time-Sense continued to paralyse Hamlet.

179

But behind the twinkling eyes was a troubled mind. Brown was distressed about Lizzie; he knew that *The House with the Green Shutters* would not sell indefinitely, and he could not rid himself of a fear that he might not be able to provide for her. He saw a danger in making a wife his conscience.

Racked by uncertainty, he decided to live at Haslemere for a while, so he collected his belongings from Penn and, with his dog, Cloigh, settled down at Briar Cottage. The familiar surroundings revived his spirits. He had read T. W. H. Crosland's book, *The Unspeakable Scot,* and in a letter to Melrose he expressed the belief that the savagery of it was partly assumed for purposes of humour. "Still," he said, "there's a great deal of bitter truth in it, bitterly expressed. I confess I enjoyed it. But I don't believe it will sell. What I devoutly hope is that no Scottish fool will write to the papers, protesting against it. That is the very thing Crosland wants."

As his lassitude lifted, Brown figured that by one of his spectacular bursts of energy he would finish his historical novel in a matter of weeks, and he promised to send an article to the editor of *Saint Andrew*, a Scots journal of religious thought, immediately the book was finished. "Whether it be from indolence or stupidity, I don't know," he wrote, "but I find a great difficulty in working on two things at the same time—even if one of them is only a short sketch. However, by August, I'll have something to show you." The article was never written, but the editor had the melancholy privilege of publishing a posthumous fragment entitled *Popularity* in his issue of 9th October.

There are moments of mystic intuition when the whole world seems to fade away round a man and leave him alone with the Omnipotent, so that miraculous strength is poured upon his soul from that intimate communion. He feels that henceforth he has no need of men; that in all existence there are but two beings of primary import—himself and his Creator; that were all others blotted out, yet were his life fulfilled. Hence the wise arrogance which is sometimes noticed in the elect. If a man is right with the Immanent Divine, what matters the judgment of the world?

Obviously, those with whom such a view is permanent (if that be possible) will care but little for popularity. But it needs no great insight to see that this view, when absolutely stated, is sadly opposed to our highest spiritual development. For spiritual progress is only possible if we surrender ourselves to the service of our fellows (only so can we realize our best selves), and to serve them we must first persuade them that our services are worth having. Thus, for our own souls' sake, we must cultivate their good opinion. Popularity is one of the true weapons of the soul. It is the fulcrum to make rock the world.

Here, then, there would seem to be a paradox in the spiritual life.

We must act in reference to two judgments, one of them transcendental and invisible, the other visible and human.

But it is those who are seen to act in reference to the higher tribunal who must gain the verdict of the lower. Consider who it is that ranks the applausive world in behind him, and sweeps it on with an irresistible power. 'Tis the man of mystic will, the transcendental man of action, or the founder of a new religion, the Napoleon or Mahomet, who discerns a driving purpose and a meaning in life which is hidden from the multitude. He links himself to that, and being so strengthened, impels the baser world with a power far higher than his own. The will of the meanly-resolute man, whose power is like that of a narrow and driving spear-head, is material and animal; it has no strength except that which resides within its narrow self; and so it has no far-reaching effect on humanity. But to the mystic will all things are auxiliary; it is inspired from on high, and, being so inspired, attracts to its aid the further momentum of a whole world that is glad to be its ally. And thus the transcendental may, at the same time, be the most popular, because of the appeal to the spiritual imagination, an appeal that subdues us all.

In that very appeal there lurks an insidious danger for the greatest of earth's children. For the man of mystic fascination, knowing that the strength which brings the world to his side resides not in him but in something higher than himself, may be tempted to make a base yet easy use of the higher in order to secure the lower end. Knowing that his power abides in mystery, he is tempted to impose upon the world by appealing to mystery, when there is no mystic communion in his soul; and then 'tis but a juggler's trick when he poses as the man of destiny; almost ere he knows it he is made a charlatan. He has used his spiritual greatness as a material means to secure a most material end. And so his soul is poisoned at its source.

The man of common sense (who is often but a common fool) will tell you that Napoleon and Mahomet were the greatest charlatans that ever lived. Would it not be more humbling and more suggestive to go a little further into the question, and to see how easily their essential greatness became their essential baseness? *Corruptio optimi pessima*, said the ancients; they might have added, with equal truth, *Corruptio optimi facillima*. For the great virtues and the great vices lie close together; change the one but a little and you have the other. Thus some, perceiving truly that the body is divine, are tempted by that very perception to make gods of their sensual desires, so easy it is to prostitute the noblest intention. Equally easy is it to prostitute a mystic greatness. For what attracts the imagination of the world to a great leader is his inscrutability, since *omne ignotum pro magnifico:* but there is no pose more easy to affect than that of the inscrutable, and having learned the secret of his power, and knowing from his past sincerity the authentic language of the mystic, the perverted genius feigns a mystery more and more. He imposes on the world, but his soul rots in the midst of his false popularity.

On all who gain a following by something higher than themselves, there is incumbent a most stern and exigent self-watchfulness. Else, and almost ere they know it, the mantle of the prophet may become the juggling cloak of the trickster.

This posthumous article had in it something akin to a confession of faith. All his life Brown had made a quest for truth, and now, in the closing weeks of his life, he came near to finding what he sought.

8

In early August Brown paid a short visit to Newhall, the M'Lennans' home in Sydenham Road, Dowanhill Gardens, Glasgow. Here, in Lizzie's company, he found it easy to suppress his foreboding and misgivings. She was radiant and full of plans; he had arranged for Meldrum to be his best man; and all those difficulties that he had posed to himself now seemed less formidable. He even persuaded himself that, in a place of his own, he would write better than he had ever done before.

He was reluctant to go south again, and on the evening of his departure he stayed at Lizzie's home until the last minute. Then he kissed her, holding her tightly in his arms, and hurried off to catch the train at St. Enoch Station. It took him a while to find a cab: he ran down Byres Road and along part of Dumbarton Road until he was wet with perspiration. It was paradoxical that the night express should be suddenly important, considering that he had not wanted to leave, anyway. As he hurried past Kelvingrove the University on the hill was clean and hard against the sky.

On the train journey he felt hot and cold by turns; an occasional drink from his whisky flask had little effect, and sleep was impossible. If he had been fit he would have remained in London for a day or two, but, in his present state, he decided to go on to Haslemere without delay. He was uneasy rather than alarmed, and he believed that by doctoring himself he would soon be all right.

In the next fortnight, however, there was no improvement; his throat and breathing troubled him, and to his dismay he began to spit blood. His handkerchiefs were mottled with rusty red stains, a fact which afterwards gave rise to a rumour that he had ruptured a blood vessel whilst engaged in physical exercises. Constant headaches prevented him from making any effort to write, severe pains stabbed his chest, and yet somehow each morning he struggled out of bed in a desperate attempt to prove to himself that he was not a sick man.

At last he was forced to the realization that he was in a very bad way, and by the fireside he pondered—quite calmly—what he ought to do. Then, with a clear mind despite the fever that burned his brow, he crossed to his desk, selected a sheet of paper, and wrote:

To William Maybin I owe £30.
To John McFadyen I owe £50.
I am owing various small sums in Oxford and Ayr. Should I die, all my belongings are to be sold and the proceeds are to be added to my Insurance Policy of £100 odd pounds. The total will be more than sufficient to pay my debts. Any money that is left (it won't be much) may be given to the Coylton Poor.

George Douglas Brown.

He put the will in an envelope, sealed it, and wrote in a bold hand: "Last Will and Testament. G. D. Brown."

By the 24th he felt worse, and sent a note to Lizzie. "Keep your faith in the value of life," it read, "no matter what happens"; and Lizzie was both mystified and profoundly disturbed. Next day, leaving Cloigh with a neighbour, Brown went up to London. It was his fixed intention to stay with the Emanuels, and he received a shattering blow when he found the house in Queensborough Terrace locked up. The Emanuels had gone to Devon on holiday, and by ill fortune their cook, who was left in sole charge, had slipped out to do some shopping. If only she had been on hand, she often remarked with regret, she would have got Brown to bed and then sent a telegram to Mrs. Emanuel.

As it was, Brown dully turned away. He had never dreamed that the Emanuels might be from home, and he was at a loss what to do. Finally, he went to Melrose and said that he had not been well and would like to stay with him. He hid the real facts, and Melrose, who readily agreed to have him at his home in Highgate, did not guess the truth until too late.

On the 27th an alarming change came over Brown; his strength drained away, and a nurse was engaged. What happened afterwards—in the early hours of the 28th—was disclosed by Doctor P. R. Ingram in a letter to Mrs. Russell.

Kildrummy,
Muswell Hill Road,
Highgate, N.
28. 10. 02.

Dear Mrs. Russell,

I was called to see Mr. Brown about one in the early morning, knowing nothing either of him or the people he was with. His condition on being called was most alarming, his breathing being so difficult that I forbade him to speak or to attempt to do so. All I could do was to get as much oxygen as possible which seemed to relieve him a little, and it was only by the administration of oxygen and hypodermics that he was kept alive until morning. I stayed a considerable time with him and encouraged him, and as I forbade him to speak he made no attempt to do so. I was with him until just before the end when he was quite peaceable and much more comfortable although the end was near. He was quite composed and sensible almost to the end and died without any struggle. He mentioned nobody's name while I was with him. The nurse did her best under the circumstances, and he was made as comfortable as possible.

The cause of his death I cannot enter upon. He was practically in extremis when I saw him first. My examination therefore was perfunctory, my objects to relieve distress and suffering.

I am sorry for your sister.

I remain
Yours truly,
P. R. Ingram.

As soon as it had become evident that Brown's condition was critical, a telegram was sent to Lizzie; and Doctor Boyd and Mrs. Russell accompanied her to London. Ere they arrived at Melrose's house he had given the notice to the newspapers:

BROWN: At the residence of his friend, Andrew Melrose, 45 Onslow Gardens, Highgate, London, on the 28th August, George Douglas Brown, aged 33 years, author of *The House with the Green Shutters.*

Thus Lizzie and Isabella looked upon an impassive face—the brow commanding even in death—and they kissed him and turned away.

Melrose had assumed that the burial would be in London; but Lizzie insisted—and Isabella was quick in support—that Brown must lie beside his mother in Ayr churchyard. It was as if at that barren moment they shared a sympathetic intuition of what he himself would have desired.

Accordingly, his body was removed to the M'Lennans' house in Glasgow, and there on Monday, 1st September, his friends gathered to take him home: David Mack (a cousin of Brown), Doctor Boyd, J. A. Russell (Isabella's husband), Lizzie's brothers and, having travelled overnight from London, Emanuel, Macqueen, Meldrum, Melrose and Neilson. It was a happy thought—again on Lizzie's part—that the minister, the Reverend J. Fraser Graham of Belmont Church, Glasgow, was asked to read Brown's favourite thirteenth chapter of First Corinthians.

"For now," he ended, "we see through a glass, darkly; but

then face to face: now I know in part; but then shall I know even as also I am known.

"And now abideth faith, hope, charity, these three; but the greatest of these *is* charity."

After the service the coffin and mourners were conveyed to St. Enoch Station and thence by the 12.30 train to Ayr. Other friends were waiting, amongst them Tom Smith from Crocketford and Robert Wilson of Auchencloigh, and the cortège, which consisted of twelve carriages, proceeded by Holmston Road to the cemetery.

Sarah's grave was open and waiting, and two other pall-bearers now took their places: silent, bearded men who stared bleakly at the inscription, "George Douglas Brown, died 28th August 1902, aged 33 years," on the brass plate on the oak coffin. Their names were John Smith and William Maybin. . . .

So Brown was buried there beside his mother, where one day his dust would mingle with her dust in the Ayrshire earth, for at the last his life had come full circle.

Nine days later the Coylton dominie was sitting at the desk in his study. There was sorrow and infinite wisdom in his heart. It had been officially stated that Brown's death had been due to pneumonia. All the newspapers and journals had paid their tributes. The *Sunday Times* had said: "The death of the author of *The House with the Green Shutters* . . . makes a serious gap in the ranks of young writers of true literary distinction." The *Illustrated London News* had declared that "those who knew him best considered *The Green Shutters* only a stage on the road, and looked with reason for a fuller realization of the author's personality." The *Pall Mall Gazette* had pointed out that "it was generally supposed that Mr. Brown wrote *The House with the Green Shutters* as a protest against the Kailyard School." The writer had gone on: "This is a mistake. Mr. Brown wrote his book merely because the social life of a little community in Ayrshire had interested him intensely. He had the perspicacity of genius, which sees into the heart of things that dullards pass by as commonplace, and finds in commonplace things an enduring interest which dullards realize only when it is woven into art." John Smith knew that it was all true and that much more would be written and argued about Brown. But now he wanted to send a letter to his son, and he stretched out his hand, rather stiffly, for his pen.

Sept. 10th, 1902.

Dear Thomas,

I enclose a copy of G. D. Brown's Will. The Will has been proved valid by Scotch Law. I have had a great deal of correspondence about it on behalf of Coylton Poor, but I can see that the whole estate will be swallowed up by Lawyers.

First there is a Mr. Britton, Geordie's Lawyer, 15 Soho Square London, who was anxious I should be appointed Judicial Factor on the Estate. His advisers in Edinburgh, however, Messrs. Horne & Lyell, W.S., 39 Castle Street, have taken the opinion of Counsel and say that the Court of Session must be applied to in order to appoint an Administrator, and the Court will only appoint some eminent C. A. in Edinburgh. I had a call to-day from a Mr. Macrae, chief clerk to Horne & Lyell, and stating that I must call a special meeting of Coylton Parish Council for the Chairman to sign a requisition authorizing them to act and realize the estate. I have called a meeting for Friday afternoon the 12th inst.

I can see that Britton must be paid; Horne & Lyell must be paid; Counsel must be paid; Court of Session fees must be paid. Expenses of sending special messenger to me to-day for which there was occasion. Telegrams received by me every day, etc., etc.

There will be nothing for the Poor. I will, however, see if I cannot get money from his publications which are in the hands of his college friend and companion, Mr. Meldrum, who is going to publish his 2nd book. The book is ready except a concluding chapter or so, which Meldrum is preparing for publication. Geordie did not sell the copyright of his last book and some royalties are coming in. But then his publisher, Macqueen, will likely have something to say. If I can make the Poor of Coylton proprietors of his last book and of the forthcoming one and his other publications I will do it. I cannot tell how this will stand, however, till I consult Meldrum, who has charge of all his literary productions and in whom I have some confidence as I have heard Geordie speak often about him. I will let you know how I get on.

For a few moments the old dominie paused; then he brought his letter to a close.

I thought you would be anxious to see Geordie's Will—poor Geordie! how I did mourn for him! ! poor Geordie!

BIBLIOGRAPHY

The Snell Exhibitions, from the University, Glasgow, to Balliol College, Oxford, by W. Innes Addison (1901).

The Bookman (New York), 1901, Vol. XIV, pp. 546–7.

"Reminiscences of a Friendship and a Notable Novel" by Andrew Melrose, *The Bookman*, October 1902.

McClure's Magazine, November 1902, contains two articles: "George Douglas" by C. Whibley and "The Closing of the Shutters" by Robert Barr.

Scottish Art and Letters, a Quarterly Review, November 1902–January 1903, features an illustrated biographical article by the Editor, Arnold Fraser-Lovat, and "Gurrulug", a short story by Brown. Towards the end of the volume there is a revealing sketch by Hamish MacQueen, "A Night at the Hut," which is, beyond doubt, Brown's work.

George Douglas Brown, a Biographical Memoir by Cuthbert Lennox, with Introduction by Andrew Lang (1903).

Modern Scots Writers by W. M. Parker (1917).

"George Douglas," by Edwin Muir, *The Scottish Nation*, July 3, 1923.

"George Douglas Brown," a Biographical Sketch, and "The Man and his Book," both by Andrew Melrose in the Memorial Edition of *The House with the Green Shutters* (1923).

Contemporary Scottish Studies by C. M. Grieve (1926).

The Scottish Literary Tradition by John Spiers.

The Looker-On by Neil Munro (1933).

Twilight in Scotland by Norman Bruce (1934).

I Liked the Life I Lived by Eveleigh Nash (1941), p. 25.

Aberdeen University Review, No. 82, Winter 1940 and No. 83, Spring 1941: "George Douglas Brown" by A. C. Mackenzie.

Father of the Man by Sir Ernest Barker (1948).

Barrie and the Kailyard School by George Blake (1951).

APPENDIX

The following letters appeared in the *Ayrshire Post* in April 1892, and there is a possibility that Brown wrote them in defence of his father.

PATENT EVICTING MACHINE
Man's inhumanity to man makes countless thousands mourn.

Sir,
   With your kind permission and with motives of the purest sympathy, I beg you will allow me, through the medium of your paper, to bring before the notice of the public the case of Mr. George Douglas Brown, who has been tenant in Drumsmudden Farm for the long period of 32 years . . . He is still enjoying good health and looks after the interest of the farm, which he has improved to a great extent; and with years of hard labour and skill he has bettered its condition in every respect—which can be proved—and entirely at his own expense. Now in his old age he has to hand it over to that benevolent gentleman the landlord; although so far as I know, the only fault they have against him is his old age—an age that any person with the least spark of humanity in their breast would think should have some claim to veneration. But to show the esteem and regard that Mr. Brown is held in by the people in the neighbourhood of Ochiltree and the feeling and indignation for such an injustice, on the 18th March upwards of a hundred people proceeded with torchlight to a field on Drumsmudden Farm, carrying the effigy of a gentleman whom they named a "Scotch Landlord's Evicting Machine", where they erected a large bonfire, the object of which, the chairman of the meeting said, was to show our respect and heartfelt sympathy for Mr. Brown, and to show our feeling and contempt for this "Scotch Landlord's Evicting Machine", who people believed had been instrumental in evicting Mr. Brown out of his farm. By inserting this in your very popular paper, you will confer a favour on the numerous sympathisers of Mr. Brown throughout Ochiltree Parish, who are thoroughly indignant at the treatment he has received.

I am,
Your most obedient servant,
Fairplay.

Sir,

In a recent issue of your paper there appeared a letter almost unparalleled for ignorance and meanness. It is for this very reason all the more difficult to refute the absurdities of that champion of the commonweal, "Pro Bono Publico". Argument, Sir, can be met with argument; but P. B. O. never argues; he quibbles, shirks and evades, like the veriest coward. Neither is it possible to follow the scriptural adage, and answer the fool as his folly might demand. There is a stupidity, Sir, the tortuous windings of which can never be unravelled, because no sane mind could ever stop to penetrate its dulness. To that category belongs the stupidity of "Pro Bono Publico". To sink to the level of his intellect by adapting our reply to his capacities were a degradation too great for ourselves and too great for the pages of your journal. But in two points at least, we must expose his absurd and fallacious remarks.

He professes to marvel, Sir, that no one has come forward to make another and more vigorous onslaught on the "Patent Evicting Machine". To that, Sir, we answer that it is unnecessary to crush a muckworm twice beneath the heel. Incidentally we should have thought that the individual in question was sick enough already without a repetition of the doze. That, however, is no concern of ours. It is not our duty to assail Mr. Reid. It should be the duty of his toadies to defend him.

In the second place, Sir, the champion of the commonweal pretends to disbelieve that Mr. Reid is an object of popular indignation. Allow us to remark, Sir, that our first letter referred to a matter of fact, and not to a matter of opinion. It is a fact that Mr. Reid's effigy was publicly burnt with every expression of loathing and contempt. We are far from saying that Mr. Reid is a mark for the popular hatred. Hatred, Sir, is a feeling we reserve for our nobler enemies; there are creatures for which we have only the lower antipathies of abhorrence and disgust.

In conclusion, Sir, allow us to remark that Mr. Brown bears no personal grudge against his landlord. We are ignorant of the nature of his feelings towards Mr. Reid. We suppose that he surveys with good-humoured contempt the petty tyranny of the hireling whose ignorance and meanness he has often exposed with merciless rigour and punished with a galling sarcasm.

I have the honour to remain, Sir,

Your most obedient servant,

Fairplay.

INDEX

195

THE INCREDIBLE DE FOE

By WILLIAM FREEMAN

Yorkshire Post: "The great merit of Mr. Freeman's book is that he does full justice to Robinson Crusoe. It gives us, too, a spirited account of De Foe's ceaseless, and not always scrupulous, activities."

Truth: "Mr. Freeman's agreeably written biography fills a long-felt want. It shows clearly what the man was like who wrote *Robinson Crusoe*, and what were the conditions in which he lived."

Sunday Mercury: "Mr. Freeman has made of his life and times a most entertaining and acceptable book. Those who have a taste for biography with an accurate historical background will certainly enjoy it."

With a Frontispiece   15s. net

OLIVER GOLDSMITH

By WILLIAM FREEMAN

Spectator: "The general reader should welcome this full chronicle of Goldsmith's turbulent and varied life, its periods of mystery and conflicting record, its years enlightened by copious and interesting accounts . . . no one who reads Mr. Freeman's book will doubt that Master Noll is endearing and entertaining."

Manchester Daily Dispatch: A good biography of an unfairly neglected writer and poet . . . this is a well-written, scholarly and sympathetic appreciation, and its background of literary London in Johnson's time is excellent."

With a Frontispiece   18s. net

HERBERT JENKINS, LTD., 3 DUKE OF YORK STREET, S.W.1

BOTH SIDES OF THE PYRENEES

By BERNARD NEWMAN

The Pyrenees have long been a favourite touring ground for enterprising British travellers. Their mountains may not approach Alpine heights, but they are more dramatic and charming with their spectacular peaks dominating lovely valleys. Furthermore, the region teems with history, legend, romance and the intense fascination of widely-varied and interesting peoples.

Newman began his journey at Pau, plunged into the heart of the High Pyrenees, descended to take an impromptu part in a procession at Lourdes, crossed the passes of the Route des Pyrenees, visited the prehistoric caves of Niaux, and rode into Andorra, that strange medieval survival now rapidly being spoiled, by "progress". After reaching the Mediterranean, he turned south into Spain.

The account of his tour, describing as it does the return journey along the Spanish slopes, is especially important, because most books on the Pyrenees describe the French side only. Highlights are the mountain monastery of Nuria, the "inland island" of Llivia, the sleepy charm of Seo de Urgel—and a succession of appalling roads; then on to the unique National Park of Ordesa, the Valley of Noblemen, and to Pamplona gone mad at the *fiesta* of San Firmin—when the entire population dances the fandango in the streets, and when bulls chase through the city to give the young men an opportunity to show off before their girl-friends! At a bullfight Bernard Newman's attention was distracted—he was given a seat among sixteen Spanish beauty queens!

The final stage of the journey led over the romantic Pass of Roncesvalles and through the heart of the fascinating Basque country.

Whether for the armchair traveller or the voyager planning a Pyrenean journey—especially if he would travel inexpensively!—this book is a 'must'. The beautiful illustrations enhance its value.

Illustrated with maps and photographs   18s. net

HERBERT JENKINS, LTD., 3 DUKE OF YORK STREET, S.W.1